MW00607827

CREATION
UNDATED

Two Stage Biblical Creation

CREATION UNDATED

Two Stage Biblical Creation

Taking Both
"In the Beginning"
and the Six Days Literally
for a Biblically Undated Creation

Thomas Patrick Arnold

Bible Bridge Books

Copyright © 2022 by Thomas Patrick Arnold, PhD

All rights reserved. No part of this publication may be reproduced in any form, except for brief quotations such as in book reviews or quotes, without written permission from Thomas Arnold, 2bbb2ta@gmail.com.

Unless otherwise indicated, all English Scripture quotations are taken from the ESV® Bible (The Holy Bible, English Standard Version®), copyright © 2001 by Crossway, a publishing ministry of Good News Publishers. Used by permission. All rights reserved.

Scripture quotations marked NIV are taken from The Holy Bible, New International Version® NIV® Copyright © 1973 1978 1984 2011 by Biblica, Inc. TM. Used by permission. All rights reserved worldwide. (Scripture quotations marked NIV 1984 are from the 1984 version.)

Scripture quotations marked NASB are taken from the New American Standard Bible®, Copyright © 1960, 1962, 1963, 1968, 1971, 1972, 1973, 1975, 1977, 1995 by The Lockman Foundation Used by permission (www.Lockman.org).

Scripture quotations marked NKJV are taken from the New King James Version®. Copyright © 1982 by Thomas Nelson. Used by permission. All rights reserved.

Scripture quotations marked CJB are taken from the Complete Jewish Bible, Copyright © 1998 and 2016 by David H. Stern. Used by permission of Messianic Jewish Publishers. All rights reserved worldwide.

Scripture quotations marked KJV and YLT are taken from the King James Version and Young's Literal Translation. Public domain.

Nestle-Aland, Novum Testamentum Graece, 27th Revised Edition, edited by Barbara and Kurt Aland, Johannes Karavidopoulos, Carlo M. Martini, and Bruce M. Metzger in cooperation with the Institute for New Testament Textual Research, Münster/Westphalia, © 1979 Deutsche Bibelgesellschaft, Stuttgart. Used by permission.

All Hebrew text is taken from BibleWorks Leningrad Hebrew text.

Library of Congress Cataloguing-in-Publication Data
Arnold, Thomas Patrick, PhD
Creation Undated: Two Stage Biblical Creation / Thomas Patrick Arnold
Includes bibliographical references and indices.
1. Creation. 2. Creationism. 3. Biblical creation. 4. Bible. O.T. Genesis I—Interpretation. Arnold, Thomas Patrick, II. Title
Library of Congress Call Number: BS651.A46 2022
Dewey Call #: 231.7652
ISBN 978-0-9798961-1-8

Published by Bible Bridge Books, Arlington Heights, IL 60004
Printed in the United States of America

Contact the author at 2bbb2ta@gmail.com for permission to translate this book into another language.
The author, Thomas Patrick Arnold, PhD, retains all rights in English worldwide.
USA

Contents

Note from the Author

The Bible is God's inspired, inerrant Word, and as originally written, is 100 percent true (2 Tim. 3:16). Sound principles of interpretation oblige us to interpret Scripture according to each passage's words, context, genre, and grammar. The focus of our interpretation should be first on the Bible text itself as originally written in Hebrew or Greek. Once we understand the Bible text accurately, then correlations with evidence that God built into the creation naturally follow.

Two Stage Biblical Creation interprets the Bible creation texts (Genesis 1 and 2, Job 26 and 38, Psalm 104, Proverbs 8, and many shorter Bible creation texts) each according to Hebrew (or New Testament Greek) word meanings, grammar, genre (historical narrative, wisdom literature, poetry), background, and context. The genre of Genesis 1 is historical narrative (objectively indicated by the Hebrew grammar), so Genesis 1 is interpreted by the plain literal sense. The plain sense of Genesis 1 is that God created the heavens and the earth in the beginning, then He worked six literal described days.

A creation understanding—whether Young Earth, Old Earth, or Two Stage Biblical Creation—is not a fundamental of the faith or a salvation issue. People may hold different views on creation while, in Christian love and respect, striving together to approach a more Biblical understanding. My hope and prayer is that this more Biblical understanding of creation will promote greater unity in God's church (John 17:22).

While agreeing with individual points in this book, quoted Bible commentators may not fully agree or may even disagree with other parts of Two Stage Biblical Creation. I wish to express gratitude to these scholars for their insights on those individual points, even if we may not fully agree.

Throughout this book, I italicize non-English transliterations of words, such as the Hebrew word *yôm* and the Greek word *hexaemeron*. Words in a Bible quote that are not represented by a word in the Hebrew or Greek text may be italicized in the King James Version, the New King James Version, and my literal translations from the Hebrew or Greek.

Bible texts noted as "from Hebrew" are translated using Hebrew tools. I do not intend to produce another readable standard English translation but offer these rather literal translations as aids to the reader. English words separated by a hyphen indicate a compound Hebrew word. I have followed Hebrew word order where possible, except where strict Hebrew word order would not make sense in English. Words separated by a slash represent a single Hebrew word that may be translated in several possible ways.

Thank you to those who have read and evaluated this book's manuscript or edited its contents.

May this book reflect the truth of God's Word to His glory.

About the Author

Thomas Patrick Arnold (ThM, PhD) taught science for seven years, but he found no modern creation theory that fully matches both the Bible and the evidence God built into the creation. He switched from graduate studies in science to Bible, completing three master's degrees and a doctorate, with his dissertation on ten major creation theories. He found that creation in two stages, although largely overlooked today, is based on the Hebrew Bible text and has been taught since the early church. He is the author of articles and *Two Stage Biblical Creation: Uniting Biblical Insights Uncovered by Ten Notable Creation Theories.* He is a member of the American Scientific Affiliation and the Evangelical Theological Society and has presented for critique key aspects of Two Stage Biblical Creation in three papers read at the annual national meetings of the Evangelical Theological Society.

Introduction

Is Reconciliation of Creation Beliefs Possible?

For decades, Young Earth Creationism and Old Earth Creationism have been locked in a no-win battle. Reconciling creation beliefs must not come by glossing over differences, compromising Bible truth, or spiritualizing Genesis 1. Reconciliation must be based on truth.

Oddly, each side has been blocking reconciliation by holding onto a different vital Bible truth, and Bible believers cannot abandon Bible truth. Young Earth creationists believe that we should interpret "day" in the historical narrative of Genesis 1 as a literal day. Old Earth creationists recognize that God's Word is true, so they will never abandon their belief that we should take Genesis 1:1 literally. God created the literal heavens and the literal planet Earth, the universe, in the literal beginning (*b^ere'shît*, in beginning time/phase of unspecified length).

Two Stage Biblical Creation holds both Bible truths literally—that Genesis 1:1 declares God created the heavens and the earth in the beginning before the six days and that Genesis 1:3–31 declares God worked six literal days finishing earth, preparing it for life, filling it with life, and creating Adam and Eve in His image. How all this fits together—multiple Bible creation texts, literal interpretation of Bible historical narrative, God always being truthful in His Word, reliable evidence that God built into the creation, and a Biblically undated creation—is the subject of this book. The answer is not simplistic, but once it all fits together like a great creation puzzle, it is beautiful. Could this Two Stage understanding—taking both "in the beginning God created the heavens and the earth" literally and the six days literally—be the solution to the creation conflict?

Genuine reconciliation of creation beliefs must be based on an accurate understanding of the Bible texts on creation. The goal of Two Stage Biblical Creation is to continually approach, more and more closely, a precise understanding of the Bible texts about God's incredible creation work—to His glory.

PART ONE

The Question:
Can Six Literal Days and Evidence of an Older Universe Fit Together?

One of my engineer friends asked, "How can the Bible account of six literal days and the evidence of an older universe fit together? The Bible says six days, but the physical evidence points to an older universe."

God, by His nature, is unswervingly truthful. God reveals verbal truth in His inerrant Word, the Bible. He also has built into the universe reliable physical evidence: "The heavens declare the glory of God" (Psa. 19:1). But how can the evidence indicating that the universe and Earth are older and the Genesis 1 account with six literal days of God's creation work fit together? When we take all of Genesis 1 literally—"In the beginning God created the heavens and the earth" (Gen. 1:1), but Earth was unfinished (Gen. 1:2), then God worked six literal days (Gen. 1:3–31)—the Genesis 1 historical narrative and the physical evidence in the creation fit together beautifully.

Chapter 1

The Heavens Declare the Glory of God

בְּרֵאשִׁית בָּרָא אֱלֹהִים אֵת הַשָּׁמַיִם וְאֵת הָאָרֶץ:
"Bᵉreʹshît bārāʹ Elōhîm et ha-shāmāyim vᵉet ha-ārets."
"In the beginning God created the heavens and the earth."

Long ago, David—the psalmist of Israel, shepherd, and harpist—spent night after night with his sheep outside under the stars. And night after night, as he looked up, he saw the evidence in the heavens of the glory of God the Creator. David wrote:

The heavens declare the glory of God;
    the skies proclaim the work of his hands.
Day after day they pour forth speech;
    night after night they display knowledge (Psa. 19:1–2, NIV 1984).

The heavens, which God created in the beginning, continue to reveal knowledge about the work of His hands, the work of creation. This knowledge from the universe that He created never contradicts knowledge from the Bible's creation texts about the same heavens. The Creator never misleads truth seekers by either the Bible or the creation.

What a Creator!

Before time,
    before space,
    before the first atoms,
there was God alone—Father, Son, and Spirit.
Then God the Father, through God the Son, created the heavens and the earth
    in the beginning.
God alone created
    the beginning of time,
    the beginning of space,
    the beginning of energy,
    the beginning of matter,
    the beginning of the heavens and the earth.

God alone created the heavens with the galaxies and distant starlight. That distant starlight reveals truth about the Creator and knowledge about the creation. Psalm 19:2 states that the skies "display knowledge." Romans 1:20 adds:

> For since the creation of the world [κόσμου, *cosmos*] His invisible attributes, His eternal power and divine nature, have been clearly seen, being understood through what has been made, so that they [people] are without excuse (NASB).

The Bible is saying that what we see in the heavens reveals truth. The light from those distant galaxies reveals truth about God's "divine nature." Part of God's divine nature is that He "cannot lie" (Titus 1:2, KJV). The inspired, inerrant Hebrew text of the Bible and the evidence in the universe are in accord because both are from the same absolutely truthful Creator God.

> *The inspired, inerrant Hebrew text of the Bible and the evidence in the universe are in accord because both are from the same absolutely truthful Creator God.*

What a Universe!

For millennia, no one had circled our blue, green, and white-cloud-streaked planet. Then in 1519, Ferdinand Magellan, with five ships and about 250 men, sailed west from Spain to reach the Spice Islands of Indonesia. Magellan was killed in the Philippines. After three years of sailing, Captain Juan Elcano, with the one remaining ship and 18 men, finally returned to Spain, having circumnavigated planet Earth.[1]

Planet Earth is 40,070 kilometers (24,900 miles) around. Earth is huge, yet how small Earth seemed as astronomers looked out first into our solar system, then into our Milky Way galaxy, and finally into the distant universe.

In 1609, Galileo turned his newly made telescope to the sky. He saw the moons that circle Jupiter and realized that Earth might not be at the center of everything. Galileo also discovered that the number of stars is vastly beyond the limited number counted by the ancient astronomer Ptolemy. Yet the stars he saw were only a tiny fraction of the stars in the universe.

Many people in 1676 assumed that light from our sun and the stars travels instantaneously or so fast that we cannot measure its speed. Then Danish astronomer Ole Rømer (1644–1710) began timing the orbit of the moon Io around Jupiter. He discovered that as Earth moved farther from Jupiter, Io seemed to lag behind schedule, but when Earth approached Jupiter, Io seemed to move ahead of schedule.

---

1 Enrique de Malacca, Magellan's servant, may actually have been the first to circumnavigate, because he originally came from Indonesia; so when he reached Indonesia, he had circumnavigated the Earth.

Rømer realized that light was taking time to travel from Io to Earth. When Jupiter was more distant, the light took longer to reach Earth. He calculated the speed of light at 225,000 kilometers (140,000 miles) per second. Rømer's estimate was slower than the actual speed of precisely 299,792.458 kilometers/second (about 186,282 miles/second). Light has not been speeding up; Rømer's measurements were less accurate than modern measurements of the speed of light. In 1728, an English astronomer made a great advance in precision. He measured the speed of light at 298,000 kilometers (185,000 miles) per second, a measurement only 1 percent slower than today's accurate measurement.

At 186,282 miles per second, light could travel around Earth more than seven times a second. Light takes eight minutes to cross the 93,000,000 miles from the sun to Earth. The sun is eight light-minutes away, so we are seeing the sun as it was eight minutes ago. The distance from Earth to the stars is so great that we measure not in miles or light-minutes but light-years. Traveling at 299,792 kilometers/second (186,282 miles/second) in the vacuum of space, light travels over nine trillion kilometers (almost six trillion miles) in a year. The nearest star group beyond our sun is a triplet of stars called Alpha Centauri. Light from Alpha Centauri takes 4.3 years to reach planet Earth. So the Alpha Centauri star system is 4.3 light-years away, and the light is 4.3 years old when it reaches Earth. Astronomers are seeing the Centauri system as it was 4.3 years in the past.

On a dark night away from city lights, we can see the thin white veil of our galaxy spread across the high sky. To the ancients, our galaxy looked like milk splashed across the sky, so the Romans called it the *Via Lactea*, the Milky Way. Today we know that the white band of stars is our spiral galaxy. Our galaxy contains several hundred billion stars. The spiral arms of the Milky Way stretch out over 100,000 light-years. Yet far beyond our own Milky Way are a trillion more galaxies clustered in orderly array. The nearest galaxy, Andromeda, is 2,500,000 light-years away. The Great Andromeda galaxy is even larger than the Milky Way. Andromeda contains a trillion massive stars, stars like our own sun.

With every improved telescope, astronomers see more galaxies. We do not know how many galaxies are in the universe, but estimates range from one to two trillion (1,000,000,000,000 to 2,000,000,000,000), each with billions of stars. The most distant observed galaxies are an astounding thirteen billion light-years away.

Even to estimate the number of stars in the universe, the number of stars in a galaxy must be multiplied by the number of galaxies. The number of stars is staggering. What an amazing universe God created!

The Heavens Reveal True Evidence about the Universe's Past

Like King David long before, another musician—a church organist in England—looked up at the stars of the night sky to see the glory of God in His creation work. William Herschel (1738–1822) began building telescopes, much larger and more precise than any built before. His greatest telescope was forty-eight inches in diameter and forty feet long. At that time it was considered one of the wonders of the world. With that telescope he discovered the first planet not seen by the ancients, the planet Uranus. For this great discovery, King George III knighted him. Herschel realized those cloudy nebulae that we recognize as galaxies are composed of many individual stars. He discovered double stars, coined the term "asteroid," and discovered infrared radiation.

Night after night William Herschel could see God's creation revealed in the heavens. Herschel said that "the un-devout astronomer must be mad."[2] He realized he was seeing the "work of His [God's] hands."

Light does not travel instantaneously but travels at the constant speed of light. Light travels so fast that we see events near us almost as they happen, but we see events in the distant universe long after they happen. By Herschel's time, astronomers had calculated the speed of light quite accurately.

▼ **William Herschel and His Forty-Foot-Long Telescope**

William Herschel by Lemuel Francis Abbott, National Portrait Gallery, https://commons.wikimedia.org/wiki/ File:William_Herschel

"Herschel 40 Foot" by Unknown. Scanned from Leisure Hour, Nov. 2, 1867, page 729. Licensed under public domain via Wikimedia Commons.

When William Herschel looked out at the night sky, he realized he was looking back at past events. He explained to his son that as we look at the stars, we are looking back in time at what happened in the universe in the distant past. We are seeing light that finally reaches us long after that light left its distant star or nebula. Herschel saw ancient starlight, but exactly how old he did not know. The heavens display the work of God, not only His recent work but also His distant past work.

---

2 Henry M. Morris, *Men of Science; Men of God* (Green Forest, AR: Master Books, 1982), 36.

God is telling us to believe the information pouring forth from the universe day after day, knowledge displayed night after night. This knowledge from the created heavens reveals truth about the history of the universe that God made.

The heavens declare the glory of God;
   the skies proclaim the work of his hands.
Day after day they pour forth speech;
   night after night they display knowledge
(Psa. 19:1–2, NIV 1984).

God is telling us to believe the information pouring forth from the universe day after day, knowledge displayed night after night. This knowledge from the created heavens reveals truth about the history of the universe that God made.

This truth from the created heavens never contradicts knowledge from the inerrant Bible's creation texts about the same heavens. God is truthful and never misleads truth seekers by either His Word or His creation work.

Chapter 2

The Bible Is True, Including Its Declarations about the Universe

Ancient myths tell of a universe without a beginning, a world of chaos. In those myths the universe operates by chance or by whims of mythical deities. Those myths claimed Earth rested on something—Atlas, elephants, turtles. Ancient Mesopotamian myths said the Earth was flat. Ancients believed the stars were fixed in place and fixed in number (except for "wandering stars," which we now know are planets, exploding stars, or comets). They saw the stars as shining forever.

But the myths were wrong.

Bible Claims about the Universe

The Bible texts on creation were written during the same era as those myths. But the claims of the Bible's creation texts are in stark contrast to the ancient myths.

The Bible Declares the Universe Had a Beginning

God alone is eternal, the only uncaused eternal Cause.

Before the mountains were brought forth,
> or ever you had formed the earth and the world,
> from everlasting to everlasting you are God (Psa. 90:2).

Only eternal God existed before the beginning when there was
> no space,
> no time,
> no matter,
> no laws of physics.

The very first sentence of the Bible declares the universe had a beginning:

In the beginning God created the heavens and the earth (Gen. 1:1).

Many astrophysicists and astronomers today have come to realize that science demonstrates that the universe had a beginning. Logically, a universe with a beginning needed a cause, an immensely powerful, supremely intelligent, eternal cause. That Cause is the eternal God of the Bible, who long ago correctly stated that the universe had a beginning.

The Bible Declares the Universe Operates by Fixed Laws

When eternal God created the universe, He established the "laws of the heavens" (Job 38:33, NIV 1984), "the fixed laws of heaven and earth" (Jer. 33:25, NIV 1984). Because the universe operates by these mathematically precise, unchanging laws, scientists can develop theories of how the universe works. Many scientists have invested their lives in discovering physical laws and constants—gravity, thermodynamics, the speed of light. These laws are not by chance. God established them as part of the universe when He created the heavens and the earth in the beginning, as stated in Genesis 1:1. True science is a process by which humans discover what God made.

> *The match between the Bible and discoveries about creation is strong evidence that the God of the Bible is the Creator and that the Bible alone is His true and unique communication to all people.*

The Bible Indicates the Number of Stars Are Beyond Human Counting

Jeremiah 33:22 reveals that "the host of heaven cannot be numbered." The number of stars is beyond what humans can count. But God knows their number and even names them.

He counts the number of the stars; He gives names to all of them (Psa. 147:4, NASB).

As the nuclear furnaces of new stars burst into light, God adds them to His number of current stars.

The Bible Indicates Earth Is Roughly Spherical and Suspended on Nothing

The Bible explains that the earth, rather than being flat, is spherical:

He [God] sits enthroned above the circle of the earth (Isa. 40:22, NIV 1984).

From His position above the Earth, God sees "the circle of the earth." The only way Earth would appear circular from all positions above it is if it is roughly spherical.

Myths pictured the Earth resting on something—Atlas, elephants, turtles. The Bible explains that the earth, rather than resting on something, is suspended on nothing:

He stretches out the north over empty space,
And hangs [suspends] the earth on nothing (Job 26:7, NASB).

The Bible Declares the Universe Is Stretching Out or Expanding

The Bible declares that God created the heavens in the beginning and stretched them out. Eleven times the Bible tells us God has been stretching out the heavens, expanding the universe.[3] Finally, in the last century, scientists discovered that the universe is expanding, just as the Bible has said all along.

God, the LORD . . . created the heavens and stretched them out (Isa. 42:5).

Only the Creator could have known long before modern science that the universe had a beginning and has been stretching out, continually expanding since its beginning. The beginning and expansion of the universe is strong evidence that the God of the Bible is the Creator, and His Word, the Bible, is true.

The Bible Declares the Universe Will Wear Out

David, in Psalm 102, says the heavens and Earth are wearing out, running down. God does not intend this universe and Earth to be eternal:

In the beginning you laid the foundations of the earth,
    and the heavens are the work of your hands.
They will perish, but you remain;
    they will all wear out like a garment.
Like clothing you will change them
    and they will be discarded.
But you remain the same,
    and your years will never end (Psa. 102:25–27, NIV 1984).

Our sun is using up its energy. The universe is wearing out. Science has discovered what the Bible has said all along.

The Bible Already Declared Truths That Modern Science Is Now Discovering

Although the Bible was written before and during the same time as the non-Biblical myths, in stark contrast to the myths, the Bible's claims are true. Because they are true, discovery after discovery about the universe is confirming them. The universe had a beginning. It operates by unchanging laws. It contains an immense number of stars. It is expanding. And it will wear out. The match between the Bible and discoveries about creation is strong evidence that the God of the Bible is the Creator and that the Bible alone is His true and unique communication to all people.

---

3 Job 9:8; Psa. 104:2; Isa. 40:22, 42:5, 44:24, 45:12, 48:13, 51:13; Jer. 10:12, 51:15; Zech. 12:1.

The Bible Is from the Creator

The Bible is from God the Creator, who alone knew and proclaimed these truths long before modern science discovered them.

Although a correct creation theory may refer to science, it must be based on the inspired, inerrant Bible text and can be derived from the Bible alone. A correct creation theory will also match the evidence in the creation, because both the Bible and the creation are from the same truthful Creator.

A correct creation theory must be based on the inspired, inerrant Bible text. And a correct creation theory will also match the evidence in the creation, because both the Bible and the creation are from the same truthful Creator.

Chapter 3

The Bible Said, Then Science Discovers, the Universe Had a Beginning

Light.
Light is an awesome way God demonstrates His glory.

Bless the LORD, O my soul!
O LORD my God, You are very great.
You are clothed *with* splendor and majesty.
    Enveloping *in* light as with a cloak,
    Stretching out *the* heavens like a tent (Psa. 104:1–2, from Hebrew).

God created the heavens in the beginning. The light that God created reveals His glory as the Creator. That light also reveals true evidence about the creation, including that the universe had a beginning.

The Bible Declares the Universe Had a Beginning

From its very first verse, the Bible declares that the universe had a beginning. Only God is eternal. He created the heavens and planet Earth.

In the beginning God created the heavens and the earth (Gen. 1:1).

In the last century, scientists discovered that the universe had a beginning, just as the Bible has said all along. Only the Creator could have known this fact before modern science.

Science Discovers the Universe Had a Beginning

In the early 1900s, many scientists thought the universe was eternal. That all changed with a series of remarkable discoveries. Science has discovered what the Bible has said all along: the universe had a beginning and is expanding.

God, the LORD . . . created the heavens and stretched them out (Isa. 42:5).

Constant Speed of Light: A Key to Understanding the Beginning of the Universe

To understand the universe, the one thing that travels across the whole universe needs to be understood: light. Danish astronomer Ole Rømer (1644–1710) showed that light does not travel instantaneously but takes time to travel. William Herschel realized that if light takes time to travel, then we are looking back in time when we see the stars. With ever-increasing accuracy, physicists have measured the speed of light at 186,282 miles/second (precisely 299,792.458 kilometers/second).[4] The speed of light is sometimes called the "cosmic speed limit," and that speed limit is unchanging.

This strange unchanging speed of light was a puzzle that started a Swiss patent office employee thinking about why light's speed is constant. That young man was Albert Einstein.

Einstein Explains Fixed Light Speed but Hesitates to Accept Expanding Universe

From 1905 through 1916, Albert Einstein developed his famous theory of relativity, explaining how light works and how gravity works. His theory showed that the universe could not be eternally stable but must be expanding (or contracting).

If the universe is expanding, the laws of physics indicate that it must have been smaller and smaller in the past, back to its beginning point. The beginning of the universe was upsetting to Einstein because that concept suggested that God created the universe. Einstein was not happy about the idea of a personal Creator, so he added a fudge factor to his calculations that he called the "cosmological constant" to make the universe stand still—theoretically. But his cosmological constant, which would

▼ **Albert Einstein in 1921**

Wikimedia Commons: Ferdinand Schmutzer, archive.org/ web/20071026151415/ http://www.anzenbergergallery.com/en/article/134.html

---

4 Light speed is unchanging in a vacuum, but the progress of light photons can be slowed by the atoms in matter (such as glass or water) that repeatedly absorb, briefly hold, and re-emit the photons in the same direction.

make the universe static, had no hard evidence, no astronomical observations, no proof at all.

Hubble Discovers Proof That the Universe Is Expanding

The man who would prove that the universe is expanding was Edwin Hubble. His discovery in 1929 that the universe is expanding would lead to proof that the universe had a beginning.

The athletic American Edwin Hubble earned a scholarship to Oxford and served with distinction in World War I. Then he worked as an astronomer at the Mount Wilson Observatory, with its magnificent new one-hundred-inch telescope, the world's largest telescope at that time.

Two discoveries—a kind of pulsing star that is a "standard candle" and a redshift of distant galaxies—would give Hubble new scientific tools to answer two questions: Is the universe static, contracting, or expanding? And did the universe have a beginning?

▼ **Edwin Hubble (1889–1953)**

By Johan Hagemeyer, http://hdl.huntington.org/, public domain, https://commons.wikimedia.org/w/index.php?curid=38358266

▼ **Henrietta Leavitt (1868–1921)**

American Institute of Physics, Emilio Segrè Visual Archives, http://photos.aip.org/veritySearch2.jsp?item_id=Leavitt%20 Henrietta%20Swan%20B1&fname=leavitt_henrietta_b1.jpg

During those early years of the Mount Wilson Observatory, women were excluded from the all-male observatory astronomers, so Henrietta Leavitt made her discoveries by studying star photographs made by the men. By 1912 she discovered 2,400 variable or pulsing stars, including a special kind called a Cepheid variable star. Big Cepheid stars pulse slowly, but smaller Cepheid stars pulse rapidly. She realized that all Cepheid variable stars with the same pulse rate have the same absolute brightness. She had discovered a "standard candle," a kind of star that always has the same average absolute brightness if it has the same pulse rate. Hubble later said she deserved the Nobel Prize, but that prize is given only to the living, and she died in 1921.

The distance to nearby Cepheid variable stars up to one hundred light-years away can be calculated using trigonometry by the slight differences in their angle from the extreme sides of Earth's orbit. The pulse rate and apparent brightness of faraway Cepheid stars enable astronomers to calculate their distance. A candle ten feet away will appear four times brighter than an identical candle twenty feet away. A Cepheid star measured by trigonometry at one hundred light-years away will appear four times brighter than another Cepheid star with the same pulse rate two hundred light-years away. Although very dim, a Cepheid that is one million light-years away will appear four times brighter than one that is two million light-years away. Henrietta Leavitt gave Edwin Hubble the tool he needed to measure distances to Cepheid variable stars, distances in space.

The second tool Hubble used was the Doppler Effect, the "redshift" of light from distant galaxies. When a train whistle or an ambulance siren comes toward us, its sound is high pitched, but as the sound passes, it becomes lower pitched. The sound waves racing toward us are squeezed together, becoming shorter and hitting our eardrums with a higher frequency, so the pitch is higher. As the sound recedes, the waves are stretched, becoming longer and hitting our eardrums less frequently, so the pitch becomes lower.

Light also comes in waves, but light waves are in colors instead of pitch. In the visible spectrum, blue has shorter high-frequency waves, and red has longer lower-frequency waves. When a light source moves away rapidly, the light waves stretch out and shift toward lower frequency red waves—what astronomers call redshift. How far the frequency shifts toward the red tells astronomers how fast the object is moving away from us. Hubble now had two new tools: Cepheid variable stars to measure distance and redshift to measure speed away from us.

Year after year Hubble sat in the cold night air in the Mount Wilson Observatory, constantly adjusting the great telescope's aim like a patient hunter, gathering the dim ancient light of Cepheid stars onto his photographic plate. Hubble found many Cepheid variable stars within our own Milky Way galaxy. These Cepheid variable stars proved that our galaxy is vast, about a hundred thousand light-years across.

In 1924 Hubble found Cepheid variable stars much farther away among the trillion suns of our neighboring galaxy, Andromeda. He estimated its great distance from our galaxy. Today's precise instruments measure the distance at 2,500,000 light-years away, indicating Andromeda is a distant, separate galaxy far beyond our Milky Way.

Hubble measured distances to even farther galaxies, proving they are massive separate galaxies millions of light-years away. Edwin Hubble increased our view of the cosmos from only our galaxy of about 100,000 light-years across to a universe with innumerable galaxies that is billions of light-years across.

Then Hubble measured the amount of redshift or blueshift of galaxies. A blueshift means the galaxy is approaching us. A redshift means it is receding away from us. To his surprise, almost every galaxy (except Andromeda, the nearest) was redshifted. The farther a galaxy is from Earth, the greater its redshift, so the faster that galaxy is receding. If a galaxy recedes faster the more distant it is from Earth, then the universe is expanding. Hubble demonstrated what Einstein reluctantly predicted—that the universe is expanding. It is spreading out farther every second.

Einstein, Lemaître, and Hubble Realize an Expanding Universe Had a Beginning

It took a unique physicist to put it all together. Belgian physicist Georges Lemaître mentally ran the expansion backward. If the universe has been expanding and the expansion is run backward, this leads to a beginning. Einstein predicted and Hubble proved the universe is expanding. Lemaître realized an expanding universe must have had a beginning. If this proved to be true, it would match what the Bible had been declaring all along—that the universe had a beginning.

In 1931, Einstein, Hubble, and Lemaître met. As Einstein came to understand Lemaître's conclusion, he applauded and said, "This is the most beautiful and satisfactory explanation of creation to which I have ever listened."

▼ **Abbé Georges Lemaître (1894–1966)**

Wikimedia Commons: https://commons.wikimedia.org/wiki/File:Lemaitre.jpg

Then Einstein repudiated his added cosmological constant that would have indicated a static, eternal universe as the "greatest blunder of my life."[5] Einstein had mathematically predicted what Hubble discovered and Lemaître fully grasped—that the universe has been expanding, implying it had a beginning. If this proved true, it would match what the Bible had been declaring all along.

> *An expanding universe must have had a beginning. If this proved to be true, it would match what the Bible had been declaring all along.*

---

5 P. D. Smith, "*Einstein's Greatest Mistake* by David Bodanis review—the story of a fallible genius," *The Guardian*, June 9, 2017.

Fred Hoyle Mocks the Idea of a "Big Bang," Because a Beginning Implies God

British physicist Fred Hoyle (1915–2001) did not like the idea that the universe had a beginning. He wanted an eternal universe with no Creator. As a strident atheist, Fred Hoyle opposed the growing evidence that the universe had a beginning, because a beginning would strongly imply a preexisting eternal Creator. What an unsavory idea to an atheist! Hoyle theorized (with no evidence or proof) that the reason the universe has been expanding must be that new matter is steadily self-creating out of nothing and forming new galaxies, so the universe continually expands forever. He called his theory the Steady State theory. He thought his theory would eliminate the need for an eternal God as the Creator. On a BBC radio broadcast in 1949, he scoffed at the idea of a sudden beginning of the universe, derisively calling that powerful event the "Big Bang." The Big Bang is the discovery by astronomy and cosmology that our universe is not eternal but had a sudden beginning and has been expanding ever since. Atheist Fred Hoyle wanted to eliminate God, so he hated this idea that the universe had a beginning and reveled in mocking the Big Bang scientists. But who was correct?

Physicists had predicted that such a sudden beginning would leave across the universe a remnant radiation—a leftover cosmic microwave background radiation, the faint afterglow from the sudden beginning of the universe. As the universe expanded, that radiation by now should have stretched out into longer microwaves and cooled to a very low temperature (estimated at about 3° Kelvin, a very cold 3° above absolute 0°). But no one had found the predicted very low temperature cosmic microwave background radiation.

Penzias and Wilson Discover Powerful Evidence of the Beginning of the Universe

In 1964 and 1965 at Bell Labs, Arno Penzias and Robert Wilson used their large horn-shaped receiving antenna to track satellite radio communication. Bell Labs let them use the antenna for radio astronomy research on the side. But they ran into a problem, an annoying continuous low level of background microwaves picked up by their big horn antenna. Microwaves are in the same electromagnetic spectrum as visible light but with longer wavelengths that are not visible to human eyes. This 3° Kelvin temperature microwave radiation did not come from any orbiting satellites. Penzias and Wilson thought the annoying radiation might be from pigeon droppings, so the two men removed the pair of pigeons from the horn antenna and cleaned out all the droppings. But the low level of microwave background radiation continued. It was very annoying. Then they thought the microwaves might be from some nearby human-made source. But when the men pointed their great horn antenna in different directions, they discovered that the microwave background radiation came from all directions.

At the same time, astrophysicists at nearby Princeton University were building a small horn antenna. Their goal: to discover the estimated 3° Kelvin cosmic micro-wave background radiation that had been predicted as the faint afterglow left by the sudden beginning of the universe often referred to as the Big Bang.

When Penzias and Wilson heard of the Princeton research, they realized that they themselves had discovered what physics had predicted and the Princeton team was seeking. They had found the afterglow microwave radiation left over from the creation of the universe. As the universe expanded, the hot microwave radiation had stretched out and cooled all the way down to the predicted approximately 3° Kelvin temperature. Penzias and Wilson had discovered definitive evidence for the beginning of the universe! It was an amazing fulfillment of the science prediction. For their discovery of this landmark proof of the beginning and expansion of the universe, Arno Penzias and Robert Wilson were awarded the Nobel Prize in Physics.

In the movie *Hawking,* Penzias is portrayed as playing a tape recording of the microwaves converted to sound and saying, "This is the most profound thing you will hear in your entire life. . . . It's the sound from the beginning of time."

▼ **Arno Penzias (right) and Robert Wilson with the Horn Antenna**

https://commons.wikimedia.org/wiki/File:Wilson_penzias200.jpg

Mathematical calculations predicted, and Penzias and Wilson discovered, the cosmic microwave background radiation from the beginning of time, from the creation of the universe.

More and more scientists have concluded that the universe had a beginning and has been expanding ever since, just as the Big Bang model predicted. Israeli physicist Dr. Gerald Schroeder explains a paradigm shift among scientists:

In 1959, a survey was taken of leading American scientists. Among the many questions asked was, "What is your concept of the age of the universe?" Now, in 1959, astronomy was popular, but cosmology—the deep physics of understanding the universe—was just developing. . . . Two-thirds of the scientists gave the same answer: "Beginning? There was no beginning. Aristotle and Plato taught us 2400 years ago that the universe is eternal. Oh, we know the Bible says 'In the beginning.' That's a nice story, but we sophisticates know better. There was no beginning." That was 1959. In 1965, Penzias and Wilson discovered the echo of the Big Bang in the black of the sky at night, and the world paradigm changed from a universe that was eternal to a universe that had a beginning. Science had made an enormous paradigm change in its understanding of the world. Understand the impact. Science said that our universe had a beginning. I can't overestimate the import of that scientific "discovery." . . . We now understand that we had a beginning. Exactly as the Bible had claimed for three millennia.[6]

Long before this modern discovery, the Bible declared the universe had a beginning and is expanding. Science is catching up with what the Bible has declared all along.

God, the LORD . . . created the heavens and stretched them out (Isa. 42:5).

Only the Creator could have known these two facts long ago. This discovery provides exceedingly strong evidence that the God of the Bible is the Creator.

> *The Bible declares that the universe had a beginning and is expanding. Science is catching up with what the Bible declared all along.*

Cosmic Microwave Background Radiation Mapping Confirms Beginning of Universe

Even more robust evidence for the beginning of the universe would be provided by mapping the cosmic microwave background (CMB) radiation all across the universe. In a NASA experiment, the Cosmic Background Explorer (COBE) satellite developed by George Smoot mapped the CMB temperature from space. COBE measured the temperature to 2.73° Kelvin. Tiny variations in temperature beautifully fit the beginning of galaxies—almost exactly as predicted if the universe began with the Big Bang. This match provides even stronger confirmation of the universe's sudden beginning and expansion, just as the Bible declares. George Smoot said of the results, "It's like looking at God."[7] Smoot received the Nobel Prize in 2006. Scientists still argue over details. But the basic fact that the universe had a sudden hot beginning, expanded rapidly, and has been cooling ever since is now almost universally accepted by scientists.[8]

More recently, the WMAP and Plank satellites have provided even more accurate maps of the slight variations in the CMB radiation temperature. Their more accurate measurements indicate a temperature of the CMB of 2.725° Kelvin[9] and about 13.8

---

6 Gerald Schroeder, "The Age of the Universe," www.geraldschroeder.com/AgeUniverse.aspx. He has some unique ideas about creation that I and most other creationists would not agree with.

7 "It's like looking at God," *Journal Times*, April 24, 1992.

8 Astrophysicist Martin Rees expressed a widely held conclusion that his confidence "that there was indeed a Big Bang" had grown to "99%." Martin Rees, "Recipe for the Universe."

9 D. J. Fixsen, "Temperature of the Cosmic Microwave Background," *The Astrophysical Journal* 707(2): 916–92.

billion years—plus or minus a few tens of millions of years—as the estimated age of the universe.

Perlmutter Discovers Expansion Is Speeding Up, Indicating a Single Beginning of Universe

Several cosmologists hypothesized that the universe expands, slows down, contracts, then starts all over with a new Big Bang in a never-ending cycle. Such a cyclical theory would not require an eternal Creator or a single beginning.

Their idea of an eternal cyclical universe was quashed by astrophysicist Saul Perlmutter's surprising discovery of the speeding up of the expansion of the universe.[10] Everyone assumed gravity (which pulls matter together) would slow down the expansion of the universe. To the amazement of Saul Perlmutter and his team, the redshift measurements of distant supernovas were so large that they indicate that the universe's expansion is speeding up, not slowing down.[11] The universe will never collapse and reexpand in an endless cycle. The universe definitely had a single sudden beginning. The expansion is a one-way event from the onetime beginning of the universe. In 2011, Saul Perlmutter received the Nobel Prize for his discovery. Despite a few scientists' wishful speculations to the contrary, the universe really did have a single sudden beginning and has been expanding ever since, just as the Bible declares. But how did it begin?

The universe did have a beginning, but not from chance or self-creation. The answer to how the universe began is "In the beginning God created the heavens and the earth."

The Bible's Accurate Information Indicates the God of the Bible Is the Creator

Regardless of whether the Big Bang theory is an accurate model, science has correctly learned that the universe had a beginning, is huge, and is expanding—all according to fixed laws. (Two Stage Biblical Creation does not affirm a self-creating Big Bang but rather affirms that the Bible declares God began and expanded the universe.) The Bible alone, long before the discoveries by modern science, declared that the universe had a beginning; has been stretching out ever since; operates by fixed laws; and has innumerable stars, implying it is huge. Only the eternal Creator could have known these facts long before modern science discovered them. These discoveries provide compelling evidence that the eternal God of the Bible, who long ago said the universe had a beginning and is stretching out, is the Creator of the universe and that the Bible is His unique communication to humans.

---

10 At the same time, a team led by Brian Schmid in Australia independently came to the same conclusion.

11 "The Supernova Cosmology Project," Berkeley, CA, www.oarval.org/SCPen.htm.

The Bible alone, long before the discoveries by modern science, declared that the universe had a beginning; has been stretching out ever since; operates by fixed laws; and has innumerable stars, implying it is huge. Only the eternal Creator could have known these facts long before modern science discovered them. The eternal God of the Bible is the Creator of the universe.

Chapter 4

The Great Creation Puzzle

The giant shark caught off the coast of Italy in 1666 was the "Jaws" (of the giant shark movie) of the Renaissance era. Danish anatomist Nicolaus Stenonius, often called Steno, was the foremost hands-on anatomist of his time, and he was teaching nearby when the phenomenal shark was caught. So the Grand Duke of Tuscany sent the shark's head to Steno to dissect. Steno noticed that the shark's teeth were similar to what had been called "tongue stones," giant shark-tooth-shape stones encased in a sedimentary rock layer in Italy. Many people believed those fossilized tongue stones and other fossils had been created in the rock. But Steno realized that they were embedded fossilized shark-tooth-shape stones that had once been the teeth of giant sharks, even bigger than the one he was dissecting. How could the teeth of an extinct giant shark species be embedded in solid rock and turned into stone?

▼ **Nicolaus Stenonius (1638–1686)**

By Unknown, http://catalogue.museogalileo.it/biography/ NielsSteensenNicolasSteno.html, public domain, https://commons.wikimedia.org/w/index.php?curid=18016823

Challenges from Geology

Steno began studying how rock layers with those embedded teeth had been laid down. He proposed that sediment and teeth that sharks regularly shed settled to the sea bottom and formed a flat sediment layer containing the teeth. From his studies of fossilized shark teeth, Steno then began developing basic laws of geology:

- Steno's Law of Original Horizontality: Sediment in seas settles to the bottom, forming flat horizontal layers that harden into horizontal rock layers. The hardened rock layers may be tilted later.
- Steno's Law of Superposition: Layers of rock are in time sequence, with the oldest at the bottom and the youngest at the top, unless the sequence is overturned later.

Steno taught that solid inclusions like shark teeth (or shells or dinosaur bones) were deposited in the mud before the mud hardened into rock. A tooth grew in the shark, was shed, settled to the sea bottom, and was encased in soft sediment that over time hardened into a rock layer. The tooth was then replaced bit by bit by dissolved minerals, forming an embedded shark-tooth-shape rock fossil in the rock layer. Later the rock layers with fossils may have been uplifted out of the water and, in some cases, tilted, forming the fossil-bearing layers seen on land. Steno published his findings in 1669.[12]

Meanwhile, Bishop James Ussher, in his famous book, *The Annals of the World* (1650), had added up the years listed in the genealogies of Adam's descendants and dated not just Adam but the universe and Earth to 4004 BC. Steno did not directly challenge Ussher's 4004 BC date. But Steno's principles of geology would raise questions about how the Genesis 1 account fits with the new geology discoveries of evidence of an older Earth.

Challenges from Dinosaur Fossils

In the subsequent decades, fossils of unknown gigantic animals were discovered in sedimentary rock layers in England. An enormous Jurassic reptile became a sensation. William Buckland (1784–1856), an English clergyman, geologist, and paleontologist, named it *Megalosaurus*, meaning giant reptile. In 1822, Buckland was the first scientist to write a complete description of a fossil dinosaur in a scientific journal.

Gideon Mantell (1790–1852), an English country doctor, was also becoming an avid fossil hunter. As the story goes, his wife, Mary, went for a walk and found some huge animal teeth. After examining them, Dr. Mantell concluded that they resembled the teeth of an iguana lizard, only many times larger, indicating an extinct reptile about thirty feet long. So he named the fossil reptile Iguanodon, meaning iguana tooth. Later he found the fossilized bones of another extinct reptile, a fifteen-foot-long Hylaeosaurus. The famous anatomist Sir Richard Owen categorized Megalosaurus, Iguanodon, and Hylaeosaurus as a new class of animals: the dinosaurs.

▼ **William Buckland with Fossils**

By Unknown, public domain, https://commons. Wikimedia.org. https://commons.wikimedia.org/w/index.php?cu- rid=7741031/w/index.php?curid=516193

---

12 Nicolas Steno, *De Solido Intra Solidum Naturaliter Contento Dissertationis Prodromus.*

Others found more dinosaur fossils. Scientists soon realized that dinosaur fossils were almost exclusively in three geological layers—the Triassic, Jurassic, and Cretaceous—forming what Mantell called the Age of Reptiles, the Mesozoic Era. Paleontologists realized that each era has distinct kinds of fossils. The lowest layers (Paleozoic Era) have primitive sea fossils, middle layers (Mesozoic Era subdivided into Triassic, Jurassic, Cretaceous periods) have dinosaur fossils, and the upper geological layers have large mammal fossils (Cenozoic Era). Scientists also noticed that each of the three distinct dinosaur fossil-bearing Mesozoic layers (Triassic, Jurassic, Cretaceous) has its unique kinds of dinosaur fossils. This scientific evidence pointed to a much older Earth.

The disparity between Bishop Ussher's 4004 BC creation date and the new scientific discoveries indicating an older Earth presented a problem to Bible believers. In response to these challenges, Bible believers developed three prominent creation theories:

- The Gap Theory inserted a gap of time—including the Age of Reptiles—between Genesis 1:1 and 1:3.
- Old Earth Creationism accepts the older ages claimed by science but proposed that the six days of creation were long day-ages of millions of years.
- Young Earth Creationism rejected older ages and claimed God created an already "mature" universe and Earth about 4004 BC (at most 10,000 BC).

Do any of these three theories fully fit the Bible and solve the great creation puzzle?

Chapter 5

Has the Gap Theory Solved the Great Creation Puzzle?

The Scottish and English founders of the Gap Theory (Creation-Ruin-Restoration Theory), including William Buckland, lived during the fascinating discoveries of geologic layers and dinosaur fossils. These discoveries suggested that Earth is much older than 6,000 years.

These Gap Theory founders accepted a literal "In the beginning God created the heavens and the earth," as well as God's six literal days of work. To fit with the scientific discoveries, they added a new creation stage, a middle stage. The Gap Theory would "become so sacrosanct with some that to question it is equivalent to tampering with Sacred Scripture."[13]

Three Big Ideas: Literal "In the Beginning," Nonliteral Gap, Literal Six Days

To answer the challenges introduced by geology and dinosaur fossils, the founders of the Gap Theory proposed an additional stage in creation, forming a three stage creation theory: creation, ruin, and restoration.

1. Creation

Gap theorists affirm that "in the beginning God created the heavens and the earth" (Gen. 1:1), meaning the literal heavens and literal planet Earth. Thomas Chalmers, a founder of the Gap Theory, wrote that Genesis 1:1 "forms no part of the first day, but refers to a period of indefinite antiquity when God created the worlds out of nothing." This view agrees with the Hebrew text of Genesis 1:1.

2. Ruin

Gap theorists propose that between Genesis 1:1 and 1:3 there was a time gap, not reported by the Bible, with millions of years and events. In that time gap, God created a first set of life—prehistoric plants; prehistoric animals, including dinosaurs; and pre-Adamite (their word) hominid people. Everything was perfect. Then, still in that time gap, Lucifer (Satan) rebelled against God, influenced the pre-Adamite people to sin, and ruined the Earth and its life. Gap theorists translate Genesis 1:2 as "But the earth became a waste and void, and darkness was upon the face of the deep." A

---

13 Bernard Ramm, *The Christian View of Science and Scripture* (1954) in "Gap Creationism," Wikipedia.

tremendous worldwide prehistoric flood, called Lucifer's Flood, engulfed that first life—including the dinosaurs and evil pre-Adamite people—buried them, and turned them into fossils.[14] So Earth "became a waste and void" in a time gap in Genesis 1:2.

3. Restoration

Gap theorists believe that in six literal days God restored Earth and re-created life—modern plants, modern animals, and modern humans, including Adam and Eve (Gen. 1:3–31).

Support and Opposition from the Hebrew Text of the Bible

The Hebrew text of the Bible supports the beginning and six days of creation but not ruin and restoration.

1. Creation: Biblical

Gap Theory advocates are correct that Genesis 1:1 declares the literal *ex nihilo* creation of the universe and planet Earth in the beginning time. "In the beginning God created the heavens and the earth" is Biblical.

2. Ruin: Not Biblical

A time gap—first creation of life, Earth ruined, Lucifer's Flood—is not Biblical. Contrary to the Gap Theory, the Bible does not describe a first creation of life or pre-Adamites sinning. Genesis 1:2 does not report the ruination of earth by Lucifer's flood. Genesis 1:2 is simply a description of planet Earth's condition after its creation in Genesis 1:1. Genesis 1:2 says, "Now the earth was *tōhû vᵃbōhû* [uninhabitable and uninhabited]," deep sea covered, and dark.

Response: Genesis 1:2 does not report a gap or the first creation of life, pre-Adamite sinners, or Lucifer's flood.

Contrary to the Gap Theory, the supposed events in the "gap" are not in the Bible. There was no first creation of life. Adam, not pre-Adamites, was the first human to sin. And there was no "Lucifer's Flood" forming the fossil layers.

Response: Genesis 1:2 is a description, not a ruination event.

All of Genesis 1:3–31 is historical narrative (objectively shown by the Hebrew *vav* consecutive series), reporting successive events. Genesis 1:1 reports the creation of the heavens and the earth. Genesis 1:3–31 reports God's work making Earth lighted, habitable, and inhabited. Verse 2 is the one verse in Genesis 1 in which the Hebrew grammar does not report events (objectively shown by the three Hebrew *vav* disjunctive clauses making up the verse and indicating a description).

Gap theorists (mis)translated the verb "was" (*hāyâ*) (contrary to the context and

---

14 Hugh Miller, *The Testimony of the Rocks* (Edinburgh: Constable, 1857).

Hebrew grammar) in Genesis 1:2 as "became": "But the earth *became* a waste." The Hebrew grammar (*vav* disjunctives) shows that Genesis 1:2 does not report events but describes the unfinished conditions on Earth after its creation in 1:1. The Earth was (not became) uninhabitable, uninhabited, dark, and water-covered at the end of the 1:1 creation of the heavens and the earth.

First action   In-beginning God created the-heavens and-the-earth.
Description   Now-the-earth was uninhabitable and uninhabited/empty
(*tōhû vᵃbōhû*),
    and-darkness *was* over *the* surface of *the* deep,
    and-Spirit of God *was* hovering over *the* surface of the-waters.
Next actions   And-said God, "Let-be light,"
    and-was light (Gen. 1:1–3, from Hebrew).[15]

After the initial creation in Genesis 1:1, Genesis 1:2 pauses the action with a Hebrew *vav* disjunctive prefixed noun, "Now-the-earth was uninhabitable." The rules of Hebrew grammar explain:

- A ***vav*-disjunctive**-prefixed noun starting a clause or sentence interrupts the narrative flow of actions to describe the circumstances of that noun. ("Now-the-earth was uninhabitable.")

The *vav*-disjunctive-prefixed noun "Now-the-earth" indicates 1:2 describes the conditions on Earth—"Now-the-earth was uninhabitable." The *vav* disjunctive shows 1:2 does not narrate events and does not say, "But the earth *became* a waste."

3. Restoration: Biblical and Not Biblical

Gap theorists believe that in six literal days God restored Earth and re-created life. The six days are Biblical, but not as a restoration. Genesis 1:3–31 narrates God's six described literal days of work, but not as a restoration and re-creation.

Summary and Evaluation of the Gap Theory

1. The Bible supports the "in the beginning" (Gen. 1:1) creation of the heavens and the earth before the six days.
2. A supposed time gap in Genesis 1:2—with a first creation of vast ancient life that a fictitious Lucifer's Flood ruined, forming the fossil layers—is not supported by the Bible.
3. The six literal days are supported by the Bible, although not as a re-creation.

---

15 *Vav*-consecutive-prefixed verbs starting clauses and sentences in a series narrate sequential actions ("Then-said God, 'Let-be light,' and-was light") and indicate historical narrative of sequential events in passing time.

These Bible-believing Gap advocates were sincerely trying to reconcile the Bible and scientific discoveries. But a time gap (a claimed time period between Genesis 1:1 and 1:3 not supported by the Hebrew text of the Bible) does not fit the Hebrew text. An erroneous theory can hold sway for a long time. For over a century, many Christians worldwide accepted the Gap Theory and Lucifer's Flood as the answer to Earth's fossils and apparent older age. But the idea of a time gap, with a first creation of life and its destruction by a supposed Lucifer's Flood, is not in agreement with the Bible and is not the solution to the great creation puzzle.

With the demise of the Gap Theory, creationists split between two competing creationism groups: Old Earth Creationism and Young Earth Creationism. Old Earth creationists take Genesis 1:1 literally but developed the idea of six long "day-ages" of millions of years. Young Earth creationists take the six days literally. But instead of taking literally the creation of the heavens and the earth in Genesis 1:1, they developed the idea that all creation—including the creation of the heavens and the earth—was in six days, a Creation Week. In the ensuing struggle between these two big groups, historical Two Stage Creation—taking literally both "in the beginning" and the six days—was overlooked.

Chapter 6

Has Day-Age Old Earth Creationism Solved the Creation Puzzle?

Bold truth seekers have considered the fine-tuning of the universe and the beautiful match between the Bible and the physical creation. The fine-tuning indicates a Creator, and the match between the Bible and the physical creation demonstrates that the God of the Bible is that Creator.

One Astrophysicist's Journey to Belief in the Creator

Hugh Ross as a young adult was an unbelieving astrophysicist. When he thought about the universe, he wondered, "Who did all this?" He found the answer in a gift Bible. He realized that the creation events described in the Bible "perfectly matched the established record of nature." Over the next several years, as Hugh Ross continued reading the Bible without finding "a single provable error or contradiction," he realized that the Bible's "perfection could come only from the Creator Himself." He testifies,

> I saw that my only rational option was to trust in the Bible's Inspirer to at least the same degree as I relied on the laws of physics. I realized, too, what a self-sufficient young man I had been. After a long evening of studying the salvation passages in the New Testament, I humbled myself before God, asking Him to forgive me of my self-exaltation . . . and received Christ as my Lord and Savior.[16]

Hugh Ross continued studying science and the Bible. He developed a growing list of fine-tuned aspects of the universe that make sense only if the Creator designed them. When he found a consistent match between the evidence in the created universe and the Bible creation texts, he realized that the Bible's double claim of the beginning and stretching out of the universe parallels the two main events of the Big Bang, a sudden beginning and expansion of the universe. But the Big Bang theory does not explain how that Big Bang started. The Bible does: "In the beginning God created the heavens and the earth." Continuing breakthroughs in the natural sciences have consistently made "the case for Christianity even stronger."[17] Hugh

---

16 Hugh Ross, *The Creator and the Cosmos* (Downers Grove: NavPress, 2001), 18–20.
17 Hugh Ross, *The Creator and the Cosmos* (Downers Grove: NavPress, 2001), 19–21.

Ross has become an outstanding apologist for Biblical Christianity and Day-Age Old Earth Creationism (OEC). I have attended lectures by Hugh Ross and respect him as a godly Christian man.

Seven Big Ideas of Day-Age Old Earth Creationism

Day-Age Old Earth creationists emphasize seven big ideas:

1. The fine-tuning of the universe indicates there is a Creator.
2. God gave two sources of truth about creation: the Bible and the physical creation.
3. The match between the Bible and creation indicates that the God of the Bible is the Creator.
4. God created the literal heavens and literal Earth in the literal beginning.
5. Creation evidence consistently indicates the heavens and Earth are much older than 6,000 years. The Bible is compatible with an older creation but not with blind evolution.
6. The Bible says Adam's sin began human death, but the cause of animal death is unmentioned.
7. Six long day-ages may be how Genesis 1 fits with an older creation.[18]

Old Earth creationists believe the eternal triune God of the Bible is the Creator of the universe and everything in it. God is truthful, so the Bible is true. Genesis 1 records the events of the creation. This Bible record and the physical creation will match.

Genesis 1:1 declares God created the literal heavens with its galaxies and the literal planet Earth in the beginning. The universe was fine-tuned precisely for future human life on Earth. Genesis 1:2 reports that the Earth was unfinished. Genesis 1:3–31 reports six days of God's work finishing Earth. Science evidence indicates that the Earth is older. Science tells us that the universe is about 13.8 billion years old, Earth about 4.5 billion years old, and life several billion years old. *Yôm*, "day," could mean "a period of time," so OEC developed the idea that each day was a day-age lasting millions of years. The six days must have been long day-ages of millions of years during which God finished the earth, started plant life, started animal life, and finally made the first human pair—Adam and Eve—in His image.

Support and Opposition from the Hebrew Text of the Bible

The Hebrew text of the Bible supports many key OEC ideas but not long day-ages.

---

18 Old Earth creationists may include advocates of the Framework Hypothesis and Analogical Days.

1. The fine-tuning of the universe indicates there is a Creator.

The Bible says, "The heavens declare the glory of God" (Psa. 19:1). The universe, Earth, and life are fine-tuned, indicating there is a Designer-Creator.

Old Earth creationists emphasize that the just-right laws, the fine-tuned constants, and the just-right events forming Earth point to a Creator instead of blind chance as the cause. A few of the fine-tuned items precisely suitable for life on Earth are

just right gravity,
just right electromagnetism,
just right nuclear forces,
just right density and expansion of the universe,
just right constant speed of light,
just right temperature on Earth for liquid water,
just right plate tectonics,
just right moon for Earth's tides and stabilizing Earth's tilt,
just right size of Earth,
just right distance of Earth from the sun,
just right Jupiter to sweep up many comets that might otherwise hit Earth, and
just right location of Earth in our galaxy's habitable zone.[19]

Hugh Ross has a much longer list of fine-tuned aspects of the universe and Earth.[20]

An Israeli physicist agrees that the universe is fine-tuned for life on Earth. He writes about one incredibly fine-tuned constant:

Professor Weinberg is an avowed skeptic . . . but even he agrees . . . , "Life as we know it . . . would be impossible if any one of several physical quantities had slightly different values. . . . One constant does seem to require incredibly fine-tuning." This constant has to do with the energy of the big bang. Weinberg qualifies the tuning as one part in 10^{120}. Scientific notation is an understatement and so I will expand that exponential into decimal notation. If the energy of the Big Bang were different by one part out of 100000000000000000000000000 0000000000000000000000000000000000000000000000000000000 00000000000000000000000000000000000000000 there would be no life anywhere in our universe. The universe is tuned for life from its inception.[21]

The likelihood of chance alone bringing about the exact laws, precise constants

---

19 Many of these are from Jay Richards, "List of Fine-Tuning Parameters," http://www.discovery.org/f/11011.

20 Hugh Ross, *The Fingerprint of God*, 129–131; *The Creator and the Cosmos*, 3rd edition (Colorado Springs, CO: NavPress, 2001), 145–157, 245–248; http://www.reasons.org/articles/fine-tuning-for-life-in-the-universe.

21 Steven Weinberg, "Life in the Quantum Universe," *Scientific American*, April 1995, quoted by Gerald Schroeder, *The Science of God* (New York: Broadway Books, 1997), 5.

in the universe, and just right events for life on our planet Earth is essentially zero. Many scientists have concluded that there must be a Designer-Creator.[22]

Yet many of these fine-tuned items (constant speed of light and expansion of the universe) indicate an older universe and Earth. Some of these truth seekers recognize only an Intelligent Designer, but Old Earth Creationism goes the next step and recognizes who He is—the God of the Bible.

2. God gave two sources of truth about creation: the Bible and physical creation.

Most Old Earth creationists recognize that the Bible is inspired and true. They also recognize that God created the universe and that the evidence God built into the created universe reveals truth.

Most Old Earth Creationists agree with Hugh Ross: "The Bible was supernaturally accurate and thus supernaturally inspired. Its perfection could only come from the Creator Himself." He "also recognized that the Bible stood alone in revealing God."[23] The Bible account and scientific discoveries about the creation match so precisely that the Bible uniquely must have been inspired by the Creator.

The Bible declares that the created universe reveals truth. The Bible also explains that the evidence in the creation is clear and reveals the Creator's attributes, power, and divine nature.

> For his invisible attributes, namely, his eternal power and divine nature, have been clearly perceived, ever since the creation of the world, in the things that have been made. So they are without excuse (Rom. 1:20).

God's attributes include His absolute truthfulness. Therefore, we should believe Romans 1:20 and Psalm 19:1–2, which tell us that the evidence in creation also reveals true knowledge.

---

22 Intelligent Design recognizes design in the old universe and Earth but is not the same as Old Earth Creationism (OEC). Like OEC, Intelligent Design recognizes an older universe, Earth, and life and sees the fine-tuning and evidence of design. "The theory of intelligent design holds that certain features of the universe and of living things are best explained by an intelligent cause, not an undirected process such as natural selection." However, unlike any creationism theory, "the scientific theory of intelligent design does not claim that modern biology [or any other science] can identify whether the intelligent cause detected through science is supernatural" (http://www.intelligentdesign.org). Intelligent Design investigates natural evidence of design that can be observed by the scientific method, not a supernatural ultimate cause that cannot be observed by science.

23 Hugh Ross, *The Creator and the Cosmos* (Downers Grove: NavPress, 2001), 20.

The heavens declare the glory of God,
and the sky above proclaims his handiwork.
Day to day pours out speech,
and night to night reveals knowledge (Psa. 19:1–2).

Because the evidence God built into the creation is true and reliable, we can use it to learn about God and discover information about the creation of the universe. The Bible does not date the creation, and the evidence in the creation is reliable, so the universe and Earth are as old as the physical evidence indicates.

3. The match between the Bible and creation indicates that the God of the Bible is the Creator.

Edwin Hubble discovered that the galaxies are receding away from each other, indicating that the universe is expanding. A universe that is expanding requires a time when the expansion started. In 1931, Einstein, Hubble, and Lemaître met and concluded that the universe did indeed have a beginning. The evidence God built into the universe shows it had a beginning and has been expanding ever since.

Long before modern science, the Bible already proclaimed that the universe had a beginning and has been stretching out or expanding ever since.

God, the LORD . . . created the heavens and stretched them out (Isa. 42:5).

Far from requiring atheism, the actual evidence of a sudden beginning and expansion of the universe—derisively called the Big Bang by atheist Fred Hoyle, who vehemently opposed the idea—is robust support for the God of the Bible. Moreover, the Bible alone long ago proclaimed the same two facts of the beginning and expansion of the universe, powerful evidence that the God of the Bible is the Creator.

4. God created the literal heavens and literal earth in the literal beginning.

Genesis 1:1 should be taken literally. God created the universe: the literal heavens and the literal earth, planet Earth, "in the beginning." God created all the materials of the universe, and then from those materials, He made the universe and planet Earth all "in the beginning."

5. The Bible is compatible with older creation, but not with blind evolution.

Creation evidence consistently indicates the heavens and the Earth are much older than 6,000 years. Old Earth creationists recognize that the Bible nowhere dates the creation to 4004 BC or any other date. Because the Bible does not date the universe, we may estimate its age from the truth-revealing evidence God built into the universe.

Old Earth creationists believe the Bible teaches that the evidence God built into the universe is trustworthy (Psa. 19:1–2). They point out that the most distant galaxy seen so far is over 13 billion light-years away. So its light has taken over 13 billion years to reach us and is over 13 billion years old when it arrives, based on its calculated distance and the constant speed of light. The latest calculation indicates the universe is about 13.8 billion years old.

The Earth is also old. Old Earth creationists see evidence from essentially every science—from archaeology to zoology—indicating that the Earth is older. Some of the many sources of evidence that the Earth is older are ice cores, coral reefs, crystal formation, historic volcano eruptions, plate tectonics, and meteor strikes. These "multiple independent confirmations"[24] strengthen the case that Earth is older.

Belief in an older universe does not equate to assuming chance is the source of the universe with its precise physical laws. Nor does belief in an older Earth equate to assuming blind evolution is the source of all life on Earth, including humans. Old Earth creationists vary in how much evolution they accept, from only microevolution (all dogs, wolves, and coyotes come from the specially created dog kind) to full theistic evolution. But all reject chance alone as the source of the universe and its physical laws and blind evolution alone as the source of all life, including humans.

6. The Bible says Adam's sin began human death but does not state that his sin began all animal death.

The Bible explicitly states that Adam's sin spread death to all humans. "Therefore, just as sin came into the world through one man, and death through sin, and so death spread to all men [*anthrōpŏs*, humans] because all sinned" (Rom. 5:12). Hugh Ross's website explains, "The Bible does not state that . . . animal death was introduced the moment Adam sinned."[25]

Old Earth creationists recognize that the fossil evidence reveals that animals died before Adam's Fall. But God describes His work as good. Therefore, many Old Earth advocates propose that animal death before Adam's sin was beneficial. "Carnivorous activity is the key to ecosystem regulation and stability."[26] Thus, many Old Earth creationists conclude that animal death is compatible with God's good creation. Others conclude that Bible evidence suggests Satan, after being thrown to Earth, started animal death.[27]

---

24 Craig Rusbult, "How Should We Interpret the Two Books of God, in Scripture and Nature?" www.asa3.org/ASA/education/origins/agelogic-cr.htm.

25 Krista Bontrager, "Animal Death and the Atonement," www.reasons.org/explore/publications/reasons-newsletter/read/reasons-newsletter/2012/03/02/animal-death-and-the-atonement, accessed Nov. 12, 2018.

26 Fazale Rana, "Animal Death Prevents Ecological Meltdown," www.reasons.org/explore/publications/connections/read/connections/2003/10/02/animal-death-prevents-ecological-meltdown, accessed Nov. 11, 2018.

27 Krista Bontrager, "Animal Death and the Atonement." To the assertion that animal death before Adam undermines Jesus' atonement for sin, an article in Hugh Ross's *Reasons to Believe* website answers, "The atonement applies to humans, the one and only sinful species. . . . Christians are right to want to preserve the

7. Six long day-ages may be how Genesis 1 fits an older creation.

These sincere truth seekers ask, How can the six days in Genesis 1 be compatible with an older universe and older Earth? Old Earth creationists developed the idea of day-ages—six long "days" of millions of years for God's work in Genesis 1.

The Hebrew word *yôm,* "day," can have several definitions:

- Any daytime
- Daylight hours from sunrise to sunset; daytime as opposed to nighttime
- One day consisting of daytime and nighttime; one rotation of Earth
- A period of time

This last definition, occasionally used in prophecy (e.g., "Day of the LORD"), can indicate a longer period of time. OEC says each of the six creation days may "refer to something like millions of years."[28]

Six day-ages allow for an older Earth and older life. The sixth day as a day-age of many thousands of years allows a much older date for Adam. Most Old Earth creationists believe that Adam and Eve were literal people and the first true humans, living 10,000 to 70,000 years ago. Many believe that earlier hominids (Neanderthals, Homo Erectus, Australopithecus) lived before Adam but were not actual humans.

Day-ages may not be the best solution to the creation puzzle, but to many in OEC at that time, this seemed to be the best way to reconcile the Bible account with evidence of an old Earth. Are day-ages of millions of years a sound Biblical solution to the creation puzzle?

Response: In Genesis 1, yôm *means a literal day-night day.*

Does the idea of day-ages fit the Bible text? Old Earth creationists chose "a period of time" of millions of years as the definition of *yôm* in "day one" (*yôm ehād* in Genesis 1:5). But does a day lasting millions of years fit the Genesis 1:3–5 Bible context?

A basic principle of Bible interpretation is that the correct sense of a word is the meaning intended by the author as indicated by his choice of words in the sentence and by the sentences in the surrounding context:

And-called God the light day, and the darkness He called night.
And-was evening, and-was morning, day one [*yôm ehād*] (Gen. 1:5, from Hebrew).

The context around *yôm ehād* in Genesis 1:3–5 is day and night, the latter consisting of evening until morning. This context indicates "day one" was one literal day-night day, fitting the definition "one day consisting of daytime and nighttime."[29] Day one

---

integrity of the Atonement. But to say the old-earth belief of pre-Fall animal death undermines Jesus' work on the cross is to make a serious charge based on insufficient biblical evidence."

28 Hugh Ross, *The Creation and Time* (Colorado Springs: NavPress, 1994), 45.

29 James Stambaugh, "The Days of Creation: A Semantic Approach," *CEN Tech. J.*, vol. 5(1), 1991, 70–78.

sets the meaning of *yôm* ("day") for all six numbered days of God's work as day-night days. The idea of millions-of-years-long day-ages does not fit the context around *yôm ehād* ("day one") in Genesis 1.

The evidence for an older creation seems substantial. But how can six literal days fit with an older creation? The answer is in part two of this book.

Summary and Evaluation of Day-Age Old Earth Creationism

1. The fine-tuning of the universe does indicate a Creator.
2. God's inspired Word, the Bible, is true; His creation work reveals reliable evidence.[30]
3. The match of the two sources of truth indicates that the God of the Bible is the Creator.
4. OEC takes Genesis 1:1 literally—God created the heavens and earth in the beginning.
5. The Bible does support God, not blind evolution, as the source of life and humans.
6. A fuller answer to animal death seems needed.
7. The claim that a day (*yôm*) was millions of years does not fit the context of Genesis 1.

Old Earth creationists are to be honored for their outstanding work showing the fine-tuning requiring a Creator. OEC emphasizes that the match between the physical creation and the Bible is compelling evidence that the God of the Bible is the Creator. And OEC takes Genesis 1:1 literally as the literal creation of the universe and Earth in the beginning time. But *yôm* as millions-of-years-long day-ages does not fit the Bible context of Genesis 1:3–5. Is there a solution that includes the Biblical ideas of OEC yet understands *yôm* in its Bible context?

---

30 OEC may overreach on this point, making the two equal sources of truth.

Chapter 7

Has Six-Days-Only Young Earth Creationism Fully Solved the Creation Puzzle?

The advocates of Young Earth Creationism are faithful Bible supporters and sincere Christians whom I respect. They hold firmly to the Bible and its teachings on the Trinity, the deity of Christ Jesus, His virgin conception and birth, His substitutionary death and atonement for our sin, His bodily resurrection, the gospel of salvation by Jesus alone through faith alone according to the Bible alone, His coming again, His future Millennial reign and Judgment Day, and the eternal New Heavens and New Earth. I agree with these truths.

Four Big Ideas of Six-Days-Only Young Earth Creationism

Young Earth Creationism (YEC) affirms four big ideas on creation. First, YEC affirms that the Bible is God's inerrant Word and is 100 percent true. Genesis 1 should be interpreted by the plain literal sense. Second, YEC affirms that the eternal God of the Bible is the Creator of all things. Third, YEC affirms that the plain literal sense of *yôm*, with a number and evening and morning, is a literal day. These three beliefs are supported by the Bible, historically affirmed by the church, and held by myself.

Six-Days-Only Young Earth Creationism's fourth big idea about creation is unique. YEC advocates teach that the phrase "*in six days*" found in English translations of Exodus 20:11 means that God created all things in only the six days, in a Creation Week. This is the Six-Days-Only part of YEC.

A series of cascading ideas results from YEC's fourth big idea. Because YEC believes that everything was created "in six days," Genesis 1:1 must have taken place on day one. Key YEC leaders teach that Genesis 1:1 was in day one, "in the beginning" must mean all time, "the heavens" must mean all space, and "the earth" must mean all matter, all starting on day one.[31] If the universe is only a few days older than Adam, and Adam's descendants' genealogies date Adam to about 4000 BC,[32] then the universe and Earth are only about 6,000 years old. If the universe and Earth are about 6,000 years old but look older, they must have been created with an appearance of

---

31 Henry M. Morris, *Biblical Creationism* (Grand Rapids: Baker Book House, 1994), 17–20; Ken Ham, *Dinosaurs in Eden* (Green Forest: Master Books, 2001), 9.

32 Some YEC advocates allow up to 10,000 BC.

age. Because death is the result of sin and there was no sin before Adam's Fall, there was no death before Adam's Fall and therefore no fossils before about 6,000 years ago. Most of the geologic layers with fossils were laid down by Noah's Flood, which took place about 2348 BC.[33] All of these ideas are based primarily on "For *in* six days" found in English translations of Exodus 20:11.

Support and Opposition from the Hebrew Text of the Bible

The Bible supports the first three big ideas of Young Earth Creationism.

1. **The Bible is God's Word and 100 percent true. Interpret it in a plain literal sense.**

   Biblical authority is the foundational issue to Young Earth creationists, both for founders Henry Morris and John Whitcomb in the past and for Ken Ham today. They believe the six days were literal days because they believe the Bible is God's sole, inspired, infallible revelation and is 100 percent true and should be interpreted by the plain literal meaning, starting with Genesis 1.

   In an article titled "Why Study Hebrew Words," the founding chairman of the board for Answers in Genesis–USA, Don Landis, is quoted: "Perhaps the most basic principle of proper hermeneutics is to understand what the words themselves mean." He explained that this "is critical to those of us who hold to a literal, historical, contextual and grammatical interpretation of Scripture. *Every single word was inspired and chosen by the Holy Spirit*. . . . God guided the biblical writers to give us the exact words He wanted in the original manuscripts. . . . Our English Bibles are translations of copies of the originals. Nuances can be lost in the transmission process, and meanings of words can change over time. So it is important to study diligently what each word means" (emphasis his).[34] Scripture agrees. Two Stage Biblical Creation agrees.

2. **The eternal triune God of the Bible is the Creator of all things out of nothing.**

   YEC firmly believes that the God of the Bible is the Creator of the universe. God created all things out of nothing (*ex nihilo*). Scripture agrees. Two Stage Biblical Creation agrees.

3. **The plain sense of *yôm*, with a number and evening and morning, is a literal day.**

   YEC believes in interpreting the Bible by the plain literal sense of the words and sentences in context. The plain sense of *yôm*, in the context of a number and evening

---

33 Some YEC advocates allow up to 3300 BC.

34 John C. P. Smith, "Why Study Hebrew Words?" Answers in Genesis, April 10, 2015, accessed Nov. 27, 2021; Don Landis, "Meaningful Words," Answers in Genesis, April 1, 2013.

and morning, is a literal day.[35] "Everywhere else in the Old Testament, when the Hebrew word for 'day' (םוֹי, *yôm*) appears with 'evening' or 'morning' or is modified by a number (e.g., 'sixth day' or 'five days'), it always means a 24-hour day."[36] Scripture agrees. Two Stage Biblical Creation agrees.

YEC leaders are to be honored for upholding that the Bible is true, the God of the Bible is the Creator, and the six days were literal days. These three big YEC claims are Biblical beliefs.

4. **Exodus 20:11 and 31:17 (in English versions) say *"in* six days," so all creation was in six days.**

    Modern Six-Days-Only YEC claims that everything was created in only six days. This unique belief of modern Six-Days-Only YEC—that all creation was in only six consecutive days and none "in the beginning" before day one—is based on *"in* six days" as found in most English Bible translations of Exodus 20:11 and 31:17.

    > Six days shalt thou labour, and do all thy work: But the seventh day *is* the sabbath of the Lord thy God: *in it* thou shalt not do any work. . . . For *in six days* the Lord made heaven and earth, the sea, and all that in them *is*, and rested the seventh day (Exod. 20:9–11, KJV).

YEC understands Exodus 20:11 as follows:

- The *"in"* in many translations of Exodus 20:11 means all creation was *"in* six days."
- *"Asâh"* ("do, make, . . . work") in 20:11 means "created." "He created in six days."[37]
- The items created *"in* six days" were the heavens, earth, sea, and everything in them.

Six-Days-Only YEC, based on the *"in"* of *"in* six days" in many English translations, claims God created everything *"in* six days" with no creation "in the beginning" before the six days. A leading Six-Days-Only Young Earth creationist claims the highest authority for this:

> "For in six days the Lord made the heavens and the earth, the sea, and all that is in them, and rested the seventh day" (Exodus 20:11).
>
> Yes, Jesus did explicitly say He created in six days. Not only this, but the one who spoke the words "six days" also wrote them down for Moses: "Then the Lord delivered to me two tablets of stone written with the finger of God, and on them

---

35 Ken Ham, *The New Answers Book 1* (Green Forest: Master Books 2010), Terry Mortenson, 26; James Stambaugh, "The Days of Creation: A Semantic Approach," *CEN Tech. Journal*, vol. 5(1), 1991, 70–78.

36 Terry Mortenson, "Six Literal Days," 4/1/2010, answersingenesis.org/days-of-creation/six-literal-days.

37 Ken Ham, *The New Answers Book 1* (Green Forest: Master Books 2010), 258.

were all the words which the LORD had spoken to you on the mountain from the midst of the fire in the day of the assembly" (Deuteronomy 9:10).

Jesus said clearly that He created in six days! And He even did something He didn't do with most of Scripture—He wrote it down Himself. How more authoritative can you get than that?[38]

Recently a Six-Days-Only Young Earth creationist and astrophysicist explained, "We can come to no other conclusion than that God created supernaturally in six ordinary days, and this happened a few thousand years ago. God makes it clear that He created in six days in Genesis chapter 1, for example. This is reaffirmed in Exodus chapter 20 verse 11 where it says, 'In six days the LORD made the heavens and earth, the sea, and all that in them is,' indicating that everything that God made was made in the span of six days."[39] He based his belief on an "*in*" added to Exodus 20:11.

These sincere Six-Days-Only Young Earth creationists correctly recognize that God's Word is 100 percent true.[40] And their English Bible translation says "in six days" (Exod. 20:11). So God must have created everything "in six days," in one "Creation Week" (a term not in the Bible).

Response: "In six days" is not in the inspired Hebrew text of the Bible.

All creation "in six days" is not in the inspired, inerrant original Hebrew text of the Bible. What God wrote in the fourth of the Ten Commandments, wrote in Hebrew on the tablet of stone, and gave to Moses was (Exodus 20:11, reading Hebrew from right to left):

כי ששת־ימים עשה יהוה את־ השמים ואת־הארץ את־הים ואת־כל־ אשר־ בם
them in that all and sea the earth the and heavens the on God worked days six For

For six [*shêshet*, no "*b^e*," no "*in*"] days *the* LORD did-work [*asâh*] on the heavens and the earth, the sea, and all that *is* in them (Exod. 20:11, from Hebrew).

What God wrote was כי ששת־ימים, "*Kî shêshet yāmîm*," "For six days," not "For in six days," not "*Kî b^eshêshet yāmîm*." In the inspired Hebrew text of 20:11, there is no "in." The inerrant Hebrew text of the Bible does not say God created everything in six days. There is no basis in the Hebrew grammar or words for adding "in" to 20:11 or 31:17.

Every verse in the five books of Moses with the translation "for in" (KJV) contains the Hebrew *b^e* ("in"), except Exodus 20:11 and 31:17. There is no *b^e*, no "*in*," in the Hebrew

---

38 Ken Ham, "Did Jesus Say He Created in Six Literal Days?" Answers in Genesis, Dec. 20, 2007, accessed Oct. 6, 2019, https://answersingenesis.org/days-of-creation/did-jesus-say-he-created-in-six-literal-days.

39 *The Frank Pastore Show*, interview with Hugh Ross and Jason Lisle, March 31, 2010.

40 I agree that the Bible in the autographs is 100 percent true. But the "in" added to the Bible is not.

first phrase of Exodus 20:11 or the same phrase in 31:17. *Nowhere* does the inspired, inerrant Hebrew Bible text (or Greek NT) say God created everything "in six days."

"*In*" was added by a second-century BC Greek translation (Septuagint or LXX, generally a helpful translation, but not here) from Alexandria, Egypt. Unfortunately, most English versions copied the "*in*" added by the LXX and so translated Exodus 20:11, "For *in* six days," instead of the words God wrote: "For six days." (The KJV and NKJV italicize "*in*," indicating "*in*" is not in the inspired Hebrew text, and Young's Literal Translation correctly has no "in.") YEC interprets the entire Genesis 1 account through the lens of this errant translation of Exodus 20:11 with the added "*in*."

Continued Response: In context, asâh *means worked; God worked six days.*

Six-Days-Only YEC interprets *asâh* ("do, make, . . . work") in Exodus 20:11 as "created." "He created in six days."[41]

Does *asâh* in Exodus 20:11 mean "created" or "worked"? The standard Hebrew lexicon, *The Brown-Driver-Briggs Hebrew and English Lexicon*, states that *asâh* has the basic meaning of "do, make." Subpoint 1 explains that "do = perform a work," "work with," "of God's working with," so *asâh* means "do, make, . . . work." Lower in the list of subpoints is "of God's making (creating)."[42] "For six days *the* LORD *asâh* [created or did-work-on?] the heavens and the earth, the sea, and all that *is* in them, and rested on the seventh day" (from Hebrew). Did God create everything "*in* six days"? Or did God *bārā'*, "create," the heavens and the earth in the beginning (Gen. 1:1) and then work six days (Gen. 1:3–31) on what He had already created *ex nihilo* in Genesis 1:1 but was still uninhabitable, uninhabited, sea covered, and dark (Gen. 1:2)?

The context of Exodus 20:11 is the fourth commandment in Exodus 20:8–11. This context tells which meaning of *asâh* the Author, God Himself, intended. The context of the fourth commandment is to work six days but not work on the seventh.

> 20:9 Six days you shall labor and do [*asâh*] all your work (NASB).
> 20:10 but the seventh day . . . you shall not do any work [*asâh*]. . . .
> 20:11 [Because[43]] For six days *the* LORD did-work [*asâh*] . . . and rested on the seventh day (from Hebrew).

In three parallel statements God uses the word *asâh*: work six days; do not work the seventh; because for six days *the* LORD worked and rested on the seventh. *Asâh* ("do, make, . . . work") in the context of the fourth commandment (Exod. 20:8–11) to work six days but not work the seventh day has the sense "worked." God wrote, "For six days the LORD worked . . . and rested on the seventh day" (Exod. 20:11). The same word (*asâh*) used in three parallel statements in the same passage will have

---

41 Ken Ham, "Did Jesus Say He Created in Six Literal Days?"

42 Brown-Driver-Briggs, *Hebrew and English Lexicon*, #7468 (Strong's #6213), 793–794.

43 "*kî*, "may = because," Brown-Driver-Briggs, *Hebrew and English Lexicon*, #4833 (Strong's #3588), 471–474.

the same meaning. The first two uses of *asâh* mean "worked on," "do work," so the third is best understood as "worked on." God worked on the sea, making dry land appear. God filled sky and sea with life. He worked on the land, making it produce vegetation and filling it with life.

Asâh has the sense of "work on" or "do work" in all three verses. God created the heavens and the earth in the beginning (Gen. 1:1), but the earth was uninhabitable, uninhabited, sea covered, and dark (Gen. 1:2). Then He worked a total quantity[44] of six described literal days (Gen. 1:3–31), finishing what was declared unfinished (Gen. 1:2) after the *ex nihilo* creation (Gen. 1:1)—planet Earth. Without the added "*in*" that would force the Genesis 1:1 creation into the six days, Genesis 1:1 may be taken literally: God created the heavens and earth in the beginning.

Exodus 20:11 lists the things God worked on: "the heavens and the earth, the sea, and all that *is* in them." This list roughly matches God's work making Earth lighted, creating land and sea, and filling them with all kinds of life. Exodus 20:11 is about God's work in the six days of Genesis 1:3–31, not about the earlier *bārā'* creation of the universe "in the beginning" (Gen. 1:1).

Five YEC Ideas Cascading from Belief That All Creation Was "in Six Days"

4a. YEC: Because all creation was "in six days," Genesis 1:1 must have been in day one.

Henry Morris, cofounder of the modern Six-Days-Only YEC, states, "Exodus 20:11: '. . . in six days the LORD made heaven and earth, the sea, and all that in them is'. . . . If this verse means what it says, then the creation of the heavens and the earth was included with the work of the six days. Therefore, the initial creative act of Genesis 1:1 was a part of God's work on Day One" (ellipses his).[45]

Response: "In the beginning [b^{e}re'shît] God created the heavens and the earth."

Did God create everything in the six days of Genesis 1:3–31? Or did God first create the heavens and the earth "in the beginning" (Gen. 1:1) before day one on Earth?

The Hebrew word *b^{e}re'shît* ("in the beginning") and the unprefixed *re'shît* ("beginning"), when referring to time, consistently mean a beginning time or phase. The prefix *b^e* means "in." *The Brown-Driver-Briggs Hebrew and English Lexicon* (BDB) defines *re'shît* as the "beginning" and, when speaking of "the course of events," the "first phase."[46]

The English word "beginning" has several senses. "Beginning" in English can have

---

44 Cardinal numbers (four, five, six) count total quantity. The number "six" in Exodus 20:11 is cardinal, indicating God worked a total quantity of six days.

45 Henry M. Morris, *Scientific Creationism* (San Diego: Creation-Life Publishers, 1974), 237.

46 Brown, Driver, Briggs, *Hebrew and English Lexicon*, 912.

the sense of a starting instant or the sense of a beginning time. Because the English word "beginning" is ambiguous, we need to specify which sense of our ambiguous English word is the sense of the Hebrew word *re'shît*. In the Bible, *re'shît* ("beginning"), when referring to time, consistently means a beginning time or phase. Let it be very clear that I am not adding the word "time" or "phase" or "period" to the Bible text, but specifying which sense of our ambiguous English word is the sense of the Hebrew word *re'shît*. *Re'shît,* when referring to time, consistently has the sense of a beginning time/phase/duration/period (not a starting instant/moment).

Hebrew professor John Sailhamer explains, "The Hebrew word *re'shît,* which is the term for 'beginning' used in this chapter [Genesis 1], has a very specific sense in Scripture. In the Bible, the term always refers to an extended, yet indeterminate duration of time—*not* a specific moment. . . . The term does not refer to a point in time but to a *period* or *duration of time*" (emphasis his).[47]

*B*e*re'shît*, "in the beginning," in Genesis 1:1 means in *the* beginning time or in *the* beginning phase, unspecified in length by the word itself. *Brown-Driver-Briggs* defines *re'shît* when speaking of events as the "first phase."[48] For example, in Jeremiah 28:1, the *b*e*re'shît* of King Zedekiah's reign according to BDB was the "first phase" of his reign, including four years and five months of his eleven-year reign.

> In the beginning [*b*e*re'shît*] of the reign of Zedekiah king of Judah, in the fourth year, in the fifth month (Jer. 28:1, NASB).

Brown-Driver-Briggs defines *re'shît* when speaking of a person as their "early life."[49] Job's *re'shît* was all his life until his troubles, at least forty and likely seventy years (Job 8:7; 42:10–16). *B*e*re'shît* does not mean the first instant. *B*e*re'shît*, "in the beginning," in Genesis 1:1 means the beginning time or phase, lasting an unspecified number of years.

The Bible says, "In the beginning God created the heavens and the earth" (Gen. 1:1). Genesis 1:1 should be taken literally, that God created the heavens and the earth in the beginning time/phase/period, a time that even in the above human examples lasted years. *B*e*re'shît*, "in the beginning," in Genesis 1:1 refers to the extensive beginning time during which God created the literal heavens and the literal planet Earth (Gen. 1:1) before He worked six literal described days (Gen. 1:3–31) making Earth lighted, habitable, and inhabited. This "period or duration of time" was not part of the literal day-night day one on planet Earth in Genesis 1:3–5.

---

47 John Sailhamer, *Genesis Unbound*, 38.

48 Brown, Driver, Briggs, *Hebrew and English Lexicon*, 912.

49 Brown, Driver, Briggs, *Hebrew and English Lexicon*, 912.

Grammatical response: Hebrew grammar proves 1:1 occurred before day one in 1:3–5.

Genesis 1:1 is best understood grammatically as an independent declaration that "In the beginning God created the heavens and the earth," proclaiming the *ex nihilo* creation of the universe "in the beginning."[50] *Bārā', "*created," is in the Hebrew perfect construction (aspect). The Hebrew perfect indicates "completed action." God completed the *ex nihilo* creation of the heavens and the earth in the beginning time. Genesis 1:2 starts with a *vav*-disjunctive-prefixed noun, indicating a description: Now-the-earth was uninhabitable, uninhabited, sea covered, and dark. Then Genesis 1:3 begins day one with a series of Hebrew *vav*-consecutive-prefixed verbs, literally "Then-said-God 'Let-be light.' And-was light," starting day one on rotating planet Earth. "Then-said" is a Hebrew *vav* consecutive introducing the next consecutive action after the action of the *ex nihilo* creation in verse 1.

After the description in Genesis 1:2, all the subsequent clauses in Genesis 1 begin with *vav*-consecutive-prefixed verbs (underlined below), indicating historical narrative, events reported in the order in which they occurred:

First Action:

    In the beginning God created   ← First reported act, perfect verb, no *vav*

Description Interrupting the Actions:

    Now-the-earth was uninhabitable   ← *vav*-disjunctive-prefixed initial noun

Historical Narrative Series of Actions and Events in Sequential Order:

    <u>Then-said</u> God, "Let-be light,"   ← *vav*-consecutive-prefixed initial verb
    <u>Then-was</u> light.   ← *vav*-consecutive-prefixed initial verb
    <u>Then-saw</u> God the light   ← *vav*-consecutive-prefixed initial verb
    <u>Then-separated</u> God between   ← *vav*-consecutive-prefixed initial verb
    <u>Then-called</u> God *the* light day   ← *vav*-consecutive-prefixed initial verb
    <u>Then-was</u> evening,   ← *vav*-consecutive-prefixed initial verb
    <u>Then-was</u> morning, day one.   ← *vav*-consecutive-prefixed initial verb

The "in the beginning" creation of the heavens and the earth was before God commanded light, starting day one on Earth. God created the heavens and the earth in the beginning time/phase lasting an unspecified amount of time before the

---

50 I hold the traditional view that Genesis 1:1 is an independent statement/clause declaring the *ex nihilo* creation of the actual heavens and the actual earth in the beginning. This was the first stage/phase of God's work. *Bᵉreʹshît* is absolute ("it functions independently of any other word," Hamilton, *The Book of Genesis*, 103). Thus, I do *not* agree with translating Genesis 1:1 as a dependent clause: "When God began creating the heavens and the earth, the earth was chaos." Genesis 1:1 is an independent clause declaring God created *ex nihilo* the actual heavens and the actual planet Earth in the beginning time/phase.

command starting day one: "Let there be light." God created the heavens and the earth "in the beginning."

4b. YEC: Because Genesis 1:1 was in day one, "beginning" must mean time and "the heavens and the earth" must mean space and matter, all starting on day one.

If Genesis 1:1 doesn't mean God created the heavens and the earth in the beginning, what do YEC advocates claim that 1:1 means? Henry Morris, cofounder of Six-Days-Only YEC, stated that "In the beginning God created the heavens and the earth" means God created "all space (heaven), all time (beginning), and all matter (earth),"[51] and all this was the "*ex nihilo* creation of the universe by God <u>on the first day</u>"[52] (underlining mine). Then, on day four, God "placed these 'lights' [sun, moon, and galaxies of stars], . . . being made of the same 'earth' that had been created on Day One."[53] A recent YEC leader says Genesis 1:1 means God "made time (beginning), space (heaven), and matter (earth). This was the beginning of our universe, all part of the first day in time."[54]

Response: Genesis 1:1 reports, "In the beginning God created the heavens and the earth."

Genesis 1:1 should be interpreted literally. "In the beginning" does not mean the start of all time in day one, "heavens" (although including space) does not mean just empty space, and "earth" does not mean all matter in the universe. Genesis 1:1 does not say, "In day one God created space, time, and matter." If "earth" in 1:1 were simply matter, then Genesis 1 has no statement of the creation of planet Earth.

If instead we take Genesis 1:1 literally, then "in the beginning" God created the actual heavens and planet Earth. Genesis 1:2 describes Earth as uninhabitable, uninhabited, dark, and sea covered. Then day one began with the command, "Let there be light" (Gen. 1:3). Once we realize that Exodus 20:11 does not say "*in* six days," then we can accept that Genesis 1:1 declares God created the actual universe with its galaxies of stars and actual planet Earth "in the beginning."

4c. YEC: Because the universe was created only days before Adam, the universe is about 6,000 years old.

YEC states that "God created the universe around 6,000 years ago."[55] If all creation was "*in* six days," then the universe was created only days before Adam. "When we add up all these dates, and the dates of other events given in the Bible, we find that

---

51 Henry M. Morris, *Biblical Creationism* (Grand Rapids: Baker Book House, 1994), 17.
52 Henry M. Morris, *Biblical Creationism*, 19.
53 Henry M. Morris, *Biblical Creationism*, 20.
54 Ken Ham, *Dinosaurs in Eden* (Green Forest: Master Books, 2001), 9.
55 Ken Ham, *Dinosaurs in Eden*, 12.

God created the universe around 6,000 years ago."[56] YEC advocates added up the years in the genealogies of Adam's descendants for a date around 6,000 years ago. These YEC advocates apply that date, not just to Adam, but to the universe. If Adam was created on the sixth consecutive day about 6,000 years ago, and the creation of the universe was only a few days earlier, then the creation of the universe was also about 6,000 years ago.

Response: Bᵉreʹshît *means in the beginning time, so the universe is Biblically undated.*

Bᵉreʹshît ("in the beginning") and the unprefixed *reʹshît* ("beginning"), when referring to time, mean a "first phase" or beginning time, the length unspecified by the word itself. The heavens and the earth (Gen. 1:1) were created in the beginning. Because "the beginning" is Biblically unspecified in length, Adam's genealogies may roughly date Adam, but not the universe. The universe is Biblically undated.

4d. YEC: Because the universe (including Earth) is about 6,000 years old but appears older, it must have been created with appearance of age.

YEC claims God created the sun, moon, and stars two days before Adam, about 6,000 years ago. Yet the universe appears older, so God must have created the universe and its luminaries with the appearance of age.

A 6,000-year-old (or at most 10,000-year-old) universe results in a problem unique to YEC: the "distant starlight problem." In 6,000 years, light at its constant speed travels 6,000 light-years. So if the universe were only 6,000 years old, we should see stars only up to 6,000 light-years away, and we should see no galaxies at all. Yet we can see with the naked eye the Andromeda Galaxy, which is 2.5 million light-years away, and astronomers with today's telescopes can see billions of galaxies.

YEC recognizes that it has a "distant starlight problem." Over the years Young Earth creationists have proposed several solutions to this distant starlight problem. Henry Morris said, "The whole universe had an 'appearance of age' right from the start."[57] He further explained, "The light-trail from the star was created in transit, as it were, all the way from the star to the earth, three days before the star was created! . . . There is no reason why God could not, if he had so willed, created 'pulses' in the trails. . . . When such pulses reached the earth they would then be interpreted as, say novas, when they were in reality merely created bursts of energy in the light trails connected with various stars. Though the reason for God doing such a thing is not yet clear."[58]

A frequent speaker for Six-Days-Only YEC conferences suggested that the starlight from those distant stars and galaxies may appear old yet is only about 6,000

---

56 Ken Ham, *Dinosaurs in Eden*, 12.
57 Henry Morris, *Scientific Creationism* (San Diego: Creation-Life Publishers, 1974), 209–210.
58 Henry Morris, *The Genesis Record* (Grand Rapids: Baker, 1976), 65–66.

years old.[59] But, he says, "Even if my particular theory should eventually turn out to be wrong"—and other physicists say it is wrong—"I know that there is a correct creation model of the cosmos, because observation and Scripture both confirm that God made the universe very recently. 'For *in* six days God made the heavens and the earth.'"[60] This sincere man theorized that ancient starlight is only about 6,000 years old based on an *"in"* added to Exodus 20:11.

Response: With a Biblically undated creation, the idea of the universe having appearance of age is unneeded.

False appearance of age is not about static unchanging objects that appear older than they are, but about events that appear to have happened but never happened. If God caused events such as nova explosions to appear to have happened when they did not actually happen, that would seem to make God deceptive. But our truthful God has not created false evidence of events that never happened to deceive people into believing the universe and Earth are either younger or older than they are.

In 1604 astronomer Johannes Kepler observed a supernova star explosion in our Milky Way. Today, telescopes can photograph the beautiful remaining expanding nova shell left by that explosion about 20,000 light-years away. If the heavens declare the glory of God, then the heavens reveal what is true. So the light from Kepler's supernova is revealing the truth. Because the explosion Kepler saw (and the expanding shell left today) was 20,000 light-years away, it happened 20,000 years earlier, indicating the universe is much older than 6,000 years. If, as YEC claims, the universe is only about 6,000 years old, the light from Kepler's supernova should not reach Earth for another 14,000 years. This contradiction between the evidence in the creation and the YEC creation theory is called the distant starlight problem.

A neighboring dwarf galaxy, called the Large Magellanic Cloud, orbits our much larger Milky Way Galaxy. In 1987 astronomers saw a supernova explosion in the Large Magellanic Cloud, which is about 160,000 light-years away. "The heavens declare the glory of God" (Psa. 90:1), and God, who created the heavens, is truthful. So the light from that explosion must be revealing the truth, and that explosion in the heavens actually happened. That light from the explosion left the Large Magellanic Cloud about 160,000 years ago, so the explosion occurred long before the 6,000-year age of the universe proposed by YEC.

The nearest galaxy (except for dwarf galaxies like the Large Magellanic Cloud) is the great Andromeda Galaxy. It is 2.5 million light-years away. For a week in August 1885, the first supernova seen in the Andromeda Galaxy was observed by telescope. The unchanging speed of light that God built into the universe reveals that the supernova exploded 2.5 million years ago. With today's amazing telescopes using computers to record events in billions of galaxies, astronomers are observing

---

59 Humphreys, *Starlight and Time* (Colorado Springs: Master Books, 1995).
60 Humphreys, *Starlight and Time* DVD (Madison, WI: Evidence Press, 2005).

thousands of supernova explosions, star collisions, and pulsing stars in distant galaxies. This contradiction between the evidence of older events in the creation and the Young Earth Creationism belief in a 6,000-year-old universe presents another example of the distant starlight problem.

YEC may object, "No appearance of age? What about Adam and Eve? Weren't they mature adults even when only a few hours old?" In the case of Adam and Eve, everyone present knew how old they were, so there was no deception. But supernova events that were only "bursts of energy in the light trails" but never actually happened do appear to be deceptive.

Once we realize that there is no "*in* six days" in the inspired Hebrew text of the Bible, but instead the universe was created "in the beginning," which lasted an unspecified amount of time, then the universe and Earth can be however old they are. So there is no need for the universe or the Earth to have a false appearance of age. When we realize this, the distant starlight problem disappears.

4e. YEC: Death is a consequence of sin. Adam sinned first, so before Adam sinned, no animal died. Most fossil layers are from the worldwide Flood.

YEC explains, "There was no sin in the world before Adam sinned, and thus no death."[61] So how could there have been millions of years of animal death forming fossil layers before Adam's sin? Quoting the first half of Romans 5:12, "Therefore, just as through one man sin entered the world, and death through sin," YEC teaches that Adam's sin about 4000 BC started all animal death. Since fossils are from dead animals, YEC concludes that no fossils could have formed before Adam's sin, ruling out millions of years of animal death that would have formed the deep fossil layers covering much of the earth. The worldwide Noahic Flood, dated to around 2348 BC, must have laid down most of the many deep fossil-bearing rock layers.

A leading YEC advocate explains, "Death, bloodshed, disease and suffering are a *consequence of sin*" (emphasis his).[62] Adam was created about 4000 BC, "there was no sin in the world before Adam sinned," and death is through sin, so all animal death was after Adam's sin about 4000 BC. "It is clear that there was no sin in the world before Adam sinned, and thus no death. . . . If there were death, bloodshed, disease, and suffering before sin, then the basis for that atonement is *destroyed*" (emphasis his).[63]

YEC claims that any animal death before Adam's sin undermines Jesus' atonement for human sin, thus putting our salvation in peril. Therefore, according to YEC, all Christians should be Young Earth creationists, believing all animal death was after Adam's Fall about 4000 BC and most fossils from the Flood about 2349 BC. A

---

61 Ken Ham and Terry Mortenson, *The New Answers Book 2*, 128–129.
62 Ken Ham, *What REALLY Happened to the Dinosaurs?* answersingenesis.org, 2001, 38.
63 Ken Ham and Terry Mortenson, *The New Answers Book 2* (Green Forest: Master Books, 2008), 128–129.

prominent YEC advocate, responding to an objection, stated, "We argue that Jesus was a young-earth creationist and so we should be too, if we call Him our Lord."[64]

Response: *Adam's sin started all human death; the start of animal death is not mentioned.*

Adam's sin resulted in the start of human death (1 Cor. 15:22). But the Bible does not state that Adam's sin started all animal death about 4000 BC. Romans 5:12 is about Adam's sin resulting in all human death.

> Therefore, just as sin entered the world through one man, and death through sin, and in this way death came to all people, because all sinned (Rom 5:12, NIV).

Adam's sin resulted in death that spread to all humans. And Jesus' atonement is for humans: "Christ died for our sins" (1 Cor. 15:3). The God-Man, Jesus (Rom. 5:15), died for our sins as our substitute, paying the full death penalty for our sin, then rose from the dead. The atonement has nothing to do with animals. Neither Romans 5:12 nor any other verse says Adam's sin resulted in all animal death or that animal death undermines Jesus' atonement.

Adam's sin preceded and caused all human death. Since the first human sin (the cause) preceded the first human death (the consequence), Jesus' atonement (the payment for the sin) is not undermined in the slightest.

The Bible does not say Adam's sin began the violent animal death seen in the fossil record. No explicit explanation is given in the Bible for the start of animal death.

Summary and Evaluation of Six-Days-Only Young Earth Creationism

The Bible supports three of the four big ideas of YEC: Biblical authority, eternal God is the Creator, and the plain sense of each numbered *yôm* ("day") in Genesis 1 is a literal day. But no Bible text supports the fourth big claim, that all creation was "*in* six days." To consistently interpret the Bible narrative by the plain literal sense, YEC should take not only the six days literally but also take literally "in the beginning God created the heavens and the earth."

---

64 Terry Mortenson, "But from the Beginning of . . . the Institution of Marriage?" answersingenesis.org, Nov. 1, 2004, accessed Nov. 6, 2021.

Chapter 8

Chris Yecman Goes to College

Chris Yecman was a smart young man.[65] He was also compassionate, helping his elderly grandparents and neighbors. His grandmother prayed for him every day. She was amazed that he could be friends with all his classmates, including some she thought were bad kids, yet he almost always chose to do right. His whole family went to church every Sunday, and they were very interested in creation. Chris's grandfather grew up believing the Gap Theory. Chris's father, an engineer, was excited about Old Earth Creationism and the match between the older universe and the Bible. Chris's mother had grown up with Young Earth Creationism, viewing it as the only truly Biblical creation theory. Mealtime conversations could be fascinating.

When a Young Earth creationist spoke at the family's church, Chris, who liked science and believed the Bible is God's Word, listened intently. The speaker said God created everything in six literal days "around 6,000 years ago."[66] He said, "If there was a global Flood, as described in Genesis, what would we expect to see? Well, billions of dead things, buried in rock layers, laid down by water all over the earth. And you know what we do find? Well, billions of dead things, buried in rock layers, laid down by water all over the earth!"[67]

The speaker continued, "As the water of the Flood gouged out the Earth and deposited great layers of mud over the Earth, plants, animals, and people would be buried. . . . In other words, most of the fossils we find in the Earth's surface are the remains of creatures and plants buried during the time of the Flood. . . . As Noah's Flood occurred about 4,500 years ago, that means the fossils from the Flood are only 4,500 years old."[68]

After the service, the church's youth leader asked the young people to summarize the message. Chris wrote:

1. God created everything in six literal days.
2. Those six literal days were about 6,000 years ago.
3. The Flood laid down layers of mud with fossils all over the Earth 4,500 years ago.

---

65 All young people and professors and their experiences are fictional (except for historical scientists, such as William Herschel and Edwin Hubble). The science is not fictional. The three sites—Jurassic National Monument, Meteor Crater, and Tanis site in Hell Creek Formation—are real, but the story is fiction.

66 Ken Ham, *Dinosaurs in Eden*, 12.

67 Ken Ham, "Billions of Dead Things, Effects of the Flood," August 28, 2018; https://answersingenesis. org/media /audio/answers-with-ken-ham/volume-130/billions-of-dead-things, accessed in 2019, no longer available.

68 Ken Ham, *Dinosaurs in Eden*, 32–33.

Chris came to believe sincerely in Young Earth Creationism, especially in the six days that Genesis 1 presents as literal days. But when he shared these ideas of Young Earth Creationism (including a 6,000-year-old universe and earth) with his friends, they just looked at him as if he were from an alien planet. His classmates shortened his name to "Yec." They told him, "Hey, Yec, that's stupid!" So Chris shut up about his Young Earth belief, except with his four high school church friends, Joe, Sam, Sarah, and Naomi.

Then Chris and his friends went to a state university. By the end of their freshman year, Joe had become virulently anti-Christian, and Sam had become totally secular.

Sam explained, "I believe in evidence. A 6,000-year-old universe isn't real. So if I have to choose between Christianity with a 6,000-year-old universe and all the scientific discoveries that our universe and life on earth are older, I choose science."

"Right on!" Joe agreed.

Sarah said she believed God created everything, but she felt uncertain about how the creation events fit together. She hoped someone would have some helpful answers.

Chris continued to believe that the Bible is true and that its history should be understood literally—including that the six days with day and night in Genesis 1 were literal days. But at the university, he struggled to reconcile those six literal days with the science he was learning that showed an apparent older universe, older Earth, and older life.

Here is the story of Chris and his four friends.

Chris Questions Radiometric Dating

Chris liked science, but when he arrived at his university, he wasn't sure which science to choose as his major. High school biology had been fascinating, so he decided to try biology. Besides, both Sarah and Naomi had signed up for biology. Their first biology class started with the very intimidating Dr. Darby Winston listing all his degrees and dramatically declaring, "Evolution is the foundation of all modern biology." Toward the end of the lecture, Dr. Win mentioned that scientists using radiometric dating estimated that Earth is 4.5 billion years old and that the earliest life began over 3.5 billion years ago.

Chris remembered that the Young Earth creationist speaker had said radiocarbon (Carbon-14) dating could be inaccurate, and he had given some examples. So Chris was wary of all radiometric dating.

After class, with Sarah and Naomi listening, Chris asked Dr. Win, "I've heard that there have been some errors in Carbon-14 dating, so how do we know that radiometric dating is accurate?"

Dr. Win seemed a little annoyed, but he answered that Carbon-14 dating has improved in accuracy. Then, to Chris's surprise, Dr. Win mentioned the Bible, saying various Dead Sea Scrolls, including books from the Hebrew Bible, had been dated by Carbon-14 to about 400 to 100 BC, with an accuracy of plus or minus about forty years. Jews and Christians had accepted these dates, he said.[69]

This answer impressed Chris and Sarah.

Dr. Win also explained that scientists do not use Carbon-14 to date older materials. Instead, they use other radioactive parent-to-daughter pairs, such as uranium decaying to lead. Scientists can analyze several pairs in the same sample to double-check their dating.

Naomi abruptly left, but Chris and Sarah found it hard to dismiss all radiometric dates as bogus.

A compassionate young lady, Naomi wanted to pursue a career that would help people. She had planned to become a nurse, and that required biology classes. After that first biology lecture though, Naomi dropped out of the class and changed her major from nursing to English literature. Today she is a compassionate assistant pastor's wife. But to this day, she says she is ignorant of science and has no answers to creation questions.

While at the university, the five friends joined a campus Bible group. The group was a real help to Chris and Sarah and once hosted a lecture by an Old Earth creationist. (Naomi skipped that meeting.) The speaker emphasized that God is truth, so the Bible is true, and the creation contains reliable evidence reflecting His truthful character. The Bible, the speaker said, tells us that the universe had a beginning and is expanding. The Old Earth creationist presented evidence for a 13.8-billion-year-old universe and 4.5-billion-year-old Earth. God created literal Adam and Eve, who lived in the Middle East in the Tigris and Euphrates valley thousands of years ago. He said he believed in six creation days, but he defined those days as long day-ages of thousands, millions, or billions of years each.

Chris wasn't sure what to think. The Old Earth explanation fit the science Chris and Sarah were learning. But later that evening Chris got out his Bible and looked at Genesis 1:3–5, about day one. He could not see how a day with daylight and evening and morning could be millions of years long.

After the first semester, Joe and Sam left the campus Bible group, never to return. But Chris and Sarah stayed all four years. They often discussed how the Bible seemed to present the six days as literal days, yet every science course was full of data indicating Earth and life began millions of years ago.

With Dr. Win pushing evolutionary biology, Chris and Sarah decided not to major in biology. Chris switched majors to what seemed like a safer science: geology. Sarah decided to study astronomy. Chris also liked astronomy, so he took an introductory astronomy course with Sarah. He found that class fascinating.

---

69 *Radiocarbon*, vol. 34, no. 3, 1992, 843–849, "Radiocarbon Dating of Fourteen Dead Sea Scrolls," Georges Bonant, et al., 845.

Astronomer Edwin Hubble's Great Discoveries

The white-haired astronomy professor Dr. Astro began his introductory class by talking about his hero: Edwin Hubble. Hubble was not a nerd, Dr. Astro pointed out, but was a basketball and track star who loved astronomy. Immediately after earning his PhD in astronomy, Hubble joined the US Army to serve in World War I. After the war, he worked with the greatest telescope in the world at that time, the Mount Wilson telescope. In the early 1900s many astronomers thought our Milky Way was the entire universe and was eternal. That belief changed when Hubble announced his evidence proving that our universe is far larger than just our Milky Way galaxy and contains many other galaxies. Then he proved that our universe is expanding. Finally, in 1929 Hubble provided evidence indicating that our universe had a beginning, that it is not eternal.

In the following classes, Dr. Astro told the story of the magnificent sudden beginning and expansion of our universe, the dramatic formation of great stars, and the growth of huge spiral galaxies of millions of stars. He was excited about research on the center of our galaxy, where stars speed around a massive black hole. He mentioned that the center of our Milky Way galaxy is 8,000 parsecs away.

Chris remembered the word "parsecs" from *Star Trek* but had to check how far away 8,000 parsecs is. He found that Earth is about 26,700 light-years away from the center of our galaxy. That means the light that astronomers see from the stars circling the center of our galaxy took about 26,700 years to reach Earth. Chris was beginning to wonder about the 4004 BC creation date at the top of the page of Genesis 1 in his old family Bible. But he still believed that Genesis 1 teaches that God worked six literal days. As he and Sarah walked together in the night under the stars, they talked about the verse "The heavens declare the glory of God" (Psa. 19:1). As they shared these thoughts, their appreciation of our Creator grew.

When the class used the university's telescope, Professor Astro reminded the students that the great astronomer William Herschel had pointed out that when we look at the stars, we are looking back in time, seeing the light that left that star long ago. Professor Astro continued, "Light travels at 186,282 miles a second. So when you see a star 1,000 light-years away, you are seeing the light that left that star a thousand years ago during Earth's Middle Ages. When you see a star 4,500 light-years away, you see it as it was about the time when the Great Pyramid of Giza was being built. When you see a star go nova 20,000 light-years away, you are looking back in time 20,000 years, seeing the explosion as it occurred 20,000 years ago."

Professor Astro showed the class how to use the attached computer to align the university's telescope on the stellar object they wanted to see. Chris and Sarah teamed up for their assignment to take a widefield infrared photograph of the area around Sagittarius A* (pronounced Sagittarius A-Star) at the center of our galaxy, about 26,700 light-years away. They were astounded at the number of stars shining in the center of our Milky Way galaxy.

The next morning Sarah seemed especially thoughtful. She had been taught that the universe is about 6,000 years old. But after the first few astronomy classes, she realized the 6,000-year-old date for the creation of the universe is not actually in the Bible.

Thinking about Psalm 90:1—"The heavens declare the glory of God"—Sarah shared her thoughts with Chris.

"God's glory includes His perfect character, and part of His character is His 100 percent truthfulness," Sarah told him. "All the evidence indicates that the center of our Milky Way galaxy is about 26,700 light-years away. William Herschel's statement got me thinking. When I started studying astronomy, I thought that the light-year was just a unit measuring a long distance in space. Now I realize the light-years don't just measure long distances but also reveal how many years back in time that light event we are seeing happened. So when we see the stars, we are really looking back in time. That means seeing those stars 26,700 light-years away is looking 26,700 years back in time, seeing them as they were when they circled our galactic center 26,700 years ago."

Chris nodded in agreement.

Sarah concluded, "Because God is truthful, doesn't that mean we're seeing true evidence from those stars?"

Chris was impressed by Sarah's logical reasoning. "I get what you're saying," he responded. "The stars God made reveal the truth He built into them. So the light from those stars we saw must actually reveal how they were about 26,700 years ago."

A Field Trip to Jurassic National Monument, Meteor Crater, and Hell Creek

During their sophomore year, Chris and Sarah learned about a field trip for both astronomy and geology students—to Jurassic National Monument in Utah, Meteor Crater in Arizona, and Hell Creek Formation in Montana. The field trip was during spring break, so instead of going to the beach, Chris and Sarah jumped at the opportunity to go together on the field trip.

First stop, Utah. There they visited a "dinosaur graveyard," Jurassic National Monument. On display was a meat-eating Allosaurus and a plant-eating Stegosaurus. In addition, they saw a team working on another Allosaurus fossil skeleton. Over 15,000 fossil bones had been removed from the site, yet many thousands remained. Chris and Sarah's geology professor, Dr. Road (a.k.a. Dr. Rocky) taught that there were three eras of life: the Paleozoic (meaning "ancient life"), the Mesozoic (meaning "middle life"), and the Cenozoic (meaning "new life"). The Mesozoic, the era of dinosaurs, was divided into three periods: the Triassic, the Jurassic, and the Cretaceous.

The big predator of the Jurassic period, Allosaurus, is by far the most abundant fossilized dinosaur found at Jurassic National Monument. Dr. Rocky explained that the site might have been a predator trap, perhaps a sticky mud lake. Paleontologists assume that when an Allosaurus smelled or saw other dinosaurs trapped in the mud, it went after them and became trapped itself. The animated young professor continued, "Nine other Jurassic dinosaur kinds have been found here. I led a team here last summer hoping to find a tenth kind of dinosaur, but what we excavated was—a Jurassic turtle."

Each layer has its own kinds of fossils, Dr. Rocky pointed out. Dinosaur fossils are found only in the three Mesozoic layers: the Triassic, Jurassic, and Cretaceous periods. Paleontologists have not found any large modern mammal fossils in these ancient Jurassic layers. They have found only extinct Jurassic species, like dinosaurs.

Chris wondered, "If dinosaurs, modern mammals, and humans were living together before the Flood, and then the Flood drowned them, how could the Flood have sorted them so precisely? Why have no modern large mammal or human fossils been found mixed in with the dinosaur bones in this or any other Jurassic site?"

Next stop, Arizona. When they arrived at Meteor Crater, Chris and Sarah were astounded at how huge the impact crater was—and its geology was fascinating. Dr. Rocky explained that Meteor Crater is the best-preserved meteor impact crater on Earth. Meteor Crater is well preserved because it is relatively new, about 50,000 years old, and is in the dry Arizona desert. Most of the 190 impact craters confirmed by the Earth Impact Database are much older, Dr. Rocky explained.[70] He listed some of the largest impact craters:

Karakul in Tajikistan	32 miles wide
Kara in Russia	40 miles wide
Acraman in Australia	56 miles wide
Manicouagan in Quebec	62 miles wide
Popigai in Siberia	62 miles wide
Sudbury in Ontario	81 miles wide
Chicxulub in Mexico	93 miles wide
Vredefort in South Africa	100 miles wide

Each of these craters is millions of years old, Dr. Rocky said. His favorite crater, Chicxulub on Mexico's Gulf Coast, is about 66 million years old.

Millions of years ago? The dates hit Chris like hammer blows. Chris briefly tuned out Dr. Rocky, not knowing what to think about the ages of the craters. Millions of years ago?

Dr. Rocky was getting very animated (he could be an exciting prof), so Chris started listening again. Dr. Rocky gave a dramatic description of what happened about 66 million years ago when the 6- to 9-mile-wide Chicxulub asteroid struck the Yucatan Peninsula and formed a 93-mile-wide crater.

---

70 http://www.passc.net/EarthImpactDatabase/index.html.

"The impact energy was equal to a billion World War II atomic bombs. First came the deadly flash of heat. Megatsunamis raced outward toward the coasts of Mexico, the southern United States, Central America, northern South America, and the Caribbean islands. Impact seismic waves shook Earth, triggering earthquakes and volcanic eruptions along fault zones. The high-speed impact melted, vaporized, and pulverized the asteroid and the surrounding rock. Molten ejecta and dust sprayed outward and rained down as fiery debris. Dust, smoke, and sulfur compounds circled the Earth, blocking sunlight worldwide for years, disrupting photosynthesis, and beginning a yearslong impact winter. Plants died. Herbivores died. Then carnivores died. About three-quarters of all plant and animal species went extinct, including most of the great dinosaurs. And Chicxulub was only one of the many impacts in the history of Earth."

Chris thought about it—a billion atomic bombs, years of impact winter from just the Chicxulub impact! If the Earth is only 6,000 years old, when did this happen?

Dr. Rocky continued his description.

"The fallout of dust and debris spread around the Earth and left its evidence—a thin layer of dust that became a thin rock layer. That thin K-T boundary layer, also called the K-Pg layer,[71] is the boundary between the Cretaceous layers below (with dinosaur fossils) and the later layers that formed above (without dinosaur fossils). That K-T layer can be seen in many places around the world. You can identify the K-T boundary layer by its abrupt change in color and its contents. It has tiny glassy beads called microtektites from melted impact rock that shot into the stratosphere and hardened as they fell back down to Earth. It also has shocked quartz crystals fractured by the shock of the meteor impact. And near the top is the fallout meteor dust that settled back to earth last with a high level of the element iridium. Iridium is uncommon on Earth's surface but common in meteors. Below the K-T are dinosaur fossils."

He enthusiastically added, "When we arrive at our next site, we'll see that K-T layer. And we'll see evidence of something that happened at the time of the Chicxulub impact."

Last stop, Montana. At the Tanis site in the Hell Creek Formation, Chris and Sarah looked at the desolate landscape of almost barren rock hills. The rock of the bottom half of the hills was one shade of gray, then came the distinct thin horizontal K-T layer. Above that thin dividing layer, the rock was a different shade. Talk about excited. Dr. Rocky looked like he was in geology paradise.

"You are not just looking at a thin rock layer. You are looking at a line in time!" he told everyone. "You are looking at the death of the dinosaurs—the K-T boundary layer, the fallout from the Chicxulub impact 66 million years ago. The rock just below

---

71 The K-T boundary layer divides the Cretaceous layer at the top of the Mesozoic from the Tertiary layers at the bottom of the Cenozoic. Recently the lower Tertiary was renamed the Paleogene, so now the boundary layer between the Cretaceous and Paleogene is often called the K-Pg for Cretaceous-Paleogene.

this K-T boundary layer is the last of the three great Mesozoic layers, the Cretaceous. Paleontologists have dug up Tyrannosaurus, Triceratops, and about twenty other kinds of dinosaurs in the Cretaceous layers. Inside the thin K-T boundary layer are those tiny glassy beads of melted rock and shocked quartz crystals from the impact and a higher level of iridium from the pulverized dust of the meteor. Above the K-T, we are not finding any fossils of the great dinosaurs."

At the Tanis site, a team of paleontologists uncovered evidence from the events in the actual hour of the impact. Chris and Sarah could hardly believe how excited Dr. Rocky was. "This site was on the shore of the Western Interior Seaway that ran north-south through western North America during the Cretaceous Period. The impact of the Chicxulub meteor was 1,880 miles to the south, but we can see its actual effects right here. This site reveals the very last hours of the Cretaceous Period, the last hours of the whole Mesozoic Era."[72]

Dr. Rocky asked Chris to use his tablet to find the calculator called "Impact: Earth."[73] He helped Chris enter factors: an 8-mile-diameter asteroid traveling at 20 kilometers/second (the typical velocity of an asteroid falling from the asteroid belt to Earth), with a density of about 3,000 Kg/m^3 (the average density of a large asteroid), impact angle 51°, seawater level at the impact site ~100 meters, and a distance of 1,880 miles from the Chicxulub impact to Tanis, where they were standing.

The results told the group that the seismic shock wave from the Chicxulub impact racing through the Earth would have reached the Tanis site on the ancient seaway in about ten minutes. The "Impact: Earth" calculator also told the group that ejecta, including glassy beads up to a quarter of an inch in diameter, would have begun raining down on Tanis about seventeen minutes after the impact. Dr. Rocky said, "We'll see the evidence right here of what happened."

One of the paleontologists working on the site explained what happened. "On land, the forests burst into flame. Glassy beads of melted rock stuck to the resin of partially burned logs. In the Seaway water, the Cretaceous paddlefish were filter feeding. They fed by scooping up water and using their gill rakers to filter out bits of food. Instead of food, suddenly the paddlefish were filling their gills with glassy beads. The fast-moving shock wave from the Chicxulub impact raised a local tsunami called a seiche. When this seiche hit, perhaps twenty minutes after the impact, it swept ashore and buried the paddlefish with the glassy beads in their gills. We also found a partially burned log with beads stuck to the resin, part of a triceratops-type dinosaur, and remains of a great water-dwelling mosasaur. A second seiche wave added a second layer of debris—preserving in detail the evidence of the Chicxulub impact."

---

72 Riley Black, "Fossil Site May Capture the Dinosaur-Killing Impact, but It's Only the Beginning of the Story," smithsonian.com, April 3, 2019.

73 "Impact Earth!" Purdue University and Imperial College of London, written by Gareth Collins, H. Jay Melosh and Robert Marcus, https://www.purdue.edu/impactearth.

Pointing to the four-foot-thick K-T deposit layer clearly visible at the site, the paleontologist said, "This is the K-T event deposit layer recording the effects here from the Chicxulub impact. It contains the two seiche layers, the fossilized paddle-fish with microtektite beads in their gills, wood with beads stuck to the resin, and iridium from the Chicxulub meteor fallout."

Chris and Sarah examined a sample of the K-T layer. They could see tiny beads of melted rock that had been shot up into the stratosphere by the Chicxulub impact 1,880 miles to the south. Dr. Rocky said the glassy bead microtektites had been dated 66 million years ago, the same date as the Chicxulub impact. Chris wondered, "Did this catastrophe really happen in the last 4,500 years since the Flood, or 66 million years ago, as the physical evidence indicates?"

Volcanology

Chris felt fortunate to take a module from a visiting famous old volcanologist, Dr. Thor. Volcanology is dangerous, and there aren't very many veteran volcanologists. The tall, powerfully built volcanologist shared that two of his geology friends were at different monitoring stations around Mount St. Helens on May 18, 1980, when suddenly, at 8:32 a.m., the mountain's north face slid downward, releasing an explosion of lava, gas, and ash northward and upward. The eruption ejected a third of a cubic mile of ash. The ash column rose fifteen miles and spread over eleven states and five provinces, devastating the northwest United States and southwest Canada. One of the professor's friends was among the fifty-seven people killed, and the other barely survived.

He listed far greater volcano explosions and lava flows, describing them in detail, since he had been to most of the locations. Mount St. Helens, he said, ejected a third of a cubic mile of ash, but those larger volcanoes ejected hundreds of cubic miles of ash:

Long Valley in California	140 cubic miles of ash ejecta
Whakamaru in New Zealand	480 cubic miles of ash ejecta
Yellowstone in western USA	600 cubic miles of ash ejecta
Atana Ignimbrite in Chile	600 cubic miles of ash ejecta
Toba in Sumatra	670 cubic miles of ash ejecta
La Garita in Colorado	1,200 cubic miles of ash ejecta
Deccan Traps in India	200,000 cubic miles of lava
Siberian Traps in Russia	700,000 cubic miles of lava

In his list, Dr. Thor described the Deccan Traps in central India, which spewed out over 200,000 cubic miles of lava 66,000,000 years ago, about the same time as the Chicxulub meteor impact. He said he had an ongoing debate with Dr. Rocky over whether the Chicxulub impact was the only cause of the extinctions or if this massive vulcanism in central India also contributed to the extinction of the great dinosaurs.

At the time, Dr. Thor was investigating the last Yellowstone eruption, which geologists dated to 640,000 years ago. Chris remembered reading in the Young Earth Creationism literature that "supervolcanoes, such as Long Valley of California and Yellowstone in Wyoming, exploded just after the Flood."[74] The YEC speaker had said that the Flood wiped out Earth's original surface features and deposited most sedimentary rock layers with their fossils. Wouldn't that mean those supervolcanoes and meteor impacts had to have occurred after the Flood? But Chris realized that there is no time in the Young Earth scenario when all those immensely destructive supervolcanoes and deadly huge meteor impacts with their horrendous consequences could fit.

Chris had been thinking about the Creator and about the geology he was seeing. He shared his thoughts with Sarah.

"I agree with you, Sarah, that God is truth personified. God created the heavens you are studying and the Earth that I am learning about in geology. So if God oversaw these volcanic and meteor impact events on Earth, doesn't that mean we are seeing the truth about those past events on the Earth?"

Chris and Sarah Consider Ways of Understanding Creation

Chris was feeling down, as if all he was learning was blasting away his Young Earth Creationism. But millions-of-years-long day-ages did not fit Genesis 1.

Meanwhile, Sarah's parents would soon celebrate their thirtieth wedding anniversary with a two-week trip to the Bahamas. Sarah would join them for the second week, when her junior year spring break began. Sarah knew that Chris was feeling low. She understood and felt great sympathy for him, so she asked her parents if they would invite Chris to come. That raised quite a stir in Sarah's family! They invited Chris to join them. He gladly accepted, and his enthusiasm soon returned.

In the clear blue waters, Sarah, her parents, and Chris swam with masks, snorkels, and fins across the amazing coral reef with brightly colored fish and corals and the fragile sea fans swaying beneath the waves. They saw a small nurse shark, a spiny lobster, and dozens of barracudas lazily hanging about waiting for a meal.

Knowing he needed to write a paper for school, Chris realized he could write about the geology of the Grand Bahama reef and the Bahama Islands. He learned that the islands are on a foundation of fossil coral reefs and limestone made of broken coral and shells. Scientists had calculated the age of the Bahamas based on the depth of coral underlying the islands and the rate of growth of that coral.[75] The living coral would have laid down the underlying foundation far too slowly to have produced the Bahama Islands in the 4,500 years since the Flood.

Sarah thoughtfully commented, "Just the evidence of the older age of the Bahama

---

74 Steven A. Austin, "Supervolcanoes and the Mt. Saint Helens Eruption," *ICR Acts & Facts*, April 13, 2010.

75 Perry G. Phillips, "The Age of Coral Reefs," www.asa3.org/ASA/education/origins/coralreefs.htm.

reef might not be enough to convince me that the Earth is older. But what gets to me is that all the evidence we've studied points to an older universe and Earth. It's as if God wants us to know that His creation work is older."

"I see what you mean," Chris responded. "But how can evidence for an older creation fit with six literal days?"

Chris and Sarah really wanted answers.

In the afternoon Chris and Sarah had a serious talk about creation while eating lunch under a palm tree. They talked about several ways of seeing creation that take the Bible seriously.

The Day-Age Old Earth creationist had given scientific explanations that made sense, and Chris and Sarah appreciated that. Moreover, he was clearly a sincere Bible believer. But his idea of long creation days of millions of years just did not seem to fit the Bible.

The Young Earth creationist also was clearly a sincere Bible believer. His explanation from the Bible that the six days were literal days seemed to fit the Bible text. But Chris and Sarah realized that his two other claims—that the universe and Earth are about 6,000 years old and that the Flood produced most of Earth's fossil layers—are not in the Bible, and they do not fit the evidence from the astronomy and geology classes and the field trip.

Chris and Sarah really wanted answers to their questions about creation. Is there another way of understanding creation that recognizes both that God's Word is true and that God built reliable evidence into the creation? Is there a way of understanding creation in which both the six literal days and a Biblically undated—and apparently older—creation fit together?

Unity on the Fundamentals of Creation

In the evening, as the sunset blazed across the sky and the white breakers curled over and washed onto the sandy shore, Sarah, her parents, and Chris talked about the beautiful creation God had made. Sarah's family took a different approach to the creation theories. Instead of arguing for this theory or against that one, they had decided to seek the shared ideas among the creation theories. They explained that all the Bible-based creation theories recognize that the God of the Bible is the Creator of the universe, the Earth, and all life. They also recognized that the Bible is true and reveals the main events of the creation. All the theories affirm that the universe had a beginning.

Sarah's parents had noticed that advocates of the Bible-based creation theories all believe that Genesis 1, including the six described days, should be interpreted literally, although the theories differed on how long a day was. They all agree that God, not blind evolution, created all the physical laws and life. Most of the theories teach that Adam and Eve were literal humans and that Adam started all human death by his sin. Sarah's parents believed that in a correct understanding of creation, the Bible record and physical creation, when both are correctly understood, are compatible.

Chris and Sarah found the discussion fascinating. Recognizing unity in the essentials among most creation theories was a new idea to Chris and a great encouragement to him and Sarah. But they still had that same question: How can six literal days fit with the evidence of an older universe and older Earth?

The next morning Chris and Sarah's dad took a walk on the beach and had a long talk. And on the last evening of their Bahamas vacation, as the clouds turned from red to purple, Chris had one more question. This one was for Sarah. On the beach overlooking the beautiful Grand Bahama reef, Chris got down on one knee and asked Sarah the happiest question of their lives.

PART TWO

The Answer:
Two Stage Biblical Creation, Taking Both "In the Beginning" and the Six Days Literally

God, by His nature, is unswervingly truthful. God's inerrant Word, the Bible, as originally written, is 100 percent true. "Your word is truth" (John 17:17).

God's creation work also reveals reliable evidence.

The heavens declare the glory of God;
    the skies proclaim the work of his hands.
Day after day they pour forth speech;
    night after night they display knowledge (Psa. 19:1, NIV 1984).

God's inspired, inerrant Word, the Bible, is true. God's creation provides reliable evidence. Inerrant Scripture about creation and the reliable evidence in the creation—when both are understood correctly—will match, correspond, and be compatible because both are from the same 100 percent truthful Creator.

Two Stages of Creation

Two Stage Biblical Creation affirms that the Bible teaches "In the beginning God created the heavens and the earth" (Gen. 1:1), but Earth was uninhabitable (Gen. 1:2). Then God worked six literal days on the earth (Gen. 1:3–31). Taking both "in the beginning" and the six days literally, we find that Genesis 1 reports two stages of creation:

Stage 1: "In the beginning God created the heavens and the earth" (Gen. 1:1). God created *ex nihilo,* making the heavens and planet Earth "in the beginning." Genesis 1:2 describes Earth at the end of stage one, "Now the earth was *tōhû vᵃbōhû* [uninhabitable and uninhabited]," deep sea covered, and dark.

Stage 2: Then God worked six literal days described in Genesis 1:3–31 making Earth lighted, habitable, and inhabited, and He rested the seventh day (Gen. 2:1–3).

The inspired, inerrant Bible texts about creation reveal two stages of creation:

"In the beginning God created the heavens and the earth" (Gen. 1:1).
    Planet Earth was uninhabitable, uninhabited, sea covered, and dark
    (Gen. 1:2).
God worked six described literal days, day one through the sixth day (Gen. 1:3–31).

Two Stage Biblical Creation takes all parts of the Genesis 1 historical narrative literally. Two Stage Biblical Creation also integrates creation data from other Bible creation texts.

Chapter 9

Two Stages of Creation Recognized throughout Church History

Long before modern science, Jewish scholars and Christian Bible scholars explained that the Bible teaches God worked in two stages or parts: "In the beginning God created the heavens and the earth" (Gen. 1:1). Genesis 1:2 describes Earth as uninhabitable, uninhabited, sea covered, and dark. Then God worked six literal days finishing the Earth (Gen. 1:3–31). Those earlier Bible teachers were not trying to reconcile the Bible to modern science (which was still in the distant future) but describing what the Hebrew text of the Bible declares—the two stages of creation.

The Bible Teaches Two Stages of Creation: Genesis 1:1 and 1:3–31

The standard *Brown-Driver-Briggs Hebrew and English Lexicon* defines *b^{e}re'shît* as "beginning," the "first phase."[76] God created in two successive parts, epochs, phases, steps, or stages of creation. First, "In the beginning God created the heavens and the earth" (Gen. 1:1), at the end of which Earth is described as uninhabitable, uninhabited, water covered, and dark (Gen. 1:2). Then God worked in the six literal days making Earth lighted, habitable, and inhabited (Gen. 1:3–31).

This basic understanding of two parts, epochs, time periods, phases, steps, or stages in Genesis 1—"In the beginning God created the heavens and the earth," then God worked in the six literal days—has been a recognized, although not universally held, historical view. Not all have agreed. For example, Clement of Alexandria (152–217) and Origen (185–254) took the six days figuratively,[77] and Augustine (354–430) wrote of creation in a single day.[78] But the Bible describes, and both Jewish and Christian Bible scholars have taught, two stages or parts: first "in the beginning" during which God created the heavens and the earth, and then the six literal days.

Jewish Scholar Nachmanides

A prominent Jewish scholar recognized two stages of creation.

---

76 Brown, Driver, Briggs, *Hebrew-English Lexicon*, #8834, p. 912, Strong's #7225.

77 Origen, *The Fundamental Doctrines*, 4:1:16, www.catholic.com/qa/genesis-symbolical-or-literal.

78 Alister McGrath, "Augustine's Origin of Species," *Christianity Today*, May 8, 2009, https://www.christianitytoday.com/ct/2009/may/22.39.html.

The Jewish scholar Rabbi Moses ben Naḥman, or Nachmanides, also referred to as Ramban (1194–1270), wrote, "*In the beginning G-d created.* . . . The Holy One, blessed be He, created all things from absolute non-existence. . . . Now we have no expression in the sacred language for bringing forth something from nothing other than the word *bārā'* [created]," the verb in Genesis 1:1. "He brought forth from total and absolute nothing."[79] "Now . . . with one command [Gen. 1:1] G-d created at first the heavens and the earth and all their hosts. . . . Scripture returns to explain that the earth after this creation was *tohu*."[80] During the six days, God put things "into a finished condition."[81]

www.myjewishlearning.com/article/nahmanides-ramban/Wiki Commons, Rabbi Louis Jacobs

Ramban did not use the term "two stages" but taught two parts: the creation of matter from nothing "in the beginning," then six days when G-d fashioned that matter.

- "*In the beginning G-d created*" out of "total and absolute nothing."
- "*In the beginning*" *He formed* "first the heavens and the earth."
- But "the earth after this creation was *tohu*" (uninhabitable).
- In the six days, He "put them into a finished condition."
- The six days were "real" days "composed of hours." The numbers are "one day," then "second" through "the seventh" days[82] (italics his).

---

79 Ramban (Nachmanides), *Commentary on the Torah: Genesis,* trans. Chavel (NY: Shiloh, 1971), 17, 23. He taught the "plain meaning" (p. 57) of the Torah text, although sometimes he alluded to Kabbalistic ideas.

80 Ramban, 17, 23.

81 Ramban, *Commentary on the Torah,* 23, 25.

82 Ramban, *Commentary on the Torah,* 28, 33.

Nachmanides believed in two parts of creation: "In the beginning" and the six days.

Church Fathers and Theologians

Several church fathers and theologians recognized two stages of creation.

Basil

Basil (330–379) was born into a Christian family in Caesarea of Cappadocia (now in Turkey). As a young man, he was well educated, "highly talented, and with a high opinion of himself."[83] Then his sister explained that he needed to be right with God. Basil became a believer in the Lord Jesus Christ as his Savior and was baptized. At that time, people who wanted to devote themselves to God often became solitary ascetics, living alone in a cave or even on top of a stone pillar. Basil realized that the New Testament tells Christians to serve others, which cannot be done by living a solitary life in a cave. He founded a community that lived together, worked together, and helped others under the guidance of the church leader. Around his church, Basil built a hospice for travelers, a school, and what today we would call a soup kitchen for the poor. He served others humbly, doing the undesirable jobs himself.

Basil defended orthodox theology and preached frequently. He taught the Bible and Christian theology and was given the title Doctor of the Church. He was influential in his support of the Nicene Creed, which affirms the one God consisting of three eternal Persons— Father, Son, and Holy Spirit—accepted by Orthodox, Catholic, and Protestant churches. Church historians recognize Basil as one of the greatest early church fathers and theologians.

Basil firmly upheld both "in the beginning," during which God created the heavens and the unfinished Earth, then the six literal days. He explained creation in his famous *Hexaemeron* (Greek for "Six Days"), a series of nine sermons or homilies on Genesis 1. In the nine sermons, he

▼ **Basil, Mosaic in Kiev**

By Unknown, http://www.sedmitza.ru/index.html? sid=883&did=49554&p_comment=belief, public domain, https://commons.wikimedia.org/w/index.php? curid=4219822

---

83 John Woodbridge, *Great Leaders of the Christian Church* (Chicago: Moody Press, 1988), 70.

spoke about "in the beginning" (1:1), the "unfinished" condition of Earth (1:2), then six days finishing Earth (1:3–31).

In sermon one of his creation series, he began, "I am about to speak of the creation of heaven and earth, which was not spontaneous, as some have imagined, but drew its origin from God." He taught that Genesis 1:1, "In the beginning God created the heavens and the earth," affirms that the universe is not by chance, eternal on its own, or coeternal with God.[84] First, God created time and the universe, including the Earth, in the beginning. Basil explained that "the creation of the heavens and of the earth were like the foundation and the groundwork."[85] He taught that "in the beginning" started "in less than an instant" and continued as "the epoch when the formation of this world began."[86] The "in the beginning" "epoch" when God created the heavens and the unfinished Earth came before day one that started day-night measured time on Earth.

Basil explained that there are "different senses of the word beginning." The sense of beginning in Genesis 1:1, "in the beginning," was "the epoch when the formation of this world began."[87] A study of the use of the Hebrew word *b^{e}re'shît* ("in the beginning") and *re'shît* ("beginning") confirms that Basil was correct. In the Hebrew Old Testament, *b^{e}re'shît* and the unprefixed *re'shît,* when referring to time, consistently mean a beginning "epoch." For example, the beginning (*b^{e}re'shît*) of King Zedekiah's eleven-year reign included at least four years and five months:

In the beginning [*b^{e}re'shît*] of the reign of Zedekiah king of Judah, in the fourth year, in the fifth month (Jer. 28:1, NASB).

Basil was correct in teaching that "in the beginning" refers to a beginning "epoch." *B^{e}re'shît* in Genesis 1:1 means in the beginning time or epoch of unspecified length, during which God created the heavens and the earth.

In sermon two, Basil preached on Genesis 1:2, explaining "the unfinished condition of the earth."[88] Earth was sea covered and lay in darkness. Basil explains,

The earth lay in darkness, because of the obscurity of the air above it.[89] Thus the earth was . . . still incomplete, . . . waiting for the appointed time and the divine order to bring forth.[90]

Then at "the appointed time," with the first divine order, "Let there be light,"

---

84 Basil the Great, *Hexaemeron Homilies*, trans. Blomfield Jackson, sermon one, 4–5.
85 Basil the Great, *Hexaemeron Homilies*, sermon one, 8.
86 Basil the Great, *Hexaemeron Homilies*, sermon one, 8.
87 Basil the Great, *Hexaemeron Homilies*, sermon one, 8.
88 Basil the Great, *Hexaemeron Homilies*, sermon two, 14.
89 Basil the Great, *Hexaemeron Homilies*, sermon two, 14.
90 Basil the Great, *Hexaemeron Homilies*, sermon two, 16.

day one started on Earth (Gen. 1:3). God brought forth light that "made darkness vanish, dispelled gloom, illuminated the world. . . . The air was lighted up."[91] Thus, at God's command, day one on Earth began with light.

Basil continued by preaching sermons about a second, third, fourth, fifth, and sixth day of God's work and God's day of rest.[92] Basil explains the six described days of God's work: "Now twenty-four hours fill up the space of one day—we mean of a day and of a night."[93] Basil believed in six literal day-night days of God's work.

In summary, Basil believed in two parts of creation. "In the beginning God created the heavens and the earth" was the "epoch when the formation of this world began." But the Earth was "unfinished" or "still incomplete" and "waiting for the appointed time" of the completing work. After "waiting" an unspecified amount of time, the "appointed time" arrived. God's first command, "Let there be light," began day one on Earth with light breaking through the obscurity to Earth (Gen. 1:3–5). Each of the six days consisted "of a day and of a night." Basil taught there were two epochs of creation: the "in the beginning" foundational epoch of unspecified length, then the six day-night days of God's work finishing Earth.

Hugo St. Victor

In the Middle Ages, Hugo St. Victor (1096–1141), an Augustinian theological writer in Paris, wrote that God created "time" and "the first substance" "in the beginning" in Genesis 1:1. But Genesis 1:2 describes the Earth as unfinished. Someone may ask how long the world remained in this unfinished condition. He answers:

> For the fact that the first substance of all things arose at the very beginning of time—or rather, with time itself—is settled by the statement that, "In the beginning God created the heavens and the earth." But how long it continued in this state . . . Scripture does not clearly show.[94]

Hugo St. Victor taught, "In the beginning God created the heavens and the earth." After the initial creation during "the beginning" (Gen. 1:1), God put the earth into an "orderly arrangement" (*dispositio*) in the six literal days. Hugo St. Victor believed in two stages of creation.

Thomas Aquinas

The great Pre-Reformation theologian Thomas Aquinas (1225–1274) explains that the initial creation described in Genesis 1:1 was before the six days:

---

91 Basil the Great, *Hexaemeron Homilies*, sermon two, 20.

92 Basil correctly recognized that "day one" is cardinal, whereas days second through sixth are ordinal.

93 Basil the Great, *Hexaemeron Homilies*, sermon two, 21.

94 Hugo St. Victor, *De Sacramentis Christianae Fidei*, Book 1, part 1, ch. 6; trans. Arthur Custance, *Without Form and Void*, 21.

It seems better to maintain the view that the creation of the heavens and the earth was prior to any of the days, literally before the days.[95]

Aquinas distinguished between the *ex nihilo,* out of nothing, creation in Genesis 1:1 and the subsequent work of God during the six days.[96] Aquinas believed in two stages of creation. Baptist theologian Bernard Ramm said that evangelicals are not always aware of Aquinas's significant thought on creation but should be.[97]

> *"It seems better to maintain the view that the creation of the heavens and the earth was prior to any of the days, literally before the days."*

John Calvin

During the Reformation, theologians from both sides taught two stages of creation. Protestant theologian John Calvin (1509–1564) (although assuming a young date for the creation[98]) taught that Genesis 1:1 was the beginning commencement time when God created the world *ex nihilo*, out of nothing. But in its "commencement," "earth was empty and waste." Then God "perfected" the earth in "the space of six days."[99]

In his *Commentary on Genesis*, Calvin wrote:

1. In the beginning. . . . The world was not perfected at its very commencement. . . . When God in the beginning created the heavens and the earth, the earth was empty and waste. He [Moses] moreover teaches by the word "created," that what before did not exist was now made; for he has not used the term יצר, (*yatsar,*) which signifies to frame or form, but ברא, (*bara,*) which signifies to create. Therefore, his meaning is, that the world was made out of nothing. . . .

---

95 Thomas Aquinas, *Sententiarum*, Book II, Distinction xiii, Article 3, "Ad Terium;" trans. Custance, *Void*, 28. "Sed melior videtur dicendum quod creatio fuerit aute omnen diem."

96 Thomas Aquinas, "creatio non est mutatio," *Sententiarum*, Book II, d. 1, q. 1, a. 2, ad 2; SCG II.

97 Bernard Ramm, *The Christian View of Science and Scripture*, 20–24.

98 I take creation (until Adam) as Biblically undated, whereas Calvin assumed a recent creation date, that "a little more than five thousand years have passed since the creation of the universe" (Calvin, *Institutes of the Christian Religion 2,* ed. John T. McNeill [Philadelphia: Westminster Press, 1960], 2:925). Yet the main point is that Calvin believed God created the heavens in the beginning out of nothing, but earth was "rude and unpolished." Then God perfected His work in "the space of six days" (*Genesis,* 73, 78). Calvin took the plain sense of Scripture, so he believed in two parts of creation: "in the beginning," then six days.

99 John Calvin, *Commentary on Genesis*, trans. John King (Edinburgh: Banner of Truth Trust: 1975), 70, 73.

2. *And the earth was without form and void* . . . תוהו, (*tohu*,) and בוהו, (*bohu*). The Hebrews use them when they designate anything empty. . . .

3. *And God said.* Moses now, for the first time, introduces God in the act of speaking. . . . God commanded the light to be.[100]

Calvin explains that in that beginning time, in Genesis 1:1, "the world was made out of nothing," created *ex nihilo*. But the world was not perfected at its "commencement." The description in Genesis 1:2 reports the earth was "empty." Then Genesis 1:3–31 reports that God completed the world in "the space of six days." Footnote 2 in the translation of Calvin's *Commentary on Genesis* adds,

ברא.[*bārā'*, "created,"] It has a twofold meaning: 1. *To create out of nothing*, as is proved from these words, *In the beginning*, because nothing was made before them. 2. *To produce something excellent out of pre-existent matter*; as it is said afterwards, *He created whales*, and *man*.[101]

Calvin took the plain sense of Genesis, so he taught two parts of creation: "In the beginning" God created [ברא, *bārā'*] *ex nihilo*, but "the world was not perfected at its very commencement." Then God perfected the earth in "the space of six days."[102]

Benedict Pereira

The Spanish theologian Benedict Pereira (1536–1610) wrote a commentary on Genesis in which he explains:

Even though before the first day, the heavens and the elements were made . . . nevertheless they were not perfected and completely furnished until the period of the six days: for then was given to them furnishing, fulfillment (filling up), and completion. However, just how long that darkened state of the world lasted, i.e., whether it lasted more than one day or less than one day, this is not clear to me, nor is it clear to any other mortal man unless to one to whom it has been divinely made so.[103]

Pereira explains the sequence of creation events: First, "before the first day," God made "the heavens and the elements" (Gen. 1:1), but "they were not perfected and completely furnished." There was a "darkened state of the world" (Gen. 1:2), but we mortals do not know how long that lasted. All this was "before the first day."

---

100 John Calvin, *Commentary on Genesis*, 69–70, 73, 74, 78.

101 John Calvin, *Commentary on Genesis*, footnote 2, 70.

102 John Calvin, *Commentary on Genesis*, trans. John King (Edinburgh: Banner of Truth Trust: 1975), 70, 73.

103 Some parenthetical additions apparently added by Custance are left out. Benedict Pereira, *Commentariorum et disputationum in Genesim tomi quattuor*, trans. Custance, *Void*, 23.

Then came "the period of the six days," when there "was given to them furnishing, fulfillment (filling up), and completion" (Gen. 1:3–31).

Pereira believed that the initial creation in Genesis 1:1 was before "the period of the six days," although how long "before the first day" we mortals do not know. Although he suggested the first stage could have been short, Pereira believed in two periods or stages of creation.

> *Many of these Bible scholars lived long before modern astronomy and geology. They were not trying to reconcile the Bible text with modern science when they explained that* b\u1eb9re'shît *("in the beginning") inherently means in the beginning epoch.*

Denis Pétau

Denis Pétau (1583–1652), a professor of theology at the University of Paris, France, wrote that the initial creation "in the beginning" was an interval of time. How long that beginning time lasted, we do not know.

> The question of 'How great an interval there was', it is not possible except by inspiration to attain knowledge of.[104]

After the beginning time interval, then came day one with "the appearance of daylight."

Professor Pétau believed in time passage of unspecified length in the first stage and then the six literal days. Professor Pétau believed in two stages of creation.

Charles Hodge

Princeton theologian Charles Hodge (1797–1878) says it would be natural to take the word "day" in its ordinary sense of a literal day, but geology supports an older Earth. He presents two views of creation: the day-age view and a two stage creation with a beginning of indefinite length followed by six literal days. Hodge summarized a two stage literal days view of creation, "Some understand the first verse of Genesis to refer to the original creation of the matter of the universe in the indefinite past, and what follows [that is, the six days described in Genesis 1:3–31] to refer to the last

---

104 Denis Pétau, *Theologiae Cursus Completus: ex tractatibus omnium prefectissimus ubique . . .*, trans. Custance, *Void*, 22–23.

reorganizing change in the state of our earth to fit it for the habitation of man."[105] After the creation of the heavens and the earth in 1:1, Genesis 1:3–31 describes six days when God changed the state of our earth to fit it for the habitation of man.

Edward J. Young

Westminster Hebrew scholar Edward Young (1907–1968) says, "The first verse of Genesis is a broad, general, declaration of the fact of the creation of the heavens and the earth." Genesis 1:1 "is a narrative complete in itself." This first narrative is part one of creation. In verse 2, attention is "directed to the Earth." "We are not told how long the three-fold condition [not habitable, empty of life, dark deep water] described in verse two had been in existence before God said, 'Let there be light.'" Young continues, "Verses 2–31 likewise constitute a narrative complete in itself."[106] This second narrative is part two of creation. He concludes, "The Bible does not state how old the earth is."[107]

Bernard Northrup and Gorman Gray

Hebrew professor Bernard Northrup and Gorman Gray both recognize two parts of creation. Northrup explains, "Genesis 1:1–2 clearly indicated that the universe and the earth were in place before the first solar day."[108]

Gray writes, "The Bible teaches that the entire universe was created 'in the beginning' which could be long before a 'first day.'"[109] Both Northrup and Gray take Genesis 1:1 literally, that "in the beginning God created the heavens and the earth," the universe with its galaxies of stars, before day one on Earth. Gray explains that this results in a Biblically "undefined age of the universe."[110] He and Northrup both believe that after the beginning, God worked six literal days. While they may not use the term "two stages" or agree entirely with my full explanation, both affirm two phases of creation.

> *"Genesis 1:1–2 clearly indicated that the universe and the earth were in place before the first solar day."*

---

105 Charles Hodge, *Systematic Theology, Abr.* (Grand Rapids: Baker, 1988), 210.

106 Edward J. Young, *Studies in Genesis One* (Phillipsburg: P&R, 1964), 9–11.

107 Edward J. Young, *Studies in Genesis One*, 102.

108 Bernard Northrup, *Recognizing Messiah in the Psalms* (Fairfax, VA: Xulon Press, 2003), 93.

109 Gorman Gray, *Genesis Chapter One: Scientifically Accurate and Surprisingly Simple* (Washougal, WA: Morningstar Publications, 2015), first page of ch. 1.

110 Gorman Gray, *The Age of the Universe: What Are the Biblical Limits?* (Washougal, WA: Morningstar Publications, 2000), 14. Gray proposes an undated universe and a young biosphere.

William Lane Craig and Paul Copan

Apologists William Lane Craig and Paul Copan strongly affirm *ex nihilo* creation. They also discuss two stages of creation. Genesis 1:1 reports stage one: God created *ex nihilo* the materials of the universe from absolutely nothing. Then the rest of Genesis 1 reports stage two: God made planet Earth habitable for humans.

They explain that this is "the testimony of not only Jewish scholars such as Ramban but also early church fathers who stated or implied that God created in two stages."[111] They explain, "What is held in common by scholars such as Young, Sailhamer and also Kidner is that there is an elegant, purposeful depiction of a two-step process to creation."[112] The two steps or stages were the *ex nihilo* creation of the universe (Gen. 1:1) and the finishing work on Earth (Gen. 1:3–31). Craig and Copan do not expand their view into a complete two stage creation theory, but they believe in two stages of creation and point out that many others believe in a two step or two part or two stage creation.

> This is "the testimony of not only Jewish scholars such as Ramban but also early church fathers who stated or implied that God created in two stages."

John Sailhamer

Hebrew professor John Sailhamer (1946–2017) says, "I contend that two distinct time periods are mentioned in Genesis 1. In the first period, God created the universe; no time limitations are placed on that period."[113] In the second period, God worked six literal days.

> "I contend that two distinct time periods are mentioned in Genesis 1."

---

[111] Paul Copan and William Lane Craig, *Creation out of Nothing* (Grand Rapids: Baker, 2004), 60–65.

[112] Paul Copan and William Craig, *Creation out of Nothing*, 63.

[113] John Sailhamer, *Genesis Unbound* (Sisters, OR: Multnomah Books: 1996), 29. He is correct about two time periods, but I do not agree with his ideas about the Garden of Eden.

Recognition of Two Stages of Creation Is Not New

Many theologians throughout church history believed in two parts or epochs or stages of creation—the beginning time, then the six days. Although these theologians may not have used the specific term "two stages," they taught the concept of two parts, epochs, phases, or stages of indeterminate length—"in the beginning," then six literal days. Two stages of creation were widely, although not universally, recognized by leading Bible scholars and theologians throughout church history.

Recognition That the Bible Does Not Tell the Length of Phase One Is Not a New Idea

Several of these church fathers and theologians emphasized that the Bible does not tell us the length of the beginning time. Hugo St. Victor (1096–1141) said, "'In the beginning God created the heavens and the earth.' But how long it continued in this state . . . Scripture does not clearly show."[114] Benedict Pereira (1536–1610) wrote, "How long that darkened state of the world lasted . . . , this is not clear to me."[115] Denis Pétau (1583–1652) explained that "it is not possible except by inspiration to attain knowledge" of the length of the beginning time.[116] Recently John Sailhamer wrote that "in the first period, God created the universe; no time limitations are placed on that period."

These theologians and Bible scholars recognized that the Bible does not date the initial creation. They recognized that the "beginning" in Genesis 1:1 means an "epoch"[117] of "an extended, yet indeterminant duration of time."[118] Many of these Bible scholars lived long before modern astronomy and geology. They were not trying to reconcile the Bible text with modern science when they explained that *bᵉreʾshît* ("in the beginning") inherently means in the beginning epoch. This Biblical and historical view of two stages of creation—a literal Genesis 1:1 creation by God in the beginning time, then six literal days—has been recognized throughout church history because it is based on the inspired, inerrant Bible text.

Not All Agreed with Two Stages

Not all agreed. Some Bible believers added the years in the Bible genealogies and calculated a date. Some applied their date not just to Adam but to the creation of the universe in Genesis 1:1. A towering figure in these calculations was the scholarly

---

114 Hugo St. Victor, *De Sacramentis Christianae Fidei*, 14, 21. Hugo's statement supports two stage creation rather than the gap theory.

115 Benedict Pereira, *Commentariorum et disputationum in Genesim tomi quattuor*, trans. Arthur Custance, *Without Form and Void*, 15/22–23.

116 Denis Pétau, *Theologiae Cursus Completus: ex tractatibus omnium prefectissimus ubique . . .* , trans. Custance, Void, 22–23.

117 Basil the Great, *Hexaemeron Homilies*, sermon one, 8.

118 John Sailhamer, *Genesis Unbound*, 38.

Bishop James Ussher (1581–1656). In his great work, *The Annals of the World* (1650), he gave a creation date of 4004 BC:

> 4004 BC
> In the beginning God created the heavens and the earth. Ge 1:1 This beginning of time, according to our chronology, happened at the start of the evening preceding the 23rd day of October.

Ussher claimed that creation began on Sunday, October 23, 4004 BC, and continued through "the seventh day, (Saturday, October 29th)." He concluded that the entire creation was in one week of seven consecutive days, starting at the end of October in 4004 BC.

Ussher's dates were placed in headings or study notes in many King James Bibles. In many people's minds, those dates became almost as authoritative as Scripture itself.

In 1961 Ussher's view was brought back to prominence in *The Genesis Flood* by John Whitcomb and Henry Morris. This book has resulted in the rise of Six-Days-Only Young Earth Creationism—a one-stage creation theory claiming all creation, including the initial creation (Gen. 1:1), was entirely in the six days.

> *A Biblical and traditional view of the church has been that the Bible teaches two parts or stages of creation. The first part of creation is "In the beginning God created the heavens and the earth" (Gen. 1:1), at the end of which the Earth was uninhabitable, uninhabited, water covered, and dark (Gen. 1:2). Then, in the second part, God worked six literal days making Earth lighted, habitable, and inhabited (Gen. 1:3–31).*

Two Parts or Stages of Creation Is Taught in the Bible and Recognized by Bible Believers

A Biblical and traditional view of the church has been that the Bible teaches two parts or stages of creation. The first part of creation is "In the beginning God created the heavens and the earth" (Gen. 1:1), at the end of which the Earth was uninhabitable, uninhabited, water covered, and dark (Gen. 1:2). Then, in the second part, God worked six literal days making Earth lighted, habitable, and inhabited (Gen. 1:3–31).

Chapter 10

Elohîm, Eternal God of the Bible, Is the Creator of the Universe

The Creator of all things, the Creator of space, the Creator of time, the Creator of the heavens and the earth is the one and only eternal God, the God of the Bible. He identifies Himself in Genesis 1:1 by His title, *Elohîm*. He is the only God; there is no other. He is eternal; all else was created. He is sufficient in Himself; all else is dependent on Him.

Although Genesis 1:1 uses only the general title for God, *Elohîm*, the Creator God reveals His holy personal name in Genesis 2:4 as YHVH (also written YHWH). In reverence for the holy name, the name is often translated as "Lord." God the Creator is not a generic god but is YHVH, reverently written in ancient Hebrew with the four consonants, יהוה, YHVH, and spoken in Hebrew as "HaShem," meaning "The Name," or as *Adonai*, or in English, Lord. He is the Creator of all things, the God of Abraham, the God of Israel, the God of the Bible. *Elohîm*, God, is the third Hebrew word in Genesis 1:1. Grammatically, *Elohîm* is the acting subject of 1:1 and thematically the acting subject of the chapter. He was before all things and is the eternal Creator, so we will start with this great subject of the sentence—the Creator Himself.

Elohîm, God, Alone Is the Eternal Creator

Under the hot sun that the Egyptians considered one of their gods, the people of Israel had been reduced to slavery. The living God saw their misery, heard their cry for help, and met Moses at the burning bush. There God revealed His personal name to Moses. Then God sent Moses and his brother, Aaron, to Pharaoh, the most powerful man in the world of his time.

Moses and Aaron went to Pharaoh and said, "This is what the Lord [YHVH], the God [*Elohîm*] of Israel, says: 'Let my people go. . . .'" Pharaoh said, "Who is the Lord [YHVH], that I should obey him and let Israel go? I do not know the Lord [YHVH] and I will not let Israel go" (Exod. 5:1–2, NIV 1984).

The word translated "Lord" is not a generic title for God but His unique covenant personal name YHVH, the name of the one eternal Creator of all things. Pharaoh's question was "Who is YHVH that I should obey him and let Israel go?" Pharaoh probably assumed that the Lord God was just one of many weak little supposed gods of one of Pharaoh's groups of slaves.

The eternal Creator LORD God would answer that powerful man with far greater power than Pharaoh could have imagined! By ten plagues targeting the false gods of Egypt, the Lord God delivered Israel out of the bondage of slavery, out of a devastated land of Egypt, out from under Pharaoh's power, proving that the eternal Creator LORD God is the one and only God.

The Israelites left Egypt and began their journey to the Promised Land of Israel. God brought them to the Red Sea, but the Egyptian army pursued them. That night, in a pillar of dark cloud toward the pursuing Egyptian army and bright fire lighting the way for the Israelites ahead, God shielded His people. As Moses raised his hand, God sent a mighty east wind, driving back the waters and parting the Red Sea before the Israelites. They crossed safely to the far shore. The Egyptian army, with its horses and chariots, pursued the Israelites onto the sea floor. Then the LORD told Moses to raise his hand over the sea once more, and the sea rushed back and swallowed up the Egyptian army with its chariots.

> And when the Israelites saw the great power the LORD [YHVH] displayed against the Egyptians, the people feared the LORD [YHVH], and put their trust in him (Exod. 14:31, NIV 1984).

God had answered Pharaoh's question, "Who is the LORD [YHVH]?" He is the only true living God, the almighty LORD. He is both just in His judgment and bountiful in His mercy.

For four hundred years, the people of Israel had lived in Egypt. Now they were leaving Egypt with its many gods and were about to enter the land of Canaan with its corrupt religious system of human sacrifice and many different gods. On the way, God brought the people of Israel to Mount Sinai. God Himself came down to the mountain in fire and thunder, and the people of Israel were terrified. There before them, high on Mount Sinai in awesome glory, was the fiery presence of the LORD God. On Mount Sinai, God gave His Law to Moses. God identified Himself as the God who brought the Israelites out of Egypt.

> I am the LORD [YHVH] your God, who brought you out of Egypt, out of the house of slavery (Exod. 20:2, NIV 1984).

He is the LORD. On Sinai, He gave His good Law, beginning with:

> You shall have no other gods before me.
> You shall not make for yourself an idol in the form of anything in heaven above or on the earth beneath or in the waters below. You shall not bow down to them

or worship them. . . . You shall not misuse the name of the LORD your God (Exod. 20:3–7, NIV 1984).

Who is *Elohîm*, the LORD God?
He is the LORD God who rescued you from slavery in Egypt!
He is the only LORD God!
He is the living LORD God who cannot be represented by a carved idol!
He is so great that even His name must never be misused.
Later David would explain:

For all the gods of the nations are idols,
but the Lord [YHVH] made the heavens (Psa. 96:5, NIV 1984).

The LORD God, YHVH *Elohîm*, is the one and only eternal Creator of all things. All other so-called gods invented by the nations are no gods. No Egyptian god, no Canaanite god, no god invented by any human is the Creator. The LORD God, YHVH *Elohîm*, is the one and only eternal Creator.

Genesis 1 is the definitive statement that *Elohîm* is the one and only Creator God. Only one God is real, and He is the eternal Creator—the God of the Bible who declared His creation work in Genesis 1.

The One Eternal God

God existed eternally before creation. The first sentence in the Bible declares,

In the beginning God [*Elohîm*] created the heavens and the earth (Gen. 1:1).

Before "in the beginning," God alone existed—eternally. When Moses asked God His name,

God said to Moses, "I AM WHO I AM."
And he said, "Say this to the people of Israel, 'I AM has sent me to you'" (Exod. 3:14).

The generic title of God is *Elohîm*. The personal name of God is "I AM," or in Hebrew, YHVH. In ancient Israel, a name conveyed the character of that person. God is revealed in the rest of the Bible by His names and His actions. Israel would speak of Him as HE IS (YHVH):
HE IS the LORD, YHVH.
HE IS the King of Glory.
HE IS God Almighty.
HE IS the living God.

HE IS the holy one.
HE IS the true God.
HE IS without beginning.
HE IS without ending.
HE IS the one and only Creator.
HE IS transcendent.
HE IS present.
HE IS independent.
HE IS self-sufficient.
HE IS perfect goodness.
HE IS separate from all evil.
HE IS omnipotent, all-powerful.
HE IS omniscient, all-knowing.
HE IS omnipresent, everywhere present.
HE IS consistent, unchanging.
HE IS lacking nothing.
HE IS complete truth.
HE IS perfect beauty.
HE IS love beyond description.
HE IS life.
HE IS the righteous, holy judge.
HE IS the LORD, YHVH, our God.

God exists eternally in a sense that we cannot fully comprehend with our time-bound physical brains. Moses was saying to ancient Israel and us that before "in the beginning," before time, there was only eternal God in all His perfection without beginning or end. Moses wrote,

> Before the mountains were born,
> Or Thou didst give birth to the earth and the world,
> Even from everlasting to everlasting, Thou art God (Psa. 90:2, NASB).

Before God created the "earth and the world," God alone existed "from everlasting to everlasting." Eternal God always exists. Before "in the beginning," there was no space, no time, no matter, no physical laws, and no universe in any form—only eternal *Elohîm*, the one and only eternal God.

In Genesis 1:1, the noun *Elohîm* is plural, yet the verb *bārā'*, "created," is singular, indicating only one God. This unusual arrangement of the plural noun yet singular verb indicates the one majestic God yet also allows the plural Persons of the one and only highly exalted God. When God made humans, He again used the plural, then the singular:

Then God [*Elohîm*, plural] said [singular], "Let us make [*poiésomen*, plural of *poiéo*] man in our image, after our likeness. . . ." So God [*Elohîm*, plural] created [*bārā'*, singular] man in his own image [*tselem*, singular], in the image of God he created [*bārā'*, singular] him; male and female he created [*bārā'*, singular] them (Gen 1:26–27).

God the Creator is one God yet plural Persons—God the Father, God the Son, and the God the Holy Spirit. God is one God.

Colossians 1:16 and Hebrews 1:2 speak of eternal God the Son, who carried out the work of creating the entire universe:

For by him [eternal God the Son] all things were created: things in heaven and on earth, visible and invisible (Col. 1:16, NIV 1984).

In these last days he [God the Father] has spoken to us by his Son,
whom he appointed heir of all things, and
through whom he made the universe (Heb. 1:2, NIV 1984).

God the Son, the Lord Jesus, is the Creator.

The third Person of the one eternal God, the Spirit of God, was also present, hovering over the surface of planet Earth's deep sea waters.

And the Spirit of God was hovering over the face of the waters (Gen. 1:2).

Although the Holy Spirit of God is present everywhere (omnipresent), Genesis 1:2 states His specific location in the creation time. The Spirit was hovering over the surface of the waters covering planet Earth. Perhaps this specific location of God the Spirit indicates the narrative perspective location for the Genesis 1:3–31 creation account, the surface of planet Earth, then covered by water.

God Is Goodness, So All His Creation Work Was Good

God does not simply possess goodness. God is good. God's character is reflected in His work. Scripture reports that God evaluated His work: "And God saw that it was good."

God Is the Sole Designer and Creator of the Universe

The sudden beginning of the universe could only have been by an eternal Originator. The precise fine-tuning of the universe, discovered by science, makes sense only if the universe had a Fine-Tuner. The immense webs of galaxies in the universe make sense only if there was a Great Architect. The just-right events forming planet Earth so precisely indicate a Planner. The irreducible complexity of life can be explained only by a Designer.[119]

The God of the Bible is the eternal Originator, the Fine-Tuner, the Great Architect, the Planner, the Designer. The eternal Creator is the only rational explanation for the start and fine-tuning of the universe, for life on Earth, for the precisely right events in Earth's formation, and for the irreducible complexity in life. The God of the Bible is the only eternal Creator God, the one who created the universe and the Earth in the beginning: "In the beginning God created the heavens and the earth."

---

119 Michael Behe, *Darwin's Black Box* (New York: Free Press, 1996); William Dembski, *Intelligent Design* (1999), *Mere Creation* (1998), *The Design Revolution* (Downers Grove, IL: InterVarsity Press, 2004).

Chapter 11

The Seven Hebrew Words
of Genesis 1:1

The seven Hebrew words of Genesis 1:1 record the absolute beginning of all but the eternal Creator God Himself.[120] These are the actual words declaring that God created the heavens and the earth in the beginning (reading Hebrew from right to left):

בְּרֵאשִׁית בָּרָא אֱלֹהִים אֵת הַשָּׁמַיִם וְאֵת הָאָרֶץ
← In-beginning created *Elohîm* the-heavens and the-earth.

The heavens and the earth are not eternal. The eternal God created both the heavens and planet Earth "in the beginning." Neither time nor the universe is endless. Both were created by God "in the beginning."

Bᵉre′shît: "In the Beginning"

In the beginning [bᵉre′shît] God created the heavens and the earth (Gen. 1:1).

The root word of bᵉre′shît is re′shît. The noun re′shît commonly means "beginning, chief"[121]— "beginning" when referring to a beginning time, and "chief" when ranking people or objects. The standard *Brown-Driver-Briggs Hebrew and English Lexicon* defines "beginning" as the "first phase" and when speaking of a person, their "early life."[122] Bᵉre′shît is the same word prefixed with the "bᵉ." The bᵉ prefix means "in, within," so bᵉre′shît may be understood as "in/within *the* first phase." The first Hebrew word of Genesis 1, bᵉre′shît, "in *the* beginning," means in the beginning phase/time.

---

120 I take the traditional view that Genesis 1:1 is an independent statement/clause declaring the *ex nihilo* creation of the actual heavens and the actual earth in the beginning. This was the first stage/step of God's work. Bᵉre′shît is absolute ("it functions independently of any other word," Hamilton, *The Book of Genesis*, 103). Thus, I do *not* agree with translating Genesis 1:1 as a dependent clause: "When God began creating the heavens and the earth, the earth was chaos." Genesis 1:1 is an independent clause declaring God created *ex nihilo* in the beginning. There was no preexisting chaos. Genesis 1:2 is circumstantial to 1:1 and consists of three disjunctive dependent clauses modifying the last word of Genesis 1:1, the earth, describing four unfinished conditions on planet Earth at the end of the 1:1 beginning time. Genesis 1:2 provides the background for the items changed in 1:3–31. Genesis 1:3 is an independent clause starting the narration of God's six described days of creation work changing Earth's four unfinished conditions (Gen. 1:2) to make Earth lighted, habitable, with land, and inhabited. Only planet Earth is described as unfinished, and even it was not chaos. I am denying all precreation chaos. God created *ex nihilo*.

121 Brown, Driver, Briggs, *Hebrew and English Lexicon*, #8834, p. 912, Strong's #7225.

122 Brown, Driver, Briggs, *Hebrew and English Lexicon*, #8834, p. 912, Strong's #7225.

"In the Beginning Time," Not "At the Starting Instant"

In the Hebrew Scriptures, *b*ᵉ*re'shît*, "in the beginning," although starting with the instant of the beginning of time, does not mean just the first instant or moment of time. When used about time or events within time (rather than chief, best, or head person or object), *re'shît* consistently means a beginning time/phase. Hebrew professor John Sailhamer explains, "The Hebrew word *reshit*, which is the term for 'beginning' used in this chapter [Genesis 1], has a very specific sense in Scripture. In the Bible, the term always refers to an extended, yet indeterminate duration of time—*not* a specific moment. . . . The term does not refer to a point in time but to a *period* or *duration* of time" (emphasis his).[123] Thus, when referring to time, the Hebrew Scriptures consistently use *b*ᵉ*re'shît* and *re'shît* to mean a beginning phase/time, *not* the starting instant.

In the Bible, *b*ᵉ*re'shît* with the prefix *b*ᵉ ("in, within") is used only four more times, all in Jeremiah, referring to the beginning portions of the reigns of Judah's last kings. The *b*ᵉ*re'shît* of King Zedekiah's reign included at least four years and five months into his eleven-year reign:

> Now in the same year, in the beginning [*b*ᵉ*re'shît*] of the reign of Zedekiah king of Judah, in the fourth year, in the fifth month (Jer. 28:1, NASB).

The "beginning" of the reign of King Zedekiah was not just the first instant he was anointed king. It referred to the beginning years of his reign. Genesis 1:1 starts with the same word, *b*ᵉ*re'shît*. Just as in Jeremiah 28:1, where *b*ᵉ*re'shît* means the beginning years of Zedekiah's reign, so in Genesis 1:1 (although starting instantly) *b*ᵉ*re'shît* means the beginning time of unspecified length during which God created the heavens and the earth.

After Genesis 1:1, the next use of the unprefixed *re'shît* ("beginning") related to time is in Genesis 10:10, where Moses records:

> The beginning [*re'shît*] of his [Nimrod's] kingdom was Babel and Erech and Accad and Calneh, in the land of Shinar (NASB).

Later Nimrod built or acquired other cities, but he developed these first four cities as the "beginning" of his growing kingdom. He did not create his kingdom in an instant. It would have taken considerable time for Nimrod to establish a kingdom of four cities. A four-city kingdom was not accomplished in a moment or one day.

A clear example of the time use of *re'shît* is in the ancient book of Job. Job lived in an era when people lived longer lives. The Bible divides Job's life into two parts: his years before his troubles and his years after his troubles. Bildad said to Job in Job 8:7:

---

123 John Sailhamer, *Genesis Unbound*, 38.

Your beginnings [*re'shît*] will seem humble, so prosperous will your future be (NIV 1984).

The book ends in Job 42:12:

And the LORD blessed the latter days of Job more than his beginning [*me-re'shît*].

Job's "latter days" were his years of double blessing after his troubles. Job's double blessings are listed: double the sheep, double the camels, double the oxen, double the donkeys, ten more children, and 140 more years of life. Job's *re'shît,* or beginning, was his entire life up to when disasters came upon him. Before his misfortunes, Job sat as an honored elder in the city (Job 29:7) and had ten adult children who had their own homes in which they took turns hosting feasts for each other (Job 1:2–4). To have ten adult children indicates that Job was at least forty years old. The symmetry in the book of doubling his possessions after his testing suggests that if he lived 140 years after his testing, he likely lived seventy years before his testing. So Job's *re'shît,* his beginning, was many years, at least forty and likely seventy years.

Length of "In the Beginning" Unspecified

When referring to time, the Hebrew Scriptures consistently use *b^ere'shît* ("in the beginning") or the unprefixed *re'shît* ("beginning") to mean a beginning amount of time. The "in the beginning" creation time of Genesis 1:1 refers to the beginning time of unspecified length when God created the heavens and the earth.

How long did the beginning time last?

Basil explained that "in the beginning" was "the epoch when the formation of this world began."[124] Hugo St. Victor added that how long the world remained "in this state . . . Scripture does not clearly show."[125] Hebrew professor John Sailhamer explains, "There is no way to limit the duration of the word 'beginning' [Hebrew, *re'shît*]." He continues, "The length of time of this 'beginning' is precisely what is left unspecified by the term." Sailhamer explains that "using *reshit* to convey the concept of 'beginning' (when other terms were readily available) is to leave the duration of time unspecified."[126] He continues, "Since the Hebrew word 'beginning' refers to an indefinite period of time, we cannot say for certain when God created the world or how long He took to create it."[127]

"In the beginning" means a beginning amount of time of unspecified length.

---

124 Basil the Great, *Hexaemeron*, sermon one, 6.

125 Hugo St. Victor, *De Sacramentis Christianae Fidei*, 21.

126 John Sailhamer, *Genesis Unbound*, 28, 29. He agrees with two stages, but I do not agree with his ideas applying stage two to Eden.

127 John Sailhamer, *Genesis Unbound*, 14.

Because the beginning time was of unstated duration, the creation of the heavens and the earth is Biblically undated.

Bārā', "Created"—A Universe Out of Nothing

The second Hebrew word of Genesis 1 is the verb *bārā'*, "created." In Scripture, only God is the subject of this Hebrew word when used in the sense of "create"—only God can *bārā'*, "create," *ex nihilo*.

Bārā' as the work of God has two related senses: (1) "create,"[128] "emphasizing the absolute newness of the object"[129] in which God is always the one acting; and (2) "shape," "form,"[130] or "separate"[131] already created materials in which God is often (but not always) the one acting. The first sense—to create absolutely new—is labeled with the Latin term *creatio ex nihilo*, "creation out of nothing." The second sense—to create from already created materials—is labeled *creatio ex materia*.

Bārā' in Genesis 1:1 Has the Unique Sense of Creating Out of Nothing

Bārā' is the only Hebrew word that has the first sense used in Genesis 1:1, to create out of nothing (*ex nihilo*), "emphasizing the absolute newness of the object."[132] Jewish scholar Rabbi Moses ben Naḥman, or Nachmanides (1194–1270), wrote, "We have in our holy language no other term for the bringing forth of something out of nothing but *bārā'*."[133] "*Creatio ex nihilo*" expresses this unique sense of *bārā'* in Genesis 1:1 as the initial creation out of nothing. Before creation, eternal God alone existed. Then "in the beginning" God created (*bārā'*) all the substance, in whatever form it was initially, of the entire universe out of nothing (*creatio ex nihilo*). John Calvin wrote, "The world was made out of nothing."[134]

> *God works through both immediate acts of creation by His direct sovereign commands and through the processes and laws He built into the universe.*

The Genesis 1:1 initial creation out of nothing is an established theological concept:

---

128 Brown, Driver, Briggs, *bārā'*, *Hebrew and English Lexicon*, #1430, p. 135, Strong's #1254.

129 Harris, et al., *Theological Wordbook of the Old Testament* (Chicago: Moody Press, 1980), 1708, vol. II, 701.

130 Brown, Driver, Briggs, *bārā'*, *Hebrew and English Lexicon*, #1430, p. 135, Strong's #1254.

131 Brown, Driver, Briggs, *bārā'*, *Hebrew and English Lexicon*, #1430, p. 135, Strong's #1254.

132 Harris, *et al.*, *Theological Wordbook of the Old Testament*, 1708, vol. II, 701.

133 Mark Rooker, "Genesis 1:1–3: Creation or Re-Creation? Part II," *Bibliotheca Sacra* 149 (1992), 416–419; quoting Jacob Newman, *The Commentary of Nahmanides on Genesis Chapters 1–6* (Leiden: Brill, 1960), 33.

134 John Calvin, *Commentary on Genesis*, 70.

All things were made through him, and without him was not any thing made that was made (John 1:3).

If God created everything completely new and there was nothing but eternal God before "the beginning," then eternal God created everything out of nothing.

Jewish writings have affirmed creation out of nothing. The eminent Rabbi Nachmanides explained Genesis 1:1, "Now listen to the correct and clear explanation of the verse in its simplicity. The Holy One, blessed be He, created all things from absolute non-existence." In the Jewish history book of 2 Maccabees 7:28, the Jewish mother at the point of martyrdom declared, "I beg you, child, look at the sky and the earth; see all that is in them and realize that God made them out of nothing."[135] God created the universe as something new out of absolutely nothing.

The initial *bārā'* creation in Genesis 1:1 was out of nothing (*ex nihilo*), directly by eternal God Himself by His command. The Bible teaches, Jewish and Christian writers have affirmed, and standard theology recognizes the initial *bārā'* creation of all the substance of the entire universe out of nothing, *creatio ex nihilo*, in Genesis 1:1.

Bārā' in the Six Days Has the Second Sense of Fashion Out of Materials

During the six days, *bārā'*, "create," is used in a second sense—"shape, ... fashion, form"[136] out of materials.[137] After the Genesis 1:1 *ex nihilo* creation, two verses during the six described days use *bārā'*: the creation of great water-dwelling creatures in Genesis 1:21 and the creation of humans in Genesis 1:27. If the great water-dwelling creatures created in Genesis 1:21, including leviathan, return to dust materials (Gen. 1:21; Psa. 104:26–29), this implies they were created from dust materials. Adam's body was certainly created from dust materials (Gen. 2:7a) and would return to dust. "For you are dust, and to dust you shall return" (Gen 3:19). Other works of God in the six days were not *creatio ex nihilo* acts. For example, in Genesis 1:9, God commanded the waters to be gathered and dry land to appear. The work in Genesis 1:9 was not creating (*bārā'*) water or land *ex nihilo* but gathering the waters and causing dry land to appear.

The only creation that we can say with certainty was creation *ex nihilo* is "In the

---

135 Paul Copan and William Lane Craig, *Creation out of Nothing* (Grand Rapids: Baker, 2004), 96.

136 Brown, Driver, Briggs, *Hebrew and English Lexicon, bārā'*, 235.

137 Charles Hodge under "Mediate and Immediate Creation" writes, "While it has ever been the doctrine of the Church that God created the universe out of nothing by the word of his power, which creation was instantaneous and immediate, i.e., without the intervention of any second causes; yet it has generally been admitted that this is to be understood only of the original call of matter into existence. Theologians have, therefore, distinguished between a first and second, or immediate and mediate creation." Charles Hodge, *Systematic Theology*, vol. I (London: James Clark & Co, 1892; reprint, 1960), 556–557. Millard Erickson in his *Christian Theology*, 477–482, writes that God is both immanent and transcendent. Because He is transcendent, He can create immediately as in Genesis 1:1. Because He is immanent, He can work through divinely guided processes. God worked both by immediate *de novo* creation acts and by processes following His laws.

beginning God created [*bārā'*] the heavens and the earth" (Gen. 1:1), before which there was only God.

Bārā' in the Perfect Indicates Completed Action in Genesis 1:1

Two common forms (aspects) of Hebrew verbs are perfect and imperfect. The perfect expresses "completed action." The imperfect expresses "incomplete action."[138]

The Hebrew verb *bārā'*, "created," in Genesis 1:1 is perfect—completed action. "In the beginning God created [*bārā'* Hebrew perfect—completed action] the heavens and the earth." The phrase "the heavens and the earth" means the entire universe. God completed the *ex nihilo* creation of all the materials of the universe, and from those materials formed the heavens and the earth "in the beginning" (Gen. 1:1).

God Worked through Both Immediate Creation and Creator-Directed Processes

Eminent theologian Millard Erickson expressed a concern that two groups are going to two polar extremes, and "each view regards the other as inappropriate." Some Bible believers "seemed to require immediacy of action" "because instantaneity seems inherently more supernatural." They believe that "God, by direct act, brought into being virtually instantaneously" the items in the six days. At the opposite extreme are those who see God working in creation only by processes. Erickson believes "both emphases [immediate creation acts and God-superintended processes] should be maintained, that is, to the extent they are taught in the Bible." Erickson writes that God worked both by immediate *de novo* creation acts and by processes following His laws.[139] God works through both immediate acts of creation by His direct sovereign commands and through the processes and laws He built into the universe.

Elohîm, the One and Only Creator God

God alone exists eternally. He created everything. The plural word *Elohîm* indicates majesty, yet it also allows the plural Persons of the one God to have participated in the creation. The singular verb *bārā'* indicates that there is only one God, and He is the one and only Creator of the heavens and the earth.

Et Ha-Shamayim v^et Ha-Aretz, the Heavens and the Earth

Each of the two direct object words—the-heavens and-the-earth—is preceded by the direct object marker *et*, indicating these are the things God created—*et*

---

138 Gary D. Pratico and Miles V. Van Pelt, *Basics of Hebrew Grammar* (Grand Rapids: Zondervan, 2001), 129–130.

139 Millard Erickson, *Christian Theology* (Grand Rapids: Baker, 1983), 477–482.

ha-shamayim v^{e}et ha-ārets. Thus, God created the actual heavens and the actual planet Earth in the beginning time.

Together these two terms mean the entire universe. Hebrew professor John Sailhamer explains, "Unlike English, Hebrew does not have a single word to express the concept of 'the universe'; it must do so by a merism."[140] He continues, "A merism combines two words to express a single idea. A merism expresses 'totality' by combining two contrasts or two extremes." An example of a merism is "Young and old came to celebrate," meaning people of all ages. Sailhamer explains that *ha-shamayim* (the heavens) and *ha-ārets* (the earth) "represent two extremes" and that the merism "the heavens and the earth" in Genesis 1:1 included not only the heavens and planet Earth, but also all that the heavens contained—"the sun, the moon, and the stars."[141] But planet Earth is described as uninhabited, uninhabitable, sea covered, and dark.

---

140 John Sailhamer, *Genesis Unbound*, 56. Sailhamer applied the merism in an odd way to the "Promised Land," which I do not agree with. But most of his Hebrew insights are helpful.

141 John Sailhamer, *Genesis Unbound*, 56.

Chapter 12

In the Beginning God Created the Heavens

When a great hero is awarded a high honor—the Nobel Prize, the Medal of Honor, the King's Accolade, the President's Award—a brief highlights statement of what the hero accomplished is often recorded on an inscription for future generations. Genesis 1:1 is the brief statement of the magnificent creation of the heavens and the earth in the beginning. This statement condenses the first events into two highlights—the creation of the heavens and the creation of the earth:

In the beginning God created the heavens and the earth (Gen. 1:1).

The beginning of the universe, with its fundamental forces, mathematical precision, and the immense power that went into its formation, is elegant and beautiful to physicists.

Genesis 1:1—the Actual *Ex Nihilo* Creation of Heavens in the Beginning

Some would reduce Genesis 1:1 to merely a title or summary of the Genesis 1 creation, with no act of actual *ex nihilo* creation in 1:1. Some take it as just the creation of space and time and unformed matter, or they take it as just part of day one. Others spiritualize Genesis 1:1 or take it in some other way less than literally.

Contrary to these nonliteral views of Genesis 1:1, the first verse describes the actual creation of the heavens and planet Earth, the universe. Grammatically, Genesis 1:1 is not a mere title. In Hebrew, a title is a phrase with no verb, so no action. Genesis 1:1 has a prominent verb—*bārā'*, "created," the second word in the Hebrew Bible. Genesis 1:1 summarizes that first millisecond and everything that followed until God's command for light to start day one on Earth.

Grammatically, the first chapter, Genesis 1, is a historical narrative. Just as the six days in Genesis 1:3–31 should be taken literally, so Genesis 1:1 should also be taken literally. "In the beginning" identifies when the action took place. "God" is the literal person acting. "Created" identifies the literal action of the *ex nihilo* creation. "The heavens and the earth" is a merism meaning the entire organized universe that we now know contains a trillion galaxies, each with billions of suns, and in one of those galaxies, the Milky Way galaxy, our sun and solar system with unfinished

Earth. *Ha-ārets* means our planet Earth, although still uninhabitable, uninhabited, sea covered, and cloud darkened.

The only verse in Genesis 1 that declares God *bārā'* ("created") the heavens and the earth is 1:1: "In the beginning God created [*bārā'*] the heavens and the earth." (In a fourth described day, God would give the already-created luminaries three new functions in the expanse of Earth's sky, making the luminaries separate and rule day and night, be signs for seasons and days and years, and be lights in the expanse of Earth's sky.) Genesis 1:1 should be interpreted literally as describing God's *ex nihilo* creation of the heavens and the earth, all during the beginning time of unspecified length.

More details would be helpful. And just as a hero's outstanding deeds are told with additional details in other accounts, so other Bible texts add details of God's actions as He created the universe in that beginning time.

Details from Other Bible Texts

Bible texts other than Genesis add details about the creation of the heavens in the beginning.

In the Beginning Was an Extensive Beginning Time of Unspecified Length

Jeremiah and Job clarify the meaning of *b^ere'shît*. In the book of Jeremiah, the beginning (*b^ere'shît*) of Zedekiah's kingship was over four years of his eleven-year reign (Jer. 28:1). Job's beginning (*re'shît*) was his entire life before his testing, at least forty and likely seventy years (Job 8:7 with 42:12).

In the Beginning Time, God the Father through God the Son Created the *Aionas*

Hebrews 1:2 says God the Father through God the Son created the *aionas* [αἰῶνας].

In the past God [the Father] spoke to our forefathers through the prophets at many times and in various ways, but in these last days he has spoken to us by his Son, whom he appointed heir of all things, and through whom he made the universe [αἰῶνας, *aionas*] (Heb. 1:2, NIV 1984).

The New Testament Greek word *aionas* in Hebrews 1:2 has a fuller sense than any single English word. It is translated as "universe" (NIV, CJB), "world" or "worlds" (KJV, ESV, NASB), and "ages" (YLT). *Aionas* means "the world," the material universe, and "a long period of time," "age,"[142] "era" (a meaning carried over into our modern

---

142 Walter Bauer, Frederick Danker, William Arndt, and F. W. Gingrich (BDAG), *A Greek-English Lexicon of the New Testament, and other Early Christian Literature, 3rd* (Chicago: University of Chicago Press), 32–33.

derived word "eons"). Eternal God the Father through eternal God the Son created "the heavens and the earth," the entire universe, during the Genesis 1:1 beginning time.

In the Beginning Time, God Created the Fixed Physical Laws of the Universe

Star Trek's original chief engineer, Scotty, would say to Captain Kirk, "Ye cannae change the laws of physics." Scotty was right. But why can't we change the laws of physics?

Jeremiah and Job explain why we can't. God built "fixed laws" (e.g., gravity) and constants (e.g., speed of light) into the creation. In Job 38:33, God asks Job if he knows the "laws [*ᵏhuqqōt*] of the heavens" (NIV 1984). In Jeremiah 33:25, God says He established the "fixed laws [*ᵏhuqqōt*] of the heaven and earth" (Jer. 33:25, NIV 1984). God made the unchanging laws. When science discovers those laws, science discovers truth that God built into the universe and the Earth.

Science has discovered God's law that light travels at a fixed speed in a vacuum. Another law-based process God designed and built into the creation, first revealed long ago by the Bible and then discovered by science in the twentieth century, is the expansion of the universe.

Isaac Newton (1642–1727) formulated the law of universal gravitation and the laws of motion. He demonstrated that the universe functions by fixed laws and credited God, not chance, with those laws. He realized, "Atheism is so senseless. When I look at the solar system, I see the earth at the right distance from the sun to receive the proper amounts of heat and light. This did not happen by chance."[143]

In a world that increasingly values feelings and emotions as of higher importance than truth, the Bible and science (when objectively seeking accurate knowledge) hold to the concept of true knowledge, of "fixed laws." The great Christian author C. S. Lewis was deeply concerned that there would be a "surrender of the claim that science is true." He wrote of early scientists, "Men became scientific because they expected Law in Nature, and they expected Law in Nature because they believed in a Legislator. In most modern scientists this belief has died: it will be interesting to see how long their confidence in uniformity [unchanging laws] survives it."[144]

Are true scientific discoveries of evidence God built into the creation compatible with Christianity? Albert Mohler asks, "Are science and Christianity friends? The answer to that is an emphatic yes, for any true science will be perfectly compatible with the truths we know by God's revelation."[145] God's inerrant Word, accurately interpreted, and God's work in the universe He created are in accord because both

---

143 https://www.doesgodexist.org/JanFeb12/Scientist-Sir-Isaac.Newton.html. Newton also had some erroneous ideas.

144 C. S. Lewis, *Miracles: A Preliminary Study* (London: Collins, 1947), 110.

145 Albert Mohler, "Science and Religion Aren't Friends?" Oct. 11, 2010, accessed Feb. 6, 2019, https://albertmohler.com/2010/10/11/science-and-religion-arent-friends.

are from the same truthful Creator. And both the Bible and true science affirm "fixed laws."

In the Beginning Time, God Upheld the Universe, and He Continues to Do So

Hebrews 1:3 affirms that God continues to uphold the entire creation, including those laws: "He upholds the universe by the word of his power." The laws that are part of the universe are not independent of God but were designed and upheld by God. God is not a distant deistic god but is intimately involved with His creation work.

In the Beginning Time, God Stretched Out the Heavens

The Bible declared, and then science discovered, that the universe had a beginning and has been expanding. Using the great one-hundred-inch Hale Telescope, Edwin Hubble discovered that the galaxies are speeding away from us and each other. He realized that means the universe is stretching out or expanding. Lemaître predicted, Hubble discovered, Einstein agreed, and Penzias and Wilson confirmed that our universe had a beginning and has been expanding ever since, just as the Bible declared long ago.

God has been expanding the universe continually ever since He created the heavens in the beginning. Eleven times the Bible says God has been stretching out the heavens:

- God created the heavens and stretched them out (Isa. 42:5).
- God enveloped the heavens in light and stretched out the heavens (Psa. 104:2).
- God stretched out the heavens and founded the Earth (Isa. 51:13).
- God stretched out the heavens and founded the Earth (Zech. 12:1).
- God founded the Earth and stretched out the heavens (Isa. 48:13).
- God made and established Earth and stretched out the heavens (Jer. 10:12).
- God made and established Earth and stretched out the heavens (Jer. 51:15).
- God alone stretches out the heavens (Job 9:8).
- God made all things and stretched out the heavens (Isa. 44:24).
- God stretches out the heavens like a curtain, spreading them like a tent (Isa. 40:22).
- God created humans and stretched out the heavens (Isa. 45:12).

God has been continually stretching out the heavens since the moment of the *ex nihilo* creation at the start of creation, even into the present time.

God, the LORD, . . . created the heavens and stretched them out (Isa. 42:5).

God created the heavens—the universe had a beginning. God stretched out the heavens—the universe has been and still is continually expanding.

Psalm 104:2 uses a metaphor to explain to ancient people that the Lord God has been stretching out the heavens:

Stretching out the heavens like a tent (Psa. 104:2).

I have slept in a Bedouin tent in the country of Jordan. Traditionally, Bedouin women weave their tents from black goat or dark brown camel hair. When a Bedouin's woven dark tent canopy is raised during the day, one can see pinpricks of light through tiny holes in the goat or camel hair fabric, like stars in the night sky. As the fabric is stretched taut on poles and roped to pegs in the desert sand, these holes spread farther apart. This spreading apart of the pinpricks of light as the fabric stretches illustrates the expansion of the universe in a way that the people of Israel could have understood.

An expanding universe logically implies that the universe was more compact at the start of the expansion. Astrophysicists tell us that the universe had a sudden start from a very compact initial state. Since then, it has expanded immensely. But they do not know what started it. Astrophysicists call their model that the universe had a beginning and has been expanding ever since "the Big Bang." Bible believers call it "the creation."

In the Beginning Time, God Enveloped the Heavens in Light

Psalm 104 describes that first light enveloping the expanding heavens before God set Earth on its foundations (during Gen. 1:1) and covered it with water (the condition in Gen. 1:2).

> Bless the LORD, O my soul!
> O LORD my God, You are very great.
> You are clothed *with* splendor and majesty.
> > Enveloping [*atah,* "cover, envelop"] *in* light as with a cloak,
> > Stretching out *the* heavens like a tent. . . .
> He set/established [*yāsad*] earth on its foundations
> > *that* cannot be removed for eon upon eon.
> You [God] covered it [Earth] with the deep as with a garment;
> > the waters stood above the mountains. . . .
> Bless the LORD, O my soul! (Psa. 104:1–2, 5–6, 35b, from Hebrew).

The two participle phrases—"enveloping *in* light" and "stretching out *the* heavens"—are parallel, describing related actions. God enveloped the universe in light and stretched out the heavens, starting the expansion of the universe.

Some translations unhelpfully add "*Yourself*" or "*Thyself*" (in italics, indicating this word is not in the Hebrew text)—as if God were wrapping *Himself* in light. Hebrew verbs have reflexive forms ("wrapped yourself"), but a reflexive is not used here in either phrase. The lack of a reflexive indicates that the psalmist says God was enveloping the heavens in light and stretching out the heavens. That enveloping in light (Psa. 104:2) took place during the Genesis 1:1 creation. It was before God established Earth on its foundations (Psa. 104:5) and before Earth was covered with water (Psa. 104:6), the condition of Earth in Genesis 1:2.

The psalmist uses Hebrew parallel poetry to express the pair of related ideas. The second line builds on and expands the first line (synthetic parallelism):

Enveloping *in* light as with a cloak,
Stretching out *the* heavens like a tent (Psa. 104:2, from Hebrew).

God enveloped the universe in light and stretched it out.

The Bible's pictorial language descriptions and the science discoveries of the expansion of the universe and the formation of that early light correspond. Astrophysicists investigating the beginning of the universe calculate that as the universe expanded and cooled, light was released, enveloping the entire cosmos in light. As the universe continued stretching out, those early visible light waves also stretched out into longer invisible infrared waves and then into even longer microwaves—the cosmic microwave background radiation discovered by Penzias and Wilson.

God built into the universe the physical laws that govern the expansion of the universe from its beginning even into the present. The expansion rate is so precisely fine-tuned that the only reasonable conclusion is that the God of the Bible, who long ago revealed the stretching out of the heavens, is the Creator.

In the Beginning Time, God Precisely Fine-Tuned the Universe
Hebrews 11:3 explains that by His command, God precisely formed the universe.

By faith we understand that the universe was formed [καταρτίζω, *katartidzo*, "form precisely, fit together just right"] at God's command, so that what is seen was not made out of what was visible (Heb. 11:3, NIV 1984).

The New Testament Greek word *katartidzo* (from ἄρτιος, *artios*—"complete, adequate") is an amazing word that may mean to put in proper condition, put in order, make complete, form, make precisely, fit together just right, adjust, finish, perfect for the fulfillment of its purpose, prepare, make function precisely right for the intended use,[146] "to create, with the implication of putting into proper condition."[147]

---

146 BDAG, 526; Friberg, *Lexicon*, accessed by BibleWorks.
147 Johannes Louw and Eugene A. Nida, *Greek-English Lexicon* (New York: United Bible Societies, 1998), 42:36.

God the Father through God the Son, the Lord Jesus, created (*bārā′*) the universe by His invisible power and command. God precisely formed (*katartidzo*) the visible universe to function exactly right and fulfill its intended purpose—for Earth to be suitable for humans.

Astrophysicists have realized that the constants, such as the universe's expansion rate, are adjusted precisely for life here on Earth.[148] God created just the right amount of matter in just the right amount of space (cosmic mass density), with just the right gravity and just the right expansion rate for life to exist on Earth. A Bible-believing astrophysicist says:

> If the cosmic mass density were even slightly smaller, the universe would expand so rapidly that gravity would be unable to collapse any gas . . . to form galaxies, stars, or planets. If the cosmic mass density were even slightly greater, gravity would work too efficiently. All the stars in the universe . . . would burn up too quickly.[149]

An eminent secular astrophysicist is even more specific. He calculated that the density of matter that resulted in the precise expansion rate of the universe was fine-tuned to a "density = 447,225,917,218,507,401,284,016 gm/cc at 1 ns [nanosecond] after the Big Bang [the sudden beginning and expansion of the universe]. Adding only 0.2 gm/cc to this 447 sextillion gm/cc causes the Big Crunch [the universe contracting and smashing together] to be right now!" How precisely fine-tuned is the universe? This professor of astrophysics explains that the density of matter in space was just right to "1 part in 2235 sextillion,"[150] making life on Earth possible. That degree of precision cannot have been by chance. The density, gravity, and expansion of our universe are "exquisitely fine-tuned for life."[151] Why? The obvious answer is that the eternal Creator God precisely fine-tuned the universe from its start to function properly and fulfill its intended purpose.

In the Beginning Time, God Made the Host of Stars

Excitement rippled across Italy as the news spread of Galileo's telescope and his discoveries of Jupiter's moons, Saturn's rings, the moon's craters, and far more stars than listed in the old star catalogs. Galileo stated, "I give infinite thanks to God, who has been pleased to make me the first observer of marvelous things, unrevealed to by-gone ages."[152]

---

148 Hugh Ross, *The Creator and the Cosmos* (Colorado Springs: NavPress, 2001), 54.

149 Hugh Ross, *Improbable Planet* (Grand Rapids: Baker Books, 2016), 25.

150 Edward Wright, PhD, professor of astronomy at UCLA, http://www.astro.ucla.edu/~wright/cosmo_03.htm#FO.

151 Hugh Ross, *Improbable Planet*, 25.

152 Sister Maria Celeste, *The Private Life of Galileo* (Boston: Nichols & Noyes, 1870), 52.

The psalmist David uses parallel poetic lines to describe God making the heavens and all their starry host:

By the word of the LORD the heavens were made,
and by the breath of his mouth all their host (Psa. 33:6).

Psalm 33:6 metaphorically describes the creation of the starry host of the heavens. God made the heavens and breathed out "their host" of stars across the expanding universe during the extensive beginning time. By the word of the LORD, the expanding heavens with their starry host shone in fiery splendor, demonstrating the glory of their Creator (Gen. 1:1; Neh. 9:6; Psa. 19:1–2; 33:6).

In the Beginning Time, God Put Together the Heavens like a Building Project

David in Psalm 8 describes the heavens, including the stars, as God's works:

When I consider Your heavens, *the* works [*ma'aseh*] of Your fingers,
the moon and the stars, which You have set in place (Psa. 8:3, from Hebrew).

Ma'aseh means "works" in the sense of building projects. God can create instantaneously. But David describes making the heavens with their stars, not as an instantaneous act, but as God's works, God's building projects. *Ma'aseh*, "works," is a Hebrew word that, when used of building projects, indicates works that take considerable time to complete. The Bible highlights two of King Solomon's great building projects (*ma'aseh*): the Temple in Jerusalem taking seven years to build (1 Kings 6:38) and Solomon's own houses and gardens taking thirteen years (1 Kings 7:1):

I made my works [*ma'aseh*] great, I built myself houses, and planted myself vineyards. I made myself gardens and orchards, and I planted all kinds of fruit trees in them. I made myself water pools from which to water the growing trees of the grove. . . . Then I looked on all the works [*ma'aseh*] that my hands had done (Eccl. 2:4, 11, NKJV).

Solomon's great works—the Temple and his houses—were built over considerable time. Psalm 8:3 pictures the stars as "the works" (*ma'aseh*) of God's fingers. Just as Solomon's building projects (*ma'aseh*) took years, using the word *ma'aseh,* the psalmist suggests that God's building projects of making the heavens with their stars took a significant amount of time.

Astrophysicists now recognize that the universe had a sudden beginning, but its stars took considerable time to form. They explain that as the universe expanded and cooled, hydrogen and helium atoms formed. Enormous clouds of hydrogen and helium gases were spread thinly across space. Gravity pulled large amounts of these gases together into dense hot spots where nuclear fusion began, and the first massive stars burst forth with light. Vast numbers of stars formed huge spirals that we call galaxies.

In the Beginning Time, God Organized the Stars of the Heavens

Nehemiah emphasizes that God made "the heavens," including all their starry host.

You made the heavens, even the highest heavens, and all their starry host [*tsābā*] (Neh. 9:6, NIV 1984).

The word *tsābā* in these verses is a plural military term for armies set in orderly array. During the extensive beginning time of Genesis 1:1, God created the heavens, including the host of stars organized into galaxies.

God arranged the galaxies into clusters of galaxies. The clusters formed huge super-clusters, and the super-clusters formed filaments of immense numbers of galaxies stretching across billions of light-years of space. Astronomers estimate the universe contains over a trillion galaxies, each with several hundred billion stars for a total of a hundred to a thousand billion trillion stars (1×10^{23} to 1×10^{24})—beyond our ability to count. Our amazing universe is by the Creator's design, plan, and work. Truly "the heavens declare the glory of God" (Psa. 19:1).

God created the heavens in the beginning. He skillfully formed and fine-tuned the universe (Psa. 136:5; Heb. 11:3), arranging its stars into an organized array (Neh. 9:6). "In the beginning God created the heavens."

Chapter 13

In the Beginning God Created the Earth

When the *Apollo* astronauts went to the moon, they photographed Earth rising over the lunar horizon. The famous photo is called "Earthrise." Our blue and white-cloud-streaked planet appeared so beautiful as it rose above the gray landscape of the moon. So how did Earth become our magnificent, precisely right planet?

Some believe Earth was miraculously formed in an instant. Others believe that science—and the Bible—reveal a long process. Eminent theologian Millard Erickson expressed his concern that two groups are going to two polar extremes, and "each view regards the other as inappropriate." Some Bible believers "seemed to require immediacy of action" "because instantaneity seems inherently more supernatural." At the opposite extreme are those who see God working only by processes in creation. Erickson believes "both emphases [immediate creation acts and God-superintended processes] should be maintained, that is, to the extent they are taught in the Bible." The work of creation was God's work, regardless of how He chose to accomplish His plan.

> *Eminent theologian Millard Erickson expressed his concern that two groups are going to two polar extremes, and "each view regards the other as inappropriate." Some Bible believers "seemed to require immediacy of action" "because instantaneity seems inherently more supernatural." The work of creation was God's work, regardless of how He chose to accomplish His plan.*

Genesis 1:1 Declares God Created Planet Earth in the Beginning

Some reduce the creation of the earth in Genesis 1:1 to just the creation of unformed matter or they take 1:1 as just part of day one. Others take 1:1 nonliterally.

The Hebrew grammar (*vav* consecutive series) in Genesis 1 indicates the chapter is historical narrative. The Author intended us to understand Genesis 1 as reporting cosmic history. Genesis 1:1 explicitly states that God created the earth in the beginning:

In the beginning God created the heavens and the earth [*ha-ārets*] (Gen. 1:1).

Genesis 1:1 has no *vav* because there is no prior event for the *vav* to connect to. Genesis 1:3–31 has *vav*-consecutive-prefixed initial verbs, indicating the whole chapter is a series of sequential events in historical narrative.

Genesis 1:2 starts with "Now the earth." The subsequent description of Earth in 1:2 indicates that God had already created the Earth in the beginning time. God did not create the Earth during the six described days of Genesis 1:3–31. He created planet Earth in the extensive beginning time of Genesis 1:1.

Details from Other Bible Texts

Other Bible texts add details about the creation of the Earth in the beginning.

In the Beginning Time, God Made the Dust of the World

Proverbs 8 contains one of the great Bible passages about creation. This passage declares God was present before all that He created. Verse 26 may give fascinating insight into how God made planet Earth.

While as yet He had not made the earth or the fields [outliers[153]],
Or the primeval dust ['*āpherōt*, dusts] of the world (Prov. 8:26, NKJV).

Verse 26 speaks of a time before God created "the primeval/first (*rōsh*, "primeval" NKJV; "first" NASB, ESV) dusts ('*āpherōt*, plural) of the world (*tēbēl*, world)."[154]

Science is now discovering what God's Word stated long ago. Astronomers using the Hubble Space Telescope have found dust disks surrounding newly forming stars in nearby gas-and-dust nebulae.[155] Planetary geologists have deduced that these gas-and-dust disk-shaped clouds are in the process of forming new planet systems. They reason that planet Earth and the other planets in our solar system formed the same way. Planetary geologists say that our sun's gravity drew the heavier dust of the gas-and-dust spinning disk closer to the sun, forming the rocky planets—Mercury, Venus, Earth, and Mars. The solar wind rushing out from the sun pushed the lighter gases farther out, forming the distant gas giant planets—Jupiter, Saturn, Uranus, and Neptune. Planetary geologists conclude that our rocky planet formed from a disk

---

153 "Outliers," *khutsōt*, means "outside, outliers, out-places." In the context of a walled city, *khutsōt* indicates things outside the city, such as fields. In Proverbs 8:22–31, *khutsōt* seems better understood as referring not to the outliers of a town but to Earth's outliers, such as the moon.

154 Brown, Driver, Briggs, *Hebrew and English Lexicon*, #3753 [3754], 385 (Strong's #8398).

155 https://www.spacetelescope.org/images/opo9545d, http://www.aoc.nrao.edu/epo/powerpoint/astro.disk.talk.pdf.

of dust particles whirling around our sun. Earth formed just the right distance from the sun, just the right size, and with just the right composition for life on our planet. The formation of the rocky planet Earth from dust particles was not by chance but by God's design.

God made Earth's "outliers," plural. The moon is an outlier; comets may also be considered outliers. Interestingly, astrophysicists recently proposed that the Earth originally had two moons that merged into the one moon, explaining why the moon's far side is so different.

In the Beginning Time, God Caused the Birth of Planet Earth

Moses, in Psalm 90:2, pictures God making Earth as a birthing process. The description goes back in time from "Before the mountains were born," to the birth of Earth, to everlasting God.

Before the mountains were born [*yālad,* "to bear, bring forth, beget"],
Or Thou didst give birth [*khul,* "to writhe, whirl, travail"] to the earth and the world,
Even from everlasting to everlasting, Thou art God (Psa. 90:2, NASB).

While emphasizing that God is everlasting, this text also describes—with a very human labor and birth illustration that people of all eras could understand—how Earth came to be. The psalmist pictures Earth being born. The verb *khul* encompasses more than the instant of birth but means "to writhe" or "travail" in labor.[156] Labor and birth are not finished in an instant but take time. Birth implies a prolonged development time before the birth, then the difficult labor process culminating in the birth. The Hebrew verb *khul,* "writhe, whirl, travail," is imperfect, indicating "incomplete action." The idea is action-in-progress (rather than a "completed action"[157] that a Hebrew perfect verb would have indicated). The verb *khul* pictures the labor and birth of planet Earth as a traumatic action-in-progress during the extensive beginning time.

In the Beginning Time, God Created, Fashioned, and Formed Planet Earth

In Isaiah 45, God explains that He is the Creator, the only LORD God, and that He speaks truth. He also explains more about His work fashioning the Earth.

For this is what the LORD says—
he who created the heavens,
    he is God;

---

156 Brown, Driver, Briggs, *Hebrew and English Lexicon,* #2888, 296–297 (Strong's #2342), "writhe . . . travail."

157 Gary D. Pratico and Miles V. Van Pelt, *Basics of Biblical Hebrew,* 129, 139.

he who fashioned [*yātsar*] and made [*asâh*] the earth,
>   he founded [*kun*] it;
he did not create [*bārā'*] it to be empty [*tōhû*],
>   but formed [*yātsar*] it to be inhabited—
he says:
"I am the LORD,
>   and there is no other. . . .
I, the LORD, speak the truth;
I declare what is right" (Isa 45:18–19, NIV 1984).

- God created (*bārā'*) Earth with the intent that it not be empty but inhabited.
- God created (*bārā'*) Earth.
- God fashioned (*yātsar*) Earth.
- God made and worked (*asâh*—"do, make, . . . work") on Earth.
- God founded (*kun*) Earth.
- God formed (*yātsar*) Earth to be inhabited.

God could have created planet Earth instantaneously, but this text does not describe an instantaneous creation of a finished planet Earth. Instead, this Bible text describes God's acts as He created (*bārā'*) planet Earth, made/did-work on (*asâh*), fashioned/formed (*yātsar*) and founded (*kun*) it. These verbs—fashioned/formed, made/did-work on, founded, and created—are not stated as sequential narrative events. Instead, these verbs report the kinds of work God did. The best understanding seems to be that God created (*bārā'*) all the materials of Earth *ex nihilo*, and then He used those materials to make/work on (*asâh*) and fashion (*yātsar*) our planet. One step in fashioning Earth was to set it on its foundations.

In the Beginning Time, God Set Earth on Its Foundations
Planetary geologists say early Earth was an accumulation of trillions of orbiting dust and rock particles randomly clumped together into a ball by gravity. These geologists believe that early Earth did not have clearly defined foundational layers within it. Today we know that Earth has distinct layers: the outer crust resting on the dense mantle and an even heavier iron-nickel core at the center. So how did Earth change from clumped dust to distinct layers?

Ten times in the Bible, the psalmist and prophets speak of God setting the Earth on its foundations. These authors describe the process by several Hebrew words: *yāsad* (verb), to lay a foundation, to found, to establish; *kun* (verb), to establish, to found; *makoun* (noun), an established place or foundation. In the New Testament, Hebrews 1:10 refers to this same process—*themellioo* (verb), to found, to establish, to lay a foundation. Hebrews 1:10 identifies the time of this process as "in the beginning."

This must have been an important process during the beginning time for the Bible to speak about it so often (all verses from NIV 1984):

Psa. 89:11	you founded [*yāsad*] the world and all that is in it
Psa. 102:25	In the beginning you laid the foundations [*yāsad*] of the earth
Psa. 104:5	He set the earth on its foundations [*makoun*]
Isa. 45:18	he who created the heavens, he is God
	he who fashioned and made the earth, he founded [*kun*] it
Isa. 48:13	My own hand laid the foundations [*yāsad*] of the earth
Isa. 51:13	[God] stretched out the heavens
	and laid the foundations [*yāsad*] of the earth
Isa. 51:16	I who set the heavens in place,
	who laid the foundations [*yāsad*] of the earth
Jer. 10:12	God made the earth by his power;
	he founded [*kun*] the world by his wisdom
Jer. 51:15	He made the earth by his power;
	he founded [*kun*] the world by his wisdom
Zech. 12:1	who stretches out the heavens,
	who lays the foundation [*yāsad*] of the earth
Heb. 1:10	In the beginning, O LORD,
	you laid the foundations [*themellioo*] of the earth

God declares that we humans cannot explore "the foundations of the Earth below" (Jer. 31:37). The deepest mine shaft into the Earth, the Ashanti Mponeng gold mine in South Africa, is 2.5 miles (3.9 km) deep. The heat deep in the mine is so intense that 2.5 miles may be about as deep as humans can dig into Earth's 20-mile-deep continental crust. The "foundations of the earth" are far deeper than the 2.5 miles deep humans can explore.

Psalm 104:5 declares that God "set the earth on its foundations." The Bible does not reveal how He did it. But science may have discovered how. Geologists explain that early Earth was a ball of dust and rock particles. Then Earth was bombarded by meteors containing radioactive elements. Those impacts melted Earth's surface. The heavy radioactive elements sank into the Earth, helping melt the interior of Earth. Gravity pulled the heavy molten iron and nickel downward into the interior of molten Earth, forming Earth's iron-nickel core. Around the core, heavy molten rock formed the mantle. The core and mantle may be understood as the foundations of the Earth. Lighter rock rose to Earth's surface, forming the continents. While the Bible does not include these details, this process does seem to correspond to the Bible texts that say God "laid the foundations of the earth."

In the Beginning Time, God Wrapped Earth in Cloud

In Job 38, the stars sang as God laid Earth's foundations. This creation passage pictures water being birthed onto Earth's surface and the infant Earth being enveloped by cloud as a thick dark swaddling garment wrapping the growing sea. God asks Job:

> Where were you when I laid the earth's foundation?
>> Tell me, if you understand. . . .
> While the morning stars sang together
>> and all the angels shouted for joy?
> Who shut up the sea behind doors
>> when it burst forth from the womb,
> when I made the clouds its garment
>> and wrapped it in thick darkness? (Job 38:4–9, NIV 1984).

God caused the infant sea to burst out and wrapped the sea in clouds, producing "thick darkness" on Earth's surface.

This same cloud also obscured the moon from the perspective of Earth. Job 26 explains that after God suspended "the earth over/on nothing" (Job 26:7), He bound up Earth's water in clouds and covered the face of the full moon (Job 26:9).

> He spreads out the northern skies over empty space;
>> he suspends the earth over nothing.
> He wraps up ["binds up," ESV] the waters in his clouds,
>> yet the clouds do not burst under their weight.
> He covers the face of the full moon,[158]
>> spreading his clouds over it [producing the darkness on Earth in Gen. 1:2].
> He marks out the horizon on the face of the waters
>> for a boundary between light and darkness [day one] (Job 26:7–10, NIV 1984).

"He covers the face of the full moon" indicates that the moon had been formed by this point in the creation. This covering was before God's command brought light to Earth's dark sea surface, forming a horizon on the sea waters, starting day one.

Geologists explain how that cloud cover formed around the Earth. "Asteroids and comets smashed into the early Earth, covering our planet's surface with molten rock during its earliest days."[159] Those meteors and comets contained water, and the impact heat liberated that water, filling the atmosphere with thick clouds of water vapor. The meteor impacts also heated Earth's crust and mantle, liberating

---

158 The vowel points that were added later to the Hebrew text indicate "throne" (KJV), but that does not fit the context. Only the original consonants were inspired, and in context they indicate "moon" (NASB, ESV, NIV).

159 https://www.space.com/26685-early-earth-bombardment-water-oasis.html.

underground water. Meanwhile, carbon dioxide was vented into the atmosphere by volcanoes. As a result, the Earth became a cloud-darkened planet.

In the Beginning Time, God Covered Earth with Deep Sea

The first part of Proverbs 8 goes back in time to when there were no oceans, no springs of water, no mountains, no hills.

> When there were no ocean depths, I [Wisdom] was brought forth;
>> when there were no springs abounding with waters,
>>> before the mountains were settled,
>>>> before the hills (Prov. 8:24–25, from Hebrew).

Geologists say early Earth's surface was scorchingly hot. But outer space is frigid at about 3° Kelvin, 3° above absolute zero (-455° F, -270° C), so heat was continually lost from the hot Earth into cold space. As heat was lost into space, Earth's surface began to cool and form a solid crust with hills and mountains. Earth's atmosphere was also cooling. Eventually the growing clouds burst with rain over the cooling Earth. By then, Earth's surface was cool enough that water from the rain began to collect in lower level basins. That rain was no gentle shower but a worldwide deluge that continued not just for hours or days but millennia. Volcanoes continued to add steam, and hot water burst from springs in the earth.

> It [water] burst forth from the womb (Job 38:8, NIV 1984).

Slowly the water increased, forming the early ocean beneath the thick cloud. Finally, the "waters stood above the mountains."

> Praise the LORD . . .
> He [God] set the earth on its foundations;
>> it can never be moved.
> You [God] covered it with the deep as with a garment;
>> the waters stood above the mountains (Psa. 104:1, 5–6, NIV 1984).

Earth became water covered with an ocean so deep that the waters "stood above the mountains." The result was the water-covered, cloud-darkened Earth described in Genesis 1:2.

Now-the-earth was uninhabitable and uninhabited [*tōhû vabōhû*],
and-darkness *was* over *the* surface of *the* deep,
and-Spirit of God *was* hovering over *the* surface of the waters (Gen. 1:2, from Hebrew).

Life as we commonly know it could not have existed in that uninhabitable, water-covered, cloud-darkened world. There was no light. There were no green plants, no great marine life, no flying life, no land animal life, no humans. Earth had become a cloud-enveloped, dark, water-covered planet.

Chapter 14

Solomon's Wisdom Account of Creation

The Bible's wisdom literature contains a unique creation text: Proverbs 8:22–31. In this text, Solomon tells the drama of creation from the perspective of Wisdom. But the wise proverb-giver wraps this poetic creation text in an enigma; he encloses it in a mystery; he hides it in a wisdom-genre puzzle. How do we understand the enigma of how Solomon's poetic creation account fits with the Genesis 1 creation narrative? How do we unpack the reversal in this mystery? Can we uncover additional creation information hidden in this wisdom puzzle?

Solomon's Account of God Making the Heavens and Earth

This is the wisdom account King Solomon told. This is the poetic riddle he wrote.

The LORD possessed me [Wisdom] at *the* beginning of His way, before His works of old.
From everlasting I was appointed, from *the* beginning, before the start of earth,
When *there were* no ocean depths, I was brought forth,
When *there were* no springs abounding with waters,
Before the mountains were settled,
Before the hills, I was brought forth,
While He had not made *the* earth and its outliers,[160]
And *the* beginning dusts [*rōsh 'āpherōt*] of *the* world,
When He set in place *the* heavens,
I [Wisdom] *was* there.
When He marked out a horizon on the face of the deep,
When He established the clouds above,
When He firmly fixed *in place* the springs of the deep-sea,
When He bounded the sea, so its waters would not pass His limit,
When He marked out the foundations of the land.
Then I [Wisdom] was beside Him as a Craftsman,
And I was *a* delight day after day,
Rejoicing in His presence always; rejoicing in His inhabited world,
With delight in the children of man (Prov. 8:22–31, from Hebrew).

---

160 "Outliers," *ḥutsōt*, means outside, outliers, may mean objects outside Earth such as the moon.

Solomon's account about God and Wisdom in the creation work can add to our understanding of the sequence of creation events—if we can unlock his enigmatic wisdom poem of creation.

Unlocking the Wisdom Creation Enigma

To unlock the account, four points need to be understood.

1. Two persons—LORD God YHVH and Wisdom—are both everlasting.

Solomon presents two persons—the LORD (YHVH) and Wisdom—in this Hebrew poem on wisdom. YHVH and Wisdom existed before the creation works of old, from everlasting. Wisdom is the Craftsman of creation (see John 1:1–3). Wisdom speaks what is right and true (Prov. 8:6–7a). And in 8:22–31, Wisdom teaches about the LORD's work in creation. Although Solomon is the human author, the speaker is Wisdom, referred to as "me" or "I," while the LORD is referred to as "He." The LORD is the ultimate Person behind the creation actions, and Wisdom is the Craftsman beside the LORD.

2. The account is structured as a chiasm with two halves.

This creation text is roughly in the form of a chiasm. A chiasm is a symmetrical literary form, with a middle line and a reversal between the first and second halves. Classic epics and many Bible passages use a chiasm. An example of a longer chiasm is the Flood narrative (Gen. 6:1—9:29):

> A – God spoke a judgment warning to Noah (Gen. 6:1ff.).
> > B – Noah, his family, and the animals entered the ark.
> > > C – The waters rose.
> > > > D – "God remembered Noah" (Gen. 8:1). ← point of reversal.
> > > C' – The waters sank.
> > B' – Noah, his family, and the animals exited the ark.
> A' – God blessed Noah and his sons (Gen. 9:1ff.).

Although perhaps not a perfect chiasm, Proverbs 8:22–31 has several characteristics of a chiasm. The first half reports that God and Wisdom were present before creating the heavens and the earth in the beginning. The middle line is "I [Wisdom] was there." The second half reports that Wisdom was there during God's work finishing the Earth (Gen. 1:3–31).

> A – The LORD possessed me, Wisdom, from the beginning.
> > B – Before God created the heavens and the Earth
> > > C – I, Wisdom, was there. ← middle line, point of reversal.
> > B' – When God completed His works on Earth

A' – I, Wisdom was beside the LORD rejoicing in His inhabited world.

3. A time reversal occurs between the two halves.

A reversal characterizes a chiasm. This creation passage has a time reversal. The first half of the chiasm (Prov. 8:22–27a) is a series of descriptions stated negatively by ("when no/before") going back in time from the water-covered Earth of Genesis 1:2 to the time when God set the heavens in place (Gen. 1:1). Before the ocean depths, before gushing springs of water, before the mountains were in place, before the hills, before God made the Earth and its outliers, before the primeval dusts of the world, before the heavens were set in place—there was eternal God and Wisdom beside Him. The second half of the chiasm (Prov. 8:27b–31) goes forward in time from the first light forming a horizon on the deep sea on day one to Earth with people on the sixth described day.

4. The two halves of the chiasm are the two stages of creation.

The first half of the chiasm (Prov. 8:22–27a) is about the "beginning" (*re'shît*). *Re'shît* in Proverbs 8:22 and 23 is the root word of *b*e*re'shît* "in the beginning."

> The LORD possessed me [Wisdom] at *the* beginning [*re'shît*] of His way, before His works of old.
> From everlasting I was appointed, from *the* beginning [*re'shît*], before the start of earth (Prov. 8:22–23, from Hebrew).

By introducing the first half (Prov. 8:22–27a) with the word *re'shît*, Solomon is identifying that half with "the beginning" in Genesis 1:1.

When inverted into chronological order, the first half corresponds to the creation of the heavens and the earth in the Genesis 1:1 beginning time and the description in 1:2—stage one. First, God "set in place the heavens" (Prov. 8:27a) with its host of stars. Then God made the primeval dusts (*rōsh 'āpherōt*) of the world. He made the Earth. He made Earth's outliers (Prov. 8:26). He made Earth's first hills and mountains (Prov. 8:25). He made springs of water come out of the Earth, and He covered Earth with the deep ocean (Prov. 8:24).

Earth was in the condition described in Genesis 1:2—an uninhabitable, uninhabited, ocean-covered world. Stage one of creation was complete. At the center of the chiasm is the declaration "I [Wisdom] was there."

The second half of the chiasm (Prov. 8:27b–31) reveals in chronological order events during the six described days of Genesis 1:3–31: stage two of creation. First, God commanded light to reach planet Earth, forming a horizon on the surface of the deep, the event of day one (Prov. 8:27b; Gen. 1:3–5). Then God "established the clouds above," the event of a second day (Prov. 8:28a; Gen. 1:6–8). Next God fixed in place the springs of the sea (Prov. 8:28b; Gen. 1:9), established the boundaries for the sea, and marked out the foundations of the land (Prov. 8:29; Gen. 1:9–10). Then God filled the earth with life, and Wisdom rejoiced, the events of a fifth day (Prov. 8:31a; Gen. 1:20–25). Finally, God created people to Wisdom's delight, the event of the sixth day (Gen. 1:27; Prov. 8:31b).

In the poetic Proverbs 8:22–31, the first half of Solomon's chiasm goes back in time; the second half goes forward. When listed in chronological order, this description of God's creation work parallels the report of Genesis 1.

Stage One: "In the beginning God created the heavens and the earth."
God possessed me, Wisdom, from eternity
> before He set in place the heavens;
> before He made the primeval dusts of the world;
> before He made the Earth and its outliers;
> before He made the hills;
> before He settled the mountains;
> before He made springs abounding with water;
> before He covered Earth with the deep ocean.

Stage Two: God made Earth lighted, habitable, and inhabited.
I, Wisdom, was there, when
> He marked out with light a horizon on the surface of the deep ocean;
> He established the clouds above;
> He fixed in place the springs of the sea;
> He bounded the sea by land;
> He marked out/inscribed into stone/decreed the foundations of the land;
> He filled the world with life, and Wisdom rejoiced;
> He created humans, and Wisdom was delighted.

This passage, when listed in chronological order, parallels the historical narrative of God's creation work reported in Genesis 1. And the more science learns, the more its discoveries correspond to these same events reported long ago in these two Bible texts.

Genesis 1, Proverbs 8, Job 38, and Psalm 104 Describe Two Stages of Creation

Stage One of Creation: In the Beginning
"In the beginning" time (Gen. 1:1) God created *ex nihilo*, out of nothing (Gen. 1:1; John 1:3). He created the heavens, the *aionas*—the universe in time and space (Gen. 1:1; Heb. 1:2; 11:3). He enveloped the heavens in light early in the beginning time (Psa. 104:2). He stretched out the heavens, continually expanding them (Isa. 45:12; Psa. 104:2). He set in place the host of stars in an organized array (Neh. 9:6).

He made the primeval dusts of the world. He created the Earth (Gen. 1:1). He made Earth's outliers (Prov. 8:26). He set Earth on its foundations (Psa. 104:5; Isa. 48:13). He fashioned planet Earth, which He had made (Isa. 45:18). He made hills on the Earth. He settled the mountains in place (Psa. 104:8; Psa. 90:2). He caused Earth's growing clouds to conceal the moon from view (Job 26:9). He wrapped Earth in thick dark clouds, shutting out the light (Job 38:9–12). He filled the clouds with water (Job 26:8) that would eventually bring rain, and He made springs burst forth with water. He made the deep ocean that eventually covered Earth's mountains (Gen. 1:2; Psa. 104:6).

Condition of Planet Earth at the End of the Beginning Time

Earth was uninhabitable and uninhabited, empty of life (Gen. 1:2). Earth was dark, wrapped in thick dark cloud cover (Gen. 1:2; Job 38:9–12). And Earth was deep sea covered (Gen. 1:2), the sea even covering the mountains.

Stage Two of Creation: Six Described Days

God commanded, "Let there be light," marking out a horizon on the surface of the deep sea waters (Gen. 1:3; Prov. 8:27). He established the clouds above the sea (Gen. 1:6–8; Prov. 8:28). He fixed in place the springs of the sea, gathering the waters into one place (Gen 1:9; Prov. 8:28), and bounded the sea by land so its waters would not pass His limit (Gen. 1:9; Prov. 8:29). He marked out/cut into stone/decreed the foundations of land (Gen. 1:9; Prov. 8:29). He filled the earth with life (Gen. 1:20–27; Prov. 8:31a). He created reproducing humans (Gen. 1:26–27; Prov. 8:31).

Outline of Two Stages of Creation from Multiple Bible Creation Texts

Stage One of Creation: In the Beginning

- The eternal perfect God—Father-Son-Spirit—exists forever.
- God "in the beginning" created *ex nihilo,* out of nothing (Gen. 1:1; John 1:3).
- God "in the beginning" created the *aionas*—the time-space-energy-matter universe.
- God began stretching out the heavens, expanding the universe (Isa. 45:12).
- God enveloped the heavens in light in the beginning time (Psa. 104:2).
- God created the heavens, setting the host of stars in an organized array (Neh. 9:6).
- God made the primeval dusts of the world (Prov. 8:26).
- God created the Earth (Gen. 1:1; Prov. 8:26).
- God made Earth's outliers (Prov. 8:26), probably including the moon.
- God set Earth on its foundations, forming its interior layers (Psa. 104:5; Isa. 48:13).
- God fashioned planet Earth, which He had made (Isa. 45:18).
- God made hills on the Earth and settled the mountains in place (Psa. 104:8; 90:2).
- God caused Earth's growing clouds to conceal the moon from view (Job 26:9).
- God wrapped Earth in thick dark clouds, shutting out the light (Job 38:9–12).
- God filled the clouds with water (Job 26:8) and made springs bursting with water.
- God made the deep sea, covering Earth's first mountains (Gen. 1:2; Psa. 104:6).
- At the end of the beginning time, planet Earth was uninhabitable, uninhabited, dark, wrapped in thick dark cloud cover (Job 38:9–12), and deep sea covered (Gen. 1:2).

Stage Two of Creation: Six Described Days

- God commanded, "Let there be light," making a horizon (Gen. 1:3; Prov. 8:27).
- God separated the cloud water above from the sea water (Gen. 1:6–7; Prov. 8:28).
  - God gathered the waters, causing dry land to appear (Gen 1:9–10; Prov. 8:28).
  - God bounded sea by land; its waters would not pass His limits (Gen. 1:9; Prov. 8:29).
  - God marked out/decreed the foundations of land (Gen. 1:9; Prov. 8:29).
- God commanded the earth to produce green vegetation (Gen. 1:11–12).
- God caused the luminaries to fully function to the Earth (Gen. 1:14–19).
  - God made reproducing animals (Gen. 1:20–25; Psa. 104:11, 24).
- The sixth day, God created the pair of reproducing humans (Gen. 1:27; Prov. 8:31).
- The seventh day, God rested (Gen. 2:1–3).

God's Word and God's Work Correspond

God, by His nature, is unswervingly truthful. God's Word is truth. Both Genesis 1 and Proverbs 8 (although different genres) reveal truth about the creation. The agreement of God's Word and parallel evidence He built into His creation is robust evidence that the God of the Bible is the Creator.

Chapter 15

Genesis 1:2 Conditions on Earth and Perspective from Earth

Earth was a world of darkness, a deep-sea-covered world, a world with a cloud-shrouded atmosphere, a world with no plants, no animals, no humans. Genesis 1:2 describes planet Earth after its creation as reported in Genesis 1:1.

> In-beginning God created the heavens and the earth.
> Now-the-earth was
>   uninhabitable and uninhabited [tōhû v^a bōhû]
>   and-darkness *was* over the surface of *the* deep,
>   and-Spirit of God *was* hovering over the surface of the waters
>   (Gen. 1:1–2, from Hebrew).

Genesis 1:1 is like a highlights movie clip of the events of the creation of the heavens and the earth "in the beginning." Genesis 1:2 is like a still photograph of planet Earth, picturing its conditions at the end of that beginning time. Earth was uninhabitable and uninhabited. Earth was cloud darkened and water covered. The Spirit of God was present at the sea-covered surface of Earth. Earth was not yet functional for humans.

> Now the earth was uninhabitable and uninhabited [tōhû v^a bōhû]
>   1. tōhû, uninhabitable
>   2. bōhû, uninhabited, or empty of life
> and darkness [^k hōshek] was on the surface of the deep [t^e hôm],
>   3. ^k hōshek, darkness
>   4. t^e hôm, deep ocean
> and the Spirit of God was hovering over the surface of the waters [ha-māyim]
> (Gen. 1:2, from Hebrew).

The natural sciences portray planet Earth in a way that corresponds very closely to this short Bible description in Genesis 1:2.

Science Describes Early Planet Earth

During the Cold War space race, Soviet Russia concentrated on the planet Venus and built rugged planetary probes. Venera 4 lasted an impressive ninety-four minutes as it descended by parachute into the thick poisonous Venusian atmosphere before the noxious gases caused it to cease transmitting.[161] Early Earth's atmosphere may have resembled the atmosphere of Venus more than the pleasant blue sky of Earth today.

Scientists tell us that on early planet Earth, volcanoes belched out steam, carbon dioxide, sulfur dioxide, and traces of hydrogen sulfide, nitrogen, argon, methane, ammonia, hydrogen fluoride, and carbon monoxide, but no free oxygen (O_2). As more and more toxic gases accumulated in the atmosphere, the sky grew darker and darker.

When Mount St. Helens erupted, one striking feature was the cloud that turned daytime into darkness across several northwestern states. A far worse eruption occurred in Iceland beginning in 1783 when the Laki fissure and Grimsvötn volcano poured out lava and poisonous gases. Clouds of sulfur dioxide and hydrogen fluoride combined with water to form sulfurous and hydrofluoric acids. These darkened the sky for eight months. The poisonous clouds and darkness severely reduced plant growth, resulting in the starvation and death of over three-quarters of Iceland's sheep and a quarter of its people. As sulfur dioxide clouds spread around the world, famine raged in India and starvation ravaged Egypt. England called it the year without a summer. About six million people died worldwide. And that was from just one eruption.

Early Earth was far less habitable. Earth's atmosphere was a thick mix of water vapor and poisonous gases but no free oxygen. As Earth cooled, water burst from the earth and the dense clouds began to release rain. Eventually a vast worldwide ocean covered Earth. Planet Earth was uninhabitable, empty of life, sea covered, and darkened by thick dark clouds and continuous heavy rain.

Genesis 1:2 Is a Description, Not a Narrative of Events

Genesis 1:2, "<u>Now</u>-the-earth," starts with a special kind of Hebrew construction called a *vav* (often spelled "*waw*") disjunctive. When a *vav*-prefixed noun starts a sentence or clause, it is a Hebrew way of indicating that what follows interrupts the flow of actions with a static description of the circumstances about that *vav*-prefixed noun. Three of the ways a *vav* is used are the following:

- A ***vav* conjunction** connects two terms or clauses and means "and" ("the heavens <u>and</u> the earth").
- A ***vav*-disjunctive**-prefixed noun starting a clause or sentence interrupts the narrative flow of actions to describe the circumstances of that noun. ("<u>Now-the-earth</u> was uninhabitable.")
- A ***vav*-consecutive**-prefixed verb starting a clause or sentence in a series narrates sequential actions ("<u>Then-said</u> God, 'Let-be light,' <u>and-was</u> light") and indicates historical narrative sequential events.

---

161 Douglas M. Messier, "Soviet Venus Missions," National Science Teachers Association, http://astro.if.ufrgs.br/solar/sovvenus.htm.

In the beginning God created the heavens <u>and</u> the earth. ← *vav* conjunction joins

Now-the-earth was uninhabitable ← *vav*-disjunctive-prefixed initial noun describes

Then-said God, "Let-be light" ←*vav*-consecutive-prefixed initial verbs narrate actions/events

Genesis 1:2 consists of three *vav*-disjunctive-prefixed-noun clauses: "<u>Now-the-earth</u> was *tōhû vᵃbōhû*, <u>and-darkness</u> was on the surface of the deep, <u>and-the-Spirit</u> of God was hovering over the surface of the waters."[162] These three *vav* disjunctive-prefixed-noun clauses in Genesis 1:2 interrupt the actions of Genesis 1:1 by describing conditions on Earth before the actions resume in 1:3–31.[163] Thus, the focus switches from God's work creating the heavens and the earth in Genesis 1:1, to a description of Earth as uninhabitable and uninhabited, sea covered, and dark in 1:2. Then God worked six days changing Earth to lighted, with land, habitable, and inhabited (1:3–31).

> *Earth was uninhabitable, having no breathable air, no light, and no permanent dry land. Earth was uninhabited, having no animals and no humans. Earth was sea covered, having no dry land. And Earth was wrapped in thick dark cloud, so no light reached its deep sea surface.*

Earth Was Uninhabitable, Uninhabited, Water Covered, and Dark

Genesis 1:1 ends with "the heavens and the earth." Then Genesis 1:2 (from Hebrew) reports:

Now-the-earth was uninhabitable and uninhabited [*tōhû vᵃbōhû*],
and-darkness over *the* surface of *the* deep,
and-Spirit of God *was* hovering over *the* surface of the waters.

The universe was not deep sea covered and dark. Only planet Earth is described as uninhabitable, uninhabited, deep sea covered, and dark on the surface of its deep sea. Unfinished Earth would be the focus of God's finishing works in Genesis 1:3–31.

---

162 Gordon J. Wenham, *Word Biblical Commentary: Genesis 1—15* (Waco: Word, 1987), 15.
163 Practico and Van Pelt, *Basics of Biblical Hebrew*, 281–282.

Tōhû v^abōhû Means Uninhabitable and Uninhabited

Planet Earth was *tōhû v^abōhû*, meaning uninhabitable and uninhabited. Hebrew professor John Sailhamer says that the meaning of the Hebrew phrase *tōhû v^abōhû* is "uninhabitable" and "wilderness." He explains that in Genesis 1:2, Earth "had not yet become habitable for human beings."[164] The first word, *tōhû*, describes a place empty of what is needed for life—uninhabitable. The second word, *bōhû*, describes a place empty of life—uninhabited. Hebrew scholar David Tsumura says the phrase means "uninhabitable and uninhabited."[165] Jeremiah 4:23–26 uses the exact phrase *tōhû v^abōhû* to describe the land of Israel being "deserted and uninhabited"[166] because of the violent conquest by the Babylonian army. The Babylonians destroyed the cities and salted the fields, so the land became uninhabitable. They killed many people and deported most of the rest as captives, so the land became uninhabited. The land was dark because the Babylonians set fires that filled the air with thick dark smoke, blocking out the light. Jeremiah described the conditions in the conquered land of Israel:

I looked at the earth,
    and it was formless and empty [*tōhû v^abōhû*];
And at the heavens,
    and their light was gone (Jer. 4:23, NIV 1984).

The Babylonian conquerors made Israel unfit for life, its people deported, and its land ruined. Some modern writers have mistakenly claimed that *tōhû v^abōhû* means formless chaos. Jeremiah used the phrase *tōhû v^abōhû* as he looked out on the devastated land of southern Israel. What he described was not formless chaos but an uninhabitable wasteland empty of life, with even the light obscured by clouds of smoke.

In parallel statements, Isaiah contrasts *tōhû* (empty) and "inhabited."

He did not create [*bārā'*] it [Earth] to be empty [*tōhû*],
    but formed [*yātsar*] it to be inhabited (Isa. 45:18, NIV 1984).

The phrase *tōhû v^abōhû* means uninhabitable and uninhabited.

Rabbi Abraham Ibn Ezra (c. 1092–1167) understood that *tōhû v^abōhû* means Earth was "uninhabited because it was covered with water, not that the earth was formless chaos."[167] David Tsumura, perhaps the foremost scholar on Genesis 1:2, says,

---

164 John Sailhamer, *Genesis Unbound*, 63, 64.

165 David Toshio Tsumura, *The Earth and the Waters*, Journal for the Study of the Old Testament, Sup. Series 83.

166 John Sailhamer, *Genesis Unbound*, 65.

167 John Sailhamer, *Genesis Unbound*, 196.

"There is nothing in this passage [Genesis 1:2] that would suggest a chaotic state of the earth."[168] Hebrew scholar Edward J. Young says it would be "wise to abandon the term 'chaos.'"[169] Like Mars or Venus today, Earth back then was an uninhabitable and uninhabited planet, but it was not formless chaos. Genesis 1:2 describes planet Earth as uninhabitable and uninhabited, empty of life, its sea-covered surface dark.

Planet Earth Was Covered by Deep Ocean

Planetary geologists say that after Earth's foundational core and mantle layer were established, volcanoes vented massive amounts of steam out of Earth's interior into the atmosphere. Meteors and a few comets, often called "dirty snowballs" because they contain so much water, brought more and more water to Earth's atmosphere. At first, any rain that fell could not reach the ground because Earth's surface was too hot. Job 26 describes Earth's water as wrapped in clouds, but at first, the clouds did not drop rain to the earth:

> He spreads out the northern skies over empty space;
>> he suspends the earth over nothing.
> He wraps up the waters in his clouds,
>> yet the clouds do not burst under their weight (Job 26:7–8, NIV 1984).

Eventually the ever-increasing water vapor caused an enormous rain that continued over a very long time. In the creation passage in Job 38, God asked Job about the creation, "Where were you when I laid the foundation of the Earth?" Then in a birth motif, God pictured the water bursting out of the ground:

> Who shut up the sea behind doors
>> when it burst forth from the womb? (Job 38:8, NIV 1984).

Water flowed out of the ground in hot springs, and the clouds burst. Rain fell constantly until Earth eventually was covered by a deep sea.

Psalm 104:5 declares that God covered the Earth with the deep sea:

> He [God] set the earth on its foundations;
>> it can never be moved.
> You [God] covered it [Earth] with the deep as with a garment;
>> the waters stood above the mountains (Psa. 104:5–6, NIV 1984).

After God set Earth on its foundations, He covered Earth, including its first mountains, with the "deep" (Psa. 104:6), the same deep sea waters described in Genesis 1:2.

---

168 David Toshio Tsumura, *The Earth and the Waters*, 33, 34.

169 Young, *Studies in Genesis One* (Phillipsburg, NJ: P & R Publishing, 1964), 13.

Clouds Darkened Earth's Deep Sea Surface

The Bible does not say darkness was across the heavens. The Bible states, "In the beginning God created the heavens," which included the starry host, so the heavens were lighted. Genesis 1:2b says darkness was over Earth's deep ocean surface:

Now-the-earth was uninhabitable and uninhabited,
and-darkness over *the* surface of *the* deep (Gen. 1:2, from Hebrew).

Job 26:8 and 38:9 explain the cause of the darkness on "the surface of the deep" (Gen. 1:2)—a thick dark cloud cover. Job 26:9 says God wrapped the water-covered Earth in clouds that hid the face of the full moon. Darkness closed over the surface of Earth's deep ocean. The explanations in Job should be understood from the perspective of the surface of the Earth's deep sea, a perspective set by "Now the earth." From the perspective of the Earth's surface, thick clouds in Earth's sky covered the face of the moon:

He obscures the face of the full moon,
And spreads His cloud over it (Job 26:9, NASB).

Job 38 confirms the cloud cover. God questioned Job, using a birth metaphor, picturing the birth of the ocean (Job 38:8–9). God then pictured the infant sea wrapped in thick dark cloud like a baby wrapped in swaddling clothes:

Who shut up the sea behind doors
    when it burst forth from the womb,
when I made the clouds its garment
    and wrapped it in thick darkness? (Job 38:8–9, NIV 1984).

Darkness was over the surface of the deep (Gen. 1:2, NIV 1984).

The light from distant stars, light from our sun, and light reflected by the moon shone across the heavens. But their light could not penetrate the thick dark cloud cover enveloping our planet. No light reached Earth's deep dark sea.

All four conditions now characterized planet Earth. Earth was uninhabitable, having no breathable air, no light, and no dry land. Earth was uninhabited, having no animals and no humans. Earth was sea covered, having no permanent dry land. And Earth was wrapped in thick dark cloud, so no light reached its deep sea surface. Thus, the Earth was uninhabitable, uninhabited, deep sea covered, with darkness over the deep sea surface, just as described in Genesis 1:2.

The Perspective of the Genesis 1:3–31 Narrative

The viewpoint, or perspective, from which a narrative is given is part of the context that tells the reader how to understand the narrative. For example, during the terrible but decisive Battle of the Bulge in World War II in Europe, a few American units were caught by a surprise attack planned by Hitler on the snow-covered ground of the weakly defended front of the Ardennes Forest. Left behind at the vital road junction of Bastogne, American paratroopers desperately fought to hold the crucial town. But they lacked winter uniforms and were running out of food, ammunition, and medical supplies. And they were being attacked by huge tanks, massed artillery, and SS infantry.

Some of the survivors have reported their appalling experiences, but all the reports are from a ground-level perspective, none from the air. The Americans had large numbers of fast P-51 Mustang fighters, heavy P-38 Thunderbolt ground attack fighter-bombers, and transport aircraft. But none could help, because the German army commanders timed their surprise attack just as a thick weather system moved in, covering the battle area with dense cloud cover for over a week. All the reports of the Battle of the Bulge for over a week were from the perspective of the ground, none from the air. Then, after the paratroopers desperately fought for days in the freezing weather, as Christmas Day approached, the cloud cover broke and sunlight began shining down onto the battlefield. American fighter aircraft stormed in, the bombers pounded the SS attackers, and supply planes dropped masses of supplies to the American fighting men below. The day after Christmas, General George Patton's tanks finally reached the besieged paratroopers in Bastogne.

The entire account came from the perspective of the paratroopers fighting on the frozen ground below the cloud cover. The perspective of an account is key to understanding that account.

Genesis 1:1 was about "the heavens and the earth." Genesis 1:2 starts, "Now the earth," changing the narrative's focus to the surface of planet Earth. Genesis 1:2 concludes with these words:

And the Spirit of God was hovering over the waters (Gen. 1:2, NIV 1984).

Why would the location of the Holy Spirit be expressly stated? The Holy Spirit of God, the third Person of the one triune God, is omnipresent, everywhere. Giving a location for the Spirit informs the reader of the perspective of the upcoming narrative. Starting in Genesis 1:3, the narrative seems best understood from the perspective of the stated location of the Holy Spirit hovering just above Earth's dark sea surface. There was no light at the Spirit's location just above Earth's deep sea under the dark cloud.

Then God said, "Let there be light." Genesis 1:3 reports, "And there was light." From the perspective of the surface of Earth's dark sea, at God's command light penetrated the cloud cover reaching Earth's sea surface, starting alternating daytime and nighttime on rotating Earth's surface. The events in the Genesis 1:3–31 narrative are best understood from the perspective of Earth's surface.

Conditions That Would Change in Genesis 1:3–31

The four conditions on early planet Earth described in Genesis 1:2 would change:

- Uninhabitable (*tōhû*) changed to habitable.
- Uninhabited (*bōhû*) changed to inhabited.
- Darkness (*ᵏhōshek*) on Earth's deep sea changed to the light of day one.
- Deep ocean (*tᵉhôm*) waters (*māyim*) changed to land and sea.

God would change these conditions on planet Earth by His upcoming work in the six described days narrated in Genesis 1:3–31.

"In the beginning," stage one, was complete. But God's work on Earth was not finished. In darkness, its surface covered with water, Earth was ready for God to finish His creation work. God would change those conditions on Earth in the upcoming six described days—adding light, open air, land, plants, fully functioning luminaries, animals, and humans.

Chapter 16

A Numbered *Yôm* in Historical Narrative Means a Literal Day

Darkness.

Darkness so deep that no glimmer of light reached down to where the Spirit of God hovered just above the surface of the dark deep sea waters. During the end of the beginning time, Earth's sea surface was covered in continual darkness. How much time passed with Earth's sea surface in that continual darkness, the Bible does not say.

> And darkness was over the surface of the deep; and the Spirit of God was moving over the surface of the waters (Gen. 1:2, NASB).

Then God spoke, beginning day one on planet Earth's rotating surface:

> Then God said, "Let there be light," and there was light. And God saw that the light was good, and God separated the light from the darkness (Gen. 1:3–4, NASB).

At God's command, sunlight reached down to the surface of planet Earth, the place just declared dark. Thus, God divided the light of day from the darkness of night.

> And God called the light day, and the darkness He called night. And there was evening and there was morning, one day (Gen 1:4–5, NASB).

The daytime of the first day on Earth faded as the narrative location rotated into the sunset, and evening light faded into nighttime darkness. Then hours later, the dawn of morning ended the nighttime. God declared this "day one" (YLT) on planet Earth. But was that day and night on rotating planet Earth a literal day?

Bible Evidence That Day One Was a Literal Day

Today many people who believe the Bible is true are uncomfortable with Ussher's 4004 BC creation date, a date that is not in the Bible. A 6,000-year-old universe and Earth do not fit discoveries by archaeology, astronomy, botany, chemistry, dendrology, ecology, geology, ichthyology, limnology, oceanography, paleontology, physics, and zoology. Truth-seeking people want to know if day one was a literal day, and if so, how does the Genesis 1 account with six literal days fit the evidence of an older creation?

Was day one composed of millions of years, or was day one a literal day? Again, the context of words around *yôm*, the sequential numbering of the days, and the grammar tell the reader which sense the author intended.

The Context of *Yôm* in Genesis 1:3–5 Indicates One Daytime-Nighttime Day

In Genesis 1:3–5, *yôm* is surrounded in its context by words indicating a day and a night together forming one day: "day," "night," "light," "darkness," "evening," and "morning." God called the light "day," identifying the daylight half of a day, and the darkness He called "night," identifying the nighttime half of a day.

> Then God said, "Let there be light," and there was light. And God saw that the light was good; and God separated the light from the darkness. And God called the light day, and the darkness He called night. And there was evening and there was morning, one day [*yôm eʰhad*] (Gen. 1:3–5, NASB).

In the historical narrative context of Genesis 1, a numbered *yôm* with the light of day, then evening starting the nighttime, and morning ending the nighttime, fits this sense of one literal day-night day. Genesis 1 presents the six days as literal days—in modern terms, one rotation of planet Earth.

The Author could have used other Hebrew words and phrases to indicate a long era of time. Instead, God chose singular *yôm,* with a number, with daylight then evening and morning to indicate one specific literal day.

"When the interpreter sees the word *yôm,* used with a number, occurring several times in succession and in a specific context, this construction serves to denote a solar day."[170] The series of numbered days in Genesis 1 were literal days, starting with the day that God numbered "day one."

Six literal days is not a new idea. Martin Luther said, "The days of creation were ordinary days in length. We must understand that these days were actual days."[171]

Vav Consecutive Grammar of Genesis 1 Indicates Historical Narrative and, Therefore, Literal Days

The *vav* consecutive series in Genesis 1 indicates historical narrative.[172] The first sentence has no *vav* because there is no prior event for the *vav* to connect to. The second sentence has three *vav* disjunctive clauses indicating a description. The

---

170 Jim Stambaugh, "The Days of Creation: A Semantic Approach," JMAT 7:2 (Fall 03).

171 Martin Luther, E. Plass, *What Martin Luther Says: A Practical In-Home Anthology for the Active Christian* (St. Louis: Concordia, 1991), 1523.

172 This *vav* has a number of names—*vav* conversive, *vav* consecutive, historical narrative *vav*, *vayyiqtol*. The Hebrew *vav* (*waw*) is a complex subject. This is a very simplified introduction.

following clauses all begin with *vav*-consecutive-prefixed verbs indicating historical narrative, events reported in the order in which they occurred.

First Action:

In the beginning God created   ← First reported act, perfect verb, no *vav*

Description Interrupting the Actions:

Now-the-earth was uninhabitable   ← *vav*-disjunctive-prefixed initial noun

Historical Narrative Series of Actions and Events in Sequential Order:

<u>Then-said</u> God, "Let-be light,"   ← *vav*-consecutive-prefixed initial verb

<u>Then-was</u> light.   ← *vav*-consecutive-prefixed initial verb

<u>Then-saw</u> God the light   ← *vav*-consecutive-prefixed initial verb

<u>Then-separated</u> God between   ← *vav*-consecutive-prefixed initial verb

<u>Then-called</u> God *the* light day   ← *vav*-consecutive-prefixed initial verb

<u>Then-was</u> evening,   ← *vav*-consecutive-prefixed initial verb

<u>Then-was</u> morning, day one.   ← *vav*-consecutive-prefixed initial verb

Historical narrative reports historical events. The ultimate Author of Genesis 1 could only be God, because only God was there. By prefixing the verbs with *vav* consecutives, the Author intends us to know that we should interpret Genesis 1:3–31 as a historical narrative of a series of sequential events. This historical narrative reports daytime, then evening starting the nighttime, and morning's first light ending the nighttime, together numbered "day one." The combination of these indicators can only mean that the days were literal days, occurring in the order in which they are reported.

Are Both Six Literal Days and a Biblically Undated Universe Possible?

The Genesis 1 context and grammar around *yôm*, "day," strongly support six literal days. Yet the creation of the heavens and earth was "in the beginning," so the universe and Earth are Biblically undated, allowing them to be older. Can a creation theory hold both supported claims—a Biblically undated Genesis 1:1 creation of the heavens and earth "in the beginning," followed by six literal described days?

Most people who accept that Genesis 1 describes historical events take one of two positions:

1. Six-Days-Only Young Earth Creationism: The six days were literal days, all creation was "in six days," and Adam (who can be dated to about 4000 BC) was only a few days after the creation of the universe. Therefore, the uni-

verse and Earth necessarily are about 6,000 (to at most 10,000) years old.

2. Day-Age Old Earth Creationism: God created the heavens and the earth "in the beginning." According to current science, the universe is 13.8 billion years old, and Earth 4.5 billion. Therefore, the six days must have been millions of years long.

Both sides assume that their two claims are linked—a 6,000-year-old universe and six literal days, or a Biblically undated creation allowing an older universe and six long day-ages of millions of years. But the Bible evidence supports only one part from each pair. Two Stage Biblical Creation affirms both a Biblically undated creation until Adam and six literal described days. Two Stage Biblical Creation also affirms that God's inspired, inerrant Word and God's creation work, when both are correctly understood, will always harmonize, fit together, be in accord, and match—because both are from the same 100 percent truthful Creator.

Chapter 17

The Ordinal Numbers without Articles Indicate Sequential Days

Precise wording in Bible translation is essential. So is Bible readability. All translations are a balance between precise literal translation and readability. Intentionally readable Bible translations may obscure the key changes in the numbers of the days in Genesis 1.

The seven numbers of the days in Genesis 1 are often translated as if they were all the same kind of numbers. They may be translated as all ordinal numbers with the definite article ("the first day," "the second day," "the third day," etc.) or all cardinal numbers ("day one," "day two," "day three," etc.). But neither would be an accurate translation of all the Hebrew numbers in Genesis 1. The rather literal NASB translates all seven numbers accurately: "one day" ("day one," YLT), "a second day," "a third day," "a fourth day," "a fifth day," "the sixth day," and "the seventh day."

Day One Is Cardinal, but Days Second through Seventh Are Ordinal

In the Hebrew text, day one has a cardinal number (one—as in one, two, three). Then the text switches to ordinal numbers—"*a* second day," "*a* third day," "*a* fourth day," "*a* fifth day." A Hebrew text can use all ordinal numbers (first, second, third) for items in a series (e.g., 1 Chron. 23:19), but the creation narrative starts with the cardinal number "day one," then switches to ordinal numbers for "*a* second day," "*a* third day," through "the seventh day." This switch from cardinal number one for day one to ordinal numbers for the second through seventh days clarifies what happened in the creation.

Hebrew	Precise translation	Kind of number
yôm e^chād	"day one"	cardinal number
yôm shēnî	"*a* second day"	ordinal number
yôm shelîshî	"*a* third day"	ordinal number
yôm rebî'î	"*a* fourth day"	ordinal number
yôm ^khămîshî	"*a* fifth day"	ordinal number
yôm ha-shîshî	"the sixth day"	ordinal number with "the"
yôm ha-shebî'î	"the seventh day"	ordinal number with "the"

Cardinal Numbers Count Total Quantity

> *In numbering the days, the Genesis 1 text does not use cardinal numbers, which would have indicated the total number of days, but ordinal numbers, indicating position in a series.*

Cardinal numbers (one, two, three) count total quantity.[173] For example, "day one" (cardinal number) in this outer world for my son David was his day of birth as he blinked in the light for the first time. For him, there had been no daylight followed by nighttime as time passed within the darkness of the womb before his birth, before his day one in the light. His first daytime was followed by the dark of his first full night, with the moon dimly shining into the hospital room of my dear wife and son, and near them a slender green vase with one red rose.

Cardinal Number One Emphasizes That Day One Was One Literal Day

At God's command, on the specific literal day on Earth that God named "day one," sunlight penetrated the thinning cloud, reaching rotating Earth's dark sea surface. The hours of daytime ended with the evening, and the hours of nighttime ended with the first morning light, for a total quantity of only one daylight-nighttime day. In Genesis 1:5, God named that day "day one." That day was numbered with a cardinal number *"yôm eḥād,"* "day one," indicating a total quantity of one day had passed. Young's Literal Translation accurately translates this as "day one," and the NASB translates this as "one day," indicating a total quantity of one day had passed.

And God called the light day, and the darkness He called night.
And there was evening and there was morning, one day (Gen. 1:5, NASB).

Day one was not billions of days long. A total quantity of only one day—with daylight then evening, night, and the dawn of morning—had passed on rotating planet Earth's surface. Day one was a literal day. All seven described days were literal days.

Ordinal Numbers Report Position in a Series

Ordinal numbers indicate the position of objects in a series. The ordinal number tells us that a "second day" of God's work was sometime after "day one" in the series and before a "third day." Hebrew grammar books explain, "Ordinal numbers

---

173 Gary D. Pratico and Miles V. Van Pelt, *Basics of Biblical Hebrew*, 116; numbers are also absolute or construct and agree in gender.

are used to indicate position in a series (first, second, third, etc.)."[174] "The ordinals express degree, quality or position in a series, 'first, second, third.'"[175] "An ordinal number is used to show the order of something, or the place of that thing in a list."[176] In numbering the days, the Genesis 1 text does not use cardinal numbers, which would have indicated the total number of days, but ordinal numbers, indicating position in a series.

Each described day in Genesis 1 was in the stated order in the series of described days—day one, *a* second day, *a* third day, *a* fourth day, *a* fifth day, the sixth day, and the seventh day. But these ordinal numbers do not tell us how many nondescribed days passed between day one and *a* second described day of God's work. The ordinals tell only the position of each of the seven described days in the series. Sometime after "day one" came a "second day," and sometime later came a "third day." The ordinal numbers decidedly lean toward nonconsecutive days.

Others have recognized that the six days need not have been consecutive. For example, theologian J. Barton Payne (1922–1979) believed in six literal days, yet he recognized that "the literal text reads, 'one day' (1:5), 'a second day' (1:8), etc.; so the days need not be taken consecutively."[177]

Six Consecutive Days or Six Chronologically Sequential Days?

The word "consecutive" means "following one after the other in order," "following each other without interruption."[178] For example, 1, 2, 3 are consecutive numbers. Monday, Tuesday, Wednesday are consecutive days, following one right after the other without interruptions or skips.

"Chronologically sequential" means "following the order in which they occurred"[179] "in a series."[180] For example, Presidents Washington, Lincoln, Carter, and Reagan are in chronologically sequential historical order. The first three were not consecutive, and the last two were consecutive. Monday, Wednesday, Friday, and Saturday are in chronologically sequential order. The first three are not consecutive, and the last two are consecutive. Events listed with ordinal numbers are in chronologically sequential order but are not necessarily consecutive. The ordinal numbers indicate that the seven days in Genesis 1 were in chronologically sequential order. But ordinal numbers do not require that all seven days be consecutive, following one immediately after the other.

---

174 Gary D. Pratico and Miles V. Van Pelt, *Basics of Biblical Hebrew*, 111.

175 Bruce Waltke, *Biblical Hebrew Syntax* (Winona Lake: Eisenbrauns, 1990), 272.

176 www.ecenglish.com/learnenglish/lessons/ordinal-vs-cardinal-numbers.

177 J. Barton Payne, "Theistic Evolution and the Hebrew of Genesis 1–2," *Bulletin of the Evangelical Theological Society 8* (1965), 87. He is opposing evolution.

178 *Merriam-Webster Dictionary.*

179 *Oxford Dictionaries.*

180 *Merriam-Webster Dictionary.*

In Hebrew, the Absence of a Definite Article Indicates Indefinite Days

The ordinal numbers indicate that the six days are in chronological order but not necessarily consecutive (one immediately after the other). The first five described work days are also indefinite ("day one," "*a* second day," "*a* third day," "*a* fourth day," and "*a* fifth day").

In English, "the day" indicates a specific definite day, while "a day" indicates an indefinite day. For example, the Fourth of July holiday is on the definite fourth day of July. "Let's take a fourth fishing trip this summer on a day sometime in August" indicates an indefinite day sometime in August.

Hebrew has no indefinite article, no "a" or "an," but grammatically, a noun without the definite article "*ha*" ("the") is considered indefinite. Hebrew grammars explain, "In Hebrew, there is no indefinite article. . . . For this reason, words occurring without the definite article should be considered indefinite unless otherwise indicated."[181] "It is the absence of the definite article which indicates that a noun is indefinite."[182] In Genesis 1, day one through *a* fifth day do not have a definite article. Only the last two days have the definite article "*ha*" ("the")—*yôm ha-shishshî*, the sixth described day when God made Adam and Eve in His image and *yôm ha-shebî'î*, the seventh day, God's day of rest.

Ordinal Numbers without Definite Articles Allow Unnumbered Days Before and After

"Day one" has a cardinal number (one, two, three) for a total quantity of one day. Therefore, no daylight-nighttime days passed on Earth before day one. At the end of day one, a total quantity of only one daylight-nighttime day had passed on Earth.

Days with ordinal numbers, especially without definite articles, allow unnumbered days to have passed before and after. Unnumbered days probably passed before and after "*a* second day." Unnumbered days probably passed before and after "*a* third day" and "*a* fourth day" and "*a* fifth day," all with ordinal numbers and without definite articles. The first five days were in chronologically sequential order but were probably not consecutive.

In Genesis 1, the ordinal numbers without articles ("*a* second day" through "*a* fifth day") indicate that the six days were sequential (in order) rather than consecutive (one immediately after the other), allowing unnumbered days to have passed before and after "*a* second day" through "*a* fifth day."

---

181 Gary D. Pratico and Miles V. Van Pelt, *Basics of Biblical Hebrew*, 40.

182 Page H. Kelly, *Biblical Hebrew: An Introductory Grammar* (Grand Rapids: Eerdmans, 1992), 24.

A Bible Example of Ordinal Numbers

An example of ordinal numbers is in 1 Corinthians 15:47:

The first [ordinal] man is from the earth, earthy; the second [ordinal] man is from heaven (1 Cor. 15:47, NASB).

The first man, Adam, founded the human family on Earth but also brought sin and death. "The second man" is not Cain, Adam and Eve's firstborn son. The second man is Jesus, who came from Heaven to Earth and defeated sin, death, and the devil. The ordinal numbers "first" and "second" do not tell us the total quantity of men between Adam and Jesus, only the chronological order of these two men on Earth. They were in chronological order in their appearance in history on Earth, with Adam first, then Jesus second. The ordinal numbers (even with the definite article) "first" man and "second" man do not require that the two be consecutive men. Many unnumbered men lived between Adam and Jesus, and many more came after. These two were selected for their greater significance, and they were in the chronological order listed: Adam first, Jesus second. In the same way, day one and a second described day in Genesis 1 were chronologically sequential in Earth's history, even though there may have been many unnumbered days and years between them.

Hebrew Ordinal Numbers without Articles Indicate Chronologically Sequential Days

Accepting Biblical authority means accepting that the Hebrew ordinal numbers ("*a* second day") without definite articles (no "*ha*," no "the") tell us that the six described days were chronologically sequential (rather than necessarily consecutive). The combination of the Hebrew ordinal numbers and absence of definite articles (no "*ha*," no "the") indicate the described work days of Genesis 1 were highly likely nonconsecutive sequential days.

God's command "Let there be light" started daylight on earth, and then came evening, starting nighttime, and then the first light of morning, ending the nighttime—together forming day one. Next, God commanded an expanse of open air between cloud water above and sea water below on a specific day. God declared that day to be "*yôm shēnî*," "*a* second day." That second day was sometime after day one, but the Bible does not say how long after. *A* second through the seventh days are numbered with ordinal numbers. And until "the sixth day," they are also without definite articles. They were in chronological order but need not have been consecutive days.

Illustrating ordinal numbers, consider this list of holidays from a fictional company that I'll call The Fyzls Company:

	Date	**Holiday**
First holiday	January 1	New Year's Day
Second holiday	May 28	Memorial Day
Third holiday	July 4	Independence Day
Fourth holiday	July 29	Soccer World Cup Finals Day
Fifth holiday	November 26	Thanksgiving Day
Sixth holiday	December 24	Christmas Eve
Seventh holiday	December 25	Christmas Day

The Fyzls Company's holidays are numbered with the ordinal numbers first, second, third, fourth, fifth, sixth, and seventh, so the holidays are in chronological order, but most are not consecutive days. A fifth listed day, Thanksgiving, is not the fifth consecutive day of the year—not January 5. This day is in the fifth position in the list of Fyzls Company holidays. The holidays are in chronological order, but only the last two are consecutive.

Day One and Ordinal Days Second to Seventh Are Sequential

Day one	God commanded, "Let there be light" for day and night on Earth
a second day	God commanded an open air expanse between sea and cloud
	God gathered the waters and made dry land appear
a third day	God commanded the Earth to start growing green vegetation
a fourth day	God commanded the luminaries to mark seasons, days, years
a fifth day	God created air-breathing, water-dwelling creatures and flyers
	God commanded the land to produce three kinds of land animals
the sixth day	God created the human pair in His image
the seventh day	God rested from all His creation work

Two Stage Biblical Creation is committed to interpreting the historical narrative of Genesis 1:1—2:4a by the plain literal sense. The genealogies of Adam's descendants give an approximate chronology, so they may roughly date Adam. But interpreted literally, the inspired Hebrew ordinal numbers of the Genesis 1 days indicate they were sequential, allowing unspecified amounts of time between the days. This, in turn, means all creation events before Adam are Biblically undated.

Does the Later Work Week Force God's Original Six Days to Be Consecutive?

Egypt, where Israel had been slaves, had a ten-day week called a decan.[183] Israel was to be different with a different week. During the exodus from Egypt, God provided manna as food for Israel six days a week but not the seventh, helping Israel become accustomed to a seven-day week (Exod. 16). In Exodus 20, in the fourth commandment,

---

183 Heidi Jauhiainen, "Do Not Celebrate Your Feast without Your Neighbors," *Asian and African Studies* 10.

God blessed Israel with a six-day work week and the seventh day of rest. The example given was that God worked six days and rested the seventh day.

> Six days you shall labor and do all your work, but the seventh is a Sabbath to the LORD your God. *On it* you shall not do any work. . . .
> Because/for six days *the* LORD did-work [*asâh*] on the heavens and the earth, the sea, and all that *is* in them, and rested on the seventh day (Exod. 20:9–11, from Hebrew).

Some claim that because the future fourth commandment in Exodus 20 refers to seven consecutive days forming a work week, God's original six described work days and one rest day in Genesis 1 must have been consecutive in a "Creation Week" (a term not in the Bible).

In response, in the fourth commandment, the number six in "six days" is cardinal (as in one, two, three), indicating a total quantity of six days, so the Bible tells us that those six days of the human work week are consecutive. In contrast, the ordinal numbers without articles (*a* second, *a* third, *a* fourth, *a* fifth) of the days described in the inspired Hebrew text of Genesis 1 do not require that God's six described work days be consecutive days in a single "Creation Week." Instead, the ordinal numbers without definite articles allow an unspecified amount of time between the described days. God chose a cardinal number in Exodus 20:9, indicating a total quantity of six work days for the human work week. In Genesis 1 He chose ordinal numbers, not cardinal numbers (except "day one"), explicitly indicating that God's work days were sequential rather than consecutive.

In the Six Days of Genesis 1:3–31, the Hebrew Verbs Are Imperfect, Indicating God Started the Work That Day

The Hebrew verbs in the six days are imperfect, indicating ongoing action. The ongoing action (technically called incomplete action) is indicated by the imperfect verbs. God started each work in its described literal day, and the effects are ongoing. God started day-night days on Earth on literal day one. He started an open expanse between the sea below and cloud above on a second described day. God started vegetation on a third described day. He started three new functions by the luminaries to Earth's surface on a fourth described day. He started air-breathing flyers and sea creatures on a fifth described day. He started the human race on the sixth described literal day.

Ordinal Numbers without Articles Indicate a Biblically Undated Creation until Adam

Ordinal numbers without definite articles indicate sequential rather than consecutive days. The Bible uses ordinal numbers (except day one), indicating the days were sequential (rather than consecutive). With an "in the beginning" time, then six sequential days, the creation events before Adam are Biblically undated.

Genesis 1:1 reports that God created the heavens and the earth "in the beginning." Taking the six days literally as day-night days and the ordinal numbers without definite articles as indicating sequential days allows a Biblically undated (until Adam) creation.

Chapter 18

All of Genesis Is about Generations

In the old movie *Clouds of Witness,* the hero and amateur detective, Lord Peter Wimsey, asked a shepherd what day an event related to an apparent murder occurred. The wind-grizzled old shepherd answered, "Day? Time means naught here, lad." That gnarled shepherd would not have known a Tuesday from a Thursday. Days and weeks meant nothing to him. Only generations of family and sheep did. Shepherds care for their flocks every day, generation after generation.

Genesis records the narratives of shepherds' lives in successive accounts, generation after generation.

Adam and Eve's son Abel was a shepherd (Gen. 4:2–4).
Abraham owned large flocks and herds (Gen. 13:2).
Abraham's son Isaac was a shepherd and a farmer (Gen. 26:12–14).
Isaac's son Jacob was a shepherd (Gen. 30:36–43).
Jacob's family identified themselves to Pharaoh as shepherds (Gen. 47:3).
Moses, for forty years, was a shepherd (Exod. 3:1).
When Israel left Egypt, they took their flocks and herds (Exod. 12:32, 38).

The world of Genesis was a world of generation after generation of descendants, of shepherds like Abraham, Isaac, and Jacob. The prominent motif, the worldview, the distinctive repeated literary structure of Genesis is generations. The idea of generations is woven into the fabric and design of Genesis. From beginning to end, Genesis is about generations.

Genesis Is Composed of Generational Narratives

The Genesis units are historical narratives of successive generations. The Genesis 1:1—2:4a account is the dramatic narrative of God creating the heavens and the earth.

The next narrative is the account of Adam and Eve and their generations of descendants (Gen. 2:4b—5:1a). The Adam narrative recounts Adam and Eve's descendants Cain and Abel, several generations of Cain's descendants, and Adam and Eve's son Seth starting the next generation.

The generations from Adam to Noah and his three sons are recorded in Genesis 5. Genesis 6—9 is the narrative of Noah and the Flood judgment. Genesis 10 records the generations of descendants of Noah's three sons. The genealogy in Genesis 11 lists the generations from Shem to Terah, the father of Abraham. Genesis continues with the narrative account of Abraham and Isaac, then the narrative account of Jacob and his twelve sons, emphasizing Judah and Joseph. These are generational narratives. All of Genesis is composed of generational narratives.

Genesis Is Divided into Successive Generation Units by *Tôledôt* Phrases

These Genesis accounts are identified by *tôledôt* generations phrases. *Tôledôt* means "generations of descendants account." The *tôledôt* phrases follow the typical ancient Mesopotamian style of a closing phrase (colophon) that lacked a verb and included the name of the prominent individual. The distinctive *tôledôt* generations phrase lists the name ("heavens and earth," "Adam," "Noah"), contains the word *tôledôt*, and lacks a verb, making that set of words a phrase, not a complete sentence—for example, "These generations [*tôledôt*] *of* Noah" (Gen. 6:9). (Translations often insert a verb like "are" for readability.) The *tôledôt* generations phrase may close a narrative unit, begin a genealogy unit, and even be in the middle, as in the Abraham-Isaac unit.

About a dozen *tôledôt* generations phrases help identify the units in Genesis (except for the final Joseph unit, which is written in Egyptian style and has no *tôledôt* generations phrase). The first *tôledôt* generations phrase closes the creation narrative unit.

These generations of the heavens and the earth when created (Gen. 2:4a).
This written-account/tablet generations *of* Adam (Gen. 5:1a).
These generations of Noah (Gen. 6:9).
These generations of sons of Noah—Shem, Ham, and Japheth (Gen. 10:1).
These clans of sons of Noah by generations in their nations (Gen. 10:32).
These generations of Shem (Gen. 11:10).
These generations of Terah. Terah begot Abram (Gen. 11:27).
These generations of Ishmael (Gen. 25:12).
These generations of Isaac, son of Abraham (Gen. 25:19).
These generations of Esau (Gen. 36:1, narrative).
These generations of Esau (Gen. 36:9, genealogy).
These generations of Jacob (Gen. 37:2).

Genesis is a series of generational narratives and genealogies, identified by *tôledôt* generations phrases, telling the historical accounts of successive families and their descendants.

Genesis 1:1—2:4a Is the First Generations Narrative

Genesis 1:1 starts the creation narrative with these words:

In the beginning God created the heavens and the earth (Gen. 1:1).

This creation unit concludes with the *tôledôt* generations phrase:

> These generations [*tôledôt*] of the heavens and the earth when [*they were*] created (Gen. 2:4a, from Hebrew).

Genesis 1:1 and 2:4a Form an *Inclusio,* Enclosing This Generations Narrative

Genesis 1:1—2:4a is set apart as a unit by the literary structure called an *inclusio*. An *inclusio* forms bookends enclosing a unit by repeating similar words or clauses at the start and end of the unit:

> In the beginning God created the heavens and the earth.
> > day one.
> > *a* second day.
> > *a* third day.
> > *a* fourth day
> > *a* fifth day.
> > the sixth day.
> > the seventh day.
> These generations of the heavens and the earth when created.

Genesis 1:1 and 2:4a bookend this creation unit with similar wording. These repeated similar phrases—"created the heavens and the earth" and "the heavens and the earth when [*they were*] created"—enclose (*inclusio*) the Genesis 1:1—2:4a passage as the first generations narrative in Genesis.

The words of Genesis 2:4a are the very next words immediately after the report of the seventh day. Genesis 2:4a is the conclusion of the *inclusio* about the creation of the heavens and the earth. Genesis 1:1 is the brief dramatic narrative statement of God's work creating the heavens and the earth. It is the beginning statement of the *inclusio*. Genesis 1:2 describes the barren conditions on planet Earth. Then Genesis 1:3–31 reports six generation-starting days when God made Earth fruitful. Genesis 2:1–3 reports that God rested the seventh day. Genesis 2:4a concludes the narrative with the ending statement of the *inclusio*, "These generations of the heavens and the earth when [*they were*] created."

God Transforms Barrenness into Fruitfulness

In the ancient world, barrenness was considered a disaster. Barrenness ended the successive generations that were so important to ancient people and meant the family line would be cut off. But God alone could command an end to barrenness.

Human Barrenness, Then God-Given Fruitfulness

Abraham and his wife Sarah were barren. But God promised them a son. Sarah became pregnant, and on a specific literal day, she gave birth to Isaac:

Now the LORD was gracious to Sarah as he had said, and the LORD did for Sarah what he had promised. Sarah became pregnant and bore a son to Abraham in his old age, at the very time God had promised him (Gen. 21:1–2, NIV 1984).

Over many years Isaac matured and then married Rebekah, but they were unable to have children. Finally, Isaac prayed to the LORD, who heard his prayer, and Rebekah became pregnant and gave birth to twins, Jacob and Esau. The specific literal day of their birth is recorded in some detail in Genesis 25:24–26.

Jacob matured over many years and then married Leah and Rachel. At first Rachel was also barren, but Leah gave birth, and finally, Rachel did also.

God, by His command, can end barrenness and begin a succession of descendant generations. That is how literal birth days and generations work—birth on a specific literal day, years of maturing, then another literal birth day starting the next generation.

Each successive generation starts on a specific literal day. Then each generation continues and matures for years before the birth of the next generation. The generations overlapped. Abraham lived well into the lifetimes of his descendants, as did Isaac and Jacob.

These ideas—barrenness, God-given generations each starting on a literal day, and an ending *tôledôt* generations phrase—also fit the Genesis 1:1—2:4a creation narrative.

Earth's Barrenness, Then God-Given Fruitfulness

God created the heavens and the earth in the beginning time. Genesis 1:2 turns the focus to "Now the earth." God declared that Earth was *tōhû vᵉbōhû*, uninhabitable and barren of life, unfruitful. Genesis 1:2 pictures planet Earth with the same pathos as the description of Abraham and Sarah, who experienced great sorrow that Sarah for a long time was barren before she gave birth. Earlier, Earth was also barren. Only God could end that barrenness.

> *God ended Earth's barrenness by His work in six generation-starting literal days.*

God ended Sarah's barrenness with the birth of Isaac on one literal day. Then in the next generation, God ended Rebekah's barrenness with the birth of her twins on one literal day. Similarly, God ended the barrenness of the Earth by a succession of commands, each occurring on one specific literal day.

Through a series of six generations, each starting on a literal day, God ended the barrenness of different aspects of planet Earth. By His command, God brought light from the heavens to planet Earth on day one (Gen. 1:5), starting the first generation of days with light. On a second described day, God formed an open expanse of atmosphere between the sea water below and cloud water above, starting the second generation with an open atmosphere. During that second generation, God gathered the waters and caused dry land to appear. On a third described day, God commanded the earth to produce vegetation, starting the generation of green vegetation. On a fourth described day, God caused the two great lights in the expanse of the sky to separate day and night, be signs for seasons and days and years, and give light on Earth. On a fifth described day, God caused the water to teem with great air-breathing creatures and caused flyers to fly across the expanse of the sky. Those creatures started the generation of great air-breathing animals. After a fifth described day, God caused the land to produce livestock, smaller scrambling animals, and wild beasts of the earth, each reproducing after its kind. On the sixth described day, God made the first human pair in His image and likeness, starting the generations of humans.

God ended Earth's barrenness and made Earth fruitful by His commands on six described work days, each starting one of the "generations of the heavens and the earth when [*they were*] created" (Gen. 2:4a).[184] In other words, God ended Earth's barrenness by His work in six generation-starting literal days.

Ordinal Numbers Support Generation-Starting Days

The ordinal numbers of Genesis support generation-starting days. Those ordinal numbers, most without a definite article—*a* second day, *a* third day, *a* fourth day, *a* fifth day, the sixth day, and the seventh day—do not require the days to be consecutive in a single week. Instead, the ordinal numbers without definite articles indicate unspecified amounts of time before and after each of those days, allowing time for the six described days to start six generations of the heavens and the Earth.

The Hebrew imperfect verbs in the six days indicate the action started on that literal day yet with ongoing effects that may not have been completed on that day. The ongoing effects fit with generation-starting sequential days, allowing time after each described literal day for the ongoing effects.

Command Units Support Generation-Starting Days

The six described days of Genesis seem best understood as generation-starting sequential literal days—days when God did specific works to make Earth lighted,

---

184 Genesis 2:4b–25 may also be understood as a work of God ending barrenness, this time in Eden. The narrative describes the barren conditions, likely of the land of Eden—no plants, no rain, no humans. Then God brought water to Eden. God planted a Garden in Eden. God brought Adam to the Garden, and Adam named the animals that now abounded in the Garden, but there was no partner for Adam. So God made Eve, who was united with Adam for a fruitful future. God made Eden watered, fruitful, and inhabited.

habitable, and inhabited. Genesis 1 reports eight command units in those six described days. A command unit follows a general formula:

- Command
- Consequence or result
- Commendation as "good"
- Calling/naming
- Chronology of numbered days (day one, *a* second day, *a* third day . . .)

Two of the eight command units do not have their own numbered day. Those units seem best understood as having occurred during the generation between the two described days.

Command Unit	Described Day
1. Light to Earth's surface for day and night on Earth	day one
2. Expanse separated sea water from cloud water	*a* second day
God gathered the waters, and dry land appeared	
3. Green vegetation started	*a* third day
4. Luminaries function for seasons and days and years	*a* fourth day
5. Water-dwelling air-breathing creatures and flyers	*a* fifth day
God made three kinds of land animals	
6. Adam and Eve in God's image	the sixth day
7. God rested from His creation work	the seventh day

With each described day starting a generation, the text allows God's command for the waters to be gathered and the dry land to appear in the generation after a second described day. Therefore, this rise of land need not have been in a single day. The Genesis 1 text also allows God's command for land animals to have been in the generation after a fifth described day. From a generation's view, these two command units without a numbered day fit beautifully into the generation of time after the previous described literal day.

The Six Described Days Were Generation-Starting Sequential Literal Days

A combination of Bible evidence makes it highly probable that the six described days were generation-starting sequential literal days (rather than consecutive days forming a single week, or long day-ages). That conclusion is based on a combination of the following Bible evidences:

- "These *are the* generations of the heavens and the earth when *they were* created"
- The generations worldview of ancient shepherds (rather than a work week view)
- The generations design of Genesis, each generation starting on a literal day
- The switch from cardinal "day one" to ordinal numbers without articles ("*a* second day" through "*a* fifth day"), indicating sequential (rather than consecutive) days
- Indefinite days, "*a* second day" through "*a* fifth day," allowing time between days
- Eight command units but six described days with two events between described days
- The match of generation-starting days and ordinal numbers without definite articles, both allowing time between the days

Together these reasons make it highly probable that the six described days of Genesis 1:3–31 were generation-starting sequential literal days, not consecutive days of a single week. However, the Bible does not say how long the generations were. Therefore, all creation events before Adam are Biblically undated.

Chapter 19

Day One: Sunlight to Earth's Surface

Before Genesis 1:1, God alone—Father, Son, and Holy Spirit— existed in eternal glory and holiness. Yet God freely chose to create.

In the Beginning God Created the Heavens

Out of nothing, God created (*bārā'*) the heavens and the earth.

In the beginning [*b^{e}re'shît*] God [*Elohîm*] created [*bārā'*] the heavens and the earth [*et ha-shāmāyim v^{e}et ha-ārets*] (Gen. 1:1).

Interpreted literally, Genesis 1:1 declares that God created the heavens and the earth—a merism meaning the whole universe, including the galaxies, the sun, the moon, and planet Earth—during the Genesis 1:1 beginning time. Hebrew professor John Sailhamer explains, "The sun, moon, and stars are all included in the usual meaning of the phrase 'the heavens and the earth' and thus . . . were all created in verse 1."[185]

By the word of the LORD were the heavens made,
    their starry host by the breath of his mouth (Psa. 33:6, NIV 1984).

Making the heavens included making the host of stars. Billions of galaxies, each with billions of stars, spun across the expanding universe. And in one of those galaxies, God made what astronomers consider an exceptionally stable star, our sun, with planets orbiting it. One of those planets was our unique planet Earth. So, stage one of creation was complete. The heavens and earth were created "in the beginning" prior to day one.

Conditions on Earth: Darkness on Earth's Cloud-Wrapped Sea Surface

The focus changes from "the heavens and the earth" in Genesis 1:1 to the surface

---

185 John Sailhamer, *The Pentateuch as Narrative* (Grand Rapids: Zondervan, 1992), 87.

of planet Earth in verse 2, "Now the earth." Only Earth is described as uninhabitable, uninhabited, and dark. From the perspective of Earth's surface, the light shining across the heavens did not reach Earth's dark sea.

> Now-the-earth was uninhabitable and uninhabited [*tōhû vᵃbōhû*],
> and-darkness *was* over *the* surface of *the* deep,
> and-Spirit of God *was* hovering over *the* surface of the waters (Gen. 1:2, from Hebrew).

Earth was uninhabitable, empty of life, covered with deep ocean water, its surface dark.

The book of Job explains why Earth's deep sea surface was dark. In his sufferings, Job asked God to respond to him (Job 31:35). In Job 38, God responded with questions about creation, revealing His greatness as Creator: Where were you when I laid the foundations of the earth? Who determined Earth's measurements? God then says He wrapped the newly birthed sea in "thick darkness," making "the clouds its garment." Thick dark clouds covered Earth's sea.

> I made the clouds its [the sea's] garment
> and wrapped it in thick darkness (Job 38:9, NIV 1984).

Stars shone brightly across the universe, but one place was dark: our planet's dark sea surface. On day one, God would bring light to the surface of the place just declared dark—the cloud-darkened surface of planet Earth.

The Genesis 1 Historical Narrative Reports the Sequential Events of Literal Day One

Genesis 1:1 reports that God created the heavens and the earth "in the beginning." Verse 2 describes the conditions on Earth. Verse 3 starts with the *vav*-consecutive-prefixed verb "Then-said God."

The Hebrew grammar of Genesis chapter 1 is a series of *vav*-consecutive-prefixed verbs (underlined on the next page) starting clauses and sentences. This series indicates historical narrative reporting sequential historical actions. The *vav* may be translated as "then." "Then-said God, 'Let there be light'" occurs after the creation of the heavens and the earth.

The *vav*-consecutive-prefixed verb "Then-said God" is followed by the command (jussive) "Let-be light" (Gen. 1:3). By His command, God brought light to the dark place. The Bible does not say God created light throughout the universe. The Bible says God commanded the light to "be." Where would that light be? In context, only one place had just been described as dark: Earth's sea surface. God caused light to be at Earth's surface for the first daytime, followed by night on Earth.

In *the* beginning God created the heavens and the earth.
  Now-the-earth was uninhabitable and uninhabited,
    and-darkness over *the* surface of *the* deep. . . .
<u>Then-said</u> God, "Let-be light,"
<u>Then-was</u> light.
<u>Then-saw</u> God the light that *it was* good,
<u>Then-separated</u> God between the light and the darkness.
<u>Then-called</u> God *the* light day, and *the* darkness *He* called night.
<u>Then-was</u> evening,
<u>Then-was</u> morning, day one (Gen. 1:1–5, from Hebrew).

These *vav*-consecutive-prefixed verbs report successive events in order. First God created the heavens and the earth. Then God said, "Let-be light," bringing light to the place that had been dark, the surface of planet Earth. God evaluated the light as good, and He called the light "day" and the darkness "night." Then came evening, starting the nighttime. Then came morning, ending the nighttime—all adding up to one day.

The Day One Command Unit Follows the Repeated Genesis 1 Format
The command units in Genesis 1:3–31 follow roughly a well-recognized formula:

- Command
- Consequence or result
- Commendation as "good"
- Calling/naming
- Chronology of numbered days (day one, *a* second day, *a* third day . . .)

The day one command unit, Genesis 1:3–5, starts just as all eight Genesis 1 command units do—with God's command. Day one began with God's command "Let-be light."

Command: God Began Day One by His Command "Let There Be Light"
Each of the six days (plus two extra command units) began with God's command. Genesis 1:2 explains that darkness was on the surface of the deep ocean. Genesis 1:3 declares God's action ending the darkness on Earth's sea surface:

Darkness was over the face of the deep. . . .
And God said, "Let there be light," and there was light (Gen. 1:2b–3).

In Hebrew, God's command is only two words, "Be light." Scripture does not say that God "created" (*bārā'*) the light on day one. God's work on day one was not to create (*bārāʾ*) light but to cause the light to "be" (*yᵉhî* jussive command form of *hāyāh*, "to be") in the dark place—the surface of Earth's deep sea.

Consequence: Diffuse Sunlight to Earth's Rotating Surface Started Day and Night

The Hebrew text says, "And-was light" (Gen. 1:3b). At God's command, sunlight penetrated the thinning cloud cover to Earth's deep dark sea surface. For the first time, diffuse sunlight shone through the fog and cloud, reaching the sea surface of rotating planet Earth. God separated the light from the dark on Earth's surface:

And God separated the light from the darkness (Gen. 1:4b).

As the Earth rotated, daylight was followed by the darkness of night and, hours later, by the first glow of dawn. Day one was the light of day, followed by the darkness of night on rotating Earth. The verbs are imperfect, indicating that day would continue to be followed by night as planet Earth continued to rotate in the sunlight.

Commendation: The Light Was Good, Functioning Properly to Earth's Surface

And God saw that the light was good (Gen. 1:4a).

"Good," *tōv*, can have the sense of "something that functions properly,"[186] with the idea of "in order, usable."[187] Hebrew professor John Walton explains that ancient Israel gave greater significance to function than material objects.[188] "The light was good" means the light now fulfilled its beneficial function and purpose on Earth. Sunlight shone down to Earth's rotating surface, starting the transformation of planet Earth. God was beginning to change Earth from uninhabitable, uninhabited, dark, and sea covered to lighted, with land, habitable, and inhabited. Earth was becoming functional in preparation for plants, animals, and humans.

Calling: God Called the Light "Day" and the Darkness "Night"

In the Ancient Near East, naming an item is declaring sovereignty over it.

God called the light Day, and the darkness he called Night (Gen. 1:5a).

God is sovereign over day and night on Earth. He called the light "day," and the darkness He called "night." God declared that the first daylight followed by nighttime

---

186 Jeff A. Benner, *Ancient Hebrew Lexicon of the Bible* (College Station, TX: VBW Publishing, 2005), 134.

187 William L. Holladay, *A Concise Hebrew and Aramaic Lexicon of the Old Testament* (Leiden, Holland: Brill, 2000) #3016.

188 John Walton, *The Lost World of Genesis One*, 26–27.

was "day one." Time had passed in the universe and on planet Earth during the beginning time, but distinguishable days and nights on Earth's surface started at God's command for light to be in the place just declared dark, Earth's surface.

Chronology: Day One

"Day one" began with God's command "Let there be light," resulting in daytime, followed by evening (beginning the nighttime) and then morning (ending the nighttime)—one literal day.[189] Later, under the Law, God told the Jewish people to celebrate the Sabbath starting with the evening (Lev. 23:32). But Genesis 1:3–5 reports that day one began with "Let there be light" and ended with "And there was evening, and there was morning—day one" (Gen. 1:5b).

The Bible does not say how much time passed during the beginning time (Gen. 1:1) before the day God called "day one" on Earth or between day one and a second described day.

The Bible Account and Evidence in Creation Fit Together

The Bible teaches that in the beginning time, darkness was on Earth's cloud-darkened sea surface. Then God commanded, "Let there be light," and light penetrated to Earth's surface. Daytime then evening and morning indicate Earth was rotating in the light.

Science has discovered that Earth's early surface was dark, with thick clouds of water vapor, carbon dioxide, and toxic gases. As Earth cooled, rain fell continuously, thinning Earth's cloud layer and deepening Earth's sea. Finally, diffuse sunlight penetrated the thinning cloud to rotating Earth's foggy sea for the first day on Earth.

Scripture and creation—both correctly understood—match beautifully.

---

189 Some confusion has resulted from the King James Version's translation of verse 5, "And the evening and the morning were the first day" (Gen. 1:5, KJV), as if day one began with evening darkness followed by morning daylight. Correcting this error, John Skinner explains, "The sentence ["And there was evening . . . , Gen. 1:5] must refer to the *close* of the first day with the first evening and the night that followed" (John Skinner, *A Critical and Exegetical Commentary on Genesis*, 2nd ed. [Edinburgh: T. & T. Clark, 1910], 21; emphasis his). Derek Kidner explains that after the light of daytime in verse 3, then "evening came and morning came" (Derek Kidner, *Genesis* [Downers Grove: Intervarsity Press, 1967], 47). Bruce Waltke explains, "The idea, as expressed by the Hebrew, is that the first day ends when the darkness of the evening is dispelled by the morning light" (Bruce Waltke, *Genesis, A Commentary* [Grand Rapids: Zondervan, 2001], 61–62). Victor Hamilton explains that there is "evidence that strongly suggests that the day was considered to begin in the morning," and the concluding phrase, "And there was evening, and there was morning" (Gen. 1:5b) refers to "the end of the day" (Victor P. Hamilton, *The Book of Genesis, Chapter 1–17* [Grand Rapids: Eerdmans, 1990], 121). Later, when God gave the Law, the Jewish people were told to celebrate the Sabbath starting with evening (Lev. 23:32). But Genesis 1:3–5 reports that day one began with "Let there be light" and ended with "And there was evening, and there was morning—day one" (Gen. 1:5b).

Chapter 20

A Second Described Day: Sea Separated from Cloud

The shimmering white fog in the early morning light along the coast of Maine blends with the white foam of breaking waves, merging the sea and fog. So it must have been on early Earth.

Conditions on Earth: No Separation between Sea Water and Cloud Water

As Earth approached a second described day of God's work, the foaming sea waves mingled with wind-whipped fog with no separation. Diffuse sunlight shimmered on the foggy surface of Earth's deep sea day after day through the all-pervasive mist. But there was no open atmosphere separating the sea water below from the cloud water above.

Command: God Commanded an Open Air Expanse between Sea Below, Cloud Above

On a second described work day, God commanded an expanse (*rāqîa'*, "spread out, expanse, sky") of open air between the billowing sea water below and the water vapor in the cloud layer in the sky above:

And God said, "Let there be an expanse [*rāqîa'*] between the waters to separate water from water" (Gen. 1:6, NIV 1984).

Consequence: An Expanse of Open Air Formed between Sea and Water-Laden Cloud

On that second described day, God separated the sea water below from the unbroken overcast cloud water above, forming between them an expanse (*rāqîa'*) of open air.

So God made the expanse and separated the water under the expanse from the water above it. And it was so (Gen. 1:7, NIV 1984).

Later, on a fifth described day, God would make creatures that would fly in this same expanse (Gen. 1:20), indicating that the expanse was the open air of our atmosphere.

Calling: God Named the Expanse "Sky"

God named the expanse, expressing His sovereignty over the sky.

God called the expanse "sky" (Gen. 1:8a, NIV 1984).

The expanse (*rāqîa'*) of the sky (*ha-shāmāyim*) was the open air between the sea water below and the cloud water above.

Commendation: No Commendation Given for the Sky at This Time

Bible scholars have wondered why there is no commendation evaluating as "good" God's second day of work. The reason may be because God had not yet finished His work on the sky. On a fourth described day, God would dissipate the overcast cloud covering Earth's surface and command the sun, moon, and stars to fulfill their full God-given functions to planet Earth. Then God would pronounce this part of His work good.

Chronology: A Second Day

A second described day concluded with the evening, ending daytime, then the morning, ending night.

Then-said God, "Let-be an expanse between the waters." . . .
And-made God the expanse. . . .
And-was evening,
and-was morning, *a* second day (Gen. 1:6–8b, from Hebrew).

The Bible does not say how much time passed between day one of God's creation work and *a* second day or between this second described day and *a* third described day. Therefore, this second described day when God made an open air expanse is Biblically undated.

The Bible Account and Evidence in Creation Fit Together

Before God's second described day of work, Earth's sea water below met the cloud water above. Science tells us that Earth's early atmosphere contained as high as 30% greenhouse gases such as carbon dioxide. (Today scientists are concerned that carbon dioxide has reached about .04%.) Those greenhouse gases trapped sunlight, making the atmosphere very hot. That hotter atmosphere could hold immense amounts of water vapor. The sea was also hot. Scientists estimate that the seawater temperature was over 104° F (over 40° C). From that hot worldwide sea, vast amounts of water vapor continually evaporated and rose into the atmosphere. Early earth had no open air between the sea surface with rising vapor and the enveloping fog.

As the worldwide sea began to cool, less water vapor rose from its surface. At

God's command, an expanse of open air formed between the sea water below and the cloud water above.

> And God made the expanse, and separated the waters which were below the expanse from the waters which were above the expanse; and it was so. And God called the expanse heaven ["sky," NIV 1984]. And there was evening and there was morning, a second day (Gen 1:7–8, NASB).

God's Word is true, and His work in creation reveals reliable evidence. Scripture and creation—when both are understood correctly—will match, correspond, and be compatible.

Chapter 21

God Gathered Waters; Dry Land Appeared

The account of a second described day concludes with the chronology statement "And-was evening, and-was morning, *a* second day," ending that day. So this next command unit for dry land was after a second described day. This command unit for dry ground includes the command, consequence, calling, and commendation. It has all the components of an independent command unit (except the numbered day), so it need not be part of the following third described day. The ordinal numbers, indicating sequential (rather than consecutive) days, allow this command unit to have been in the generation of time between the second and third described days. Thus, these events need not be limited to a single day.

Conditions on Earth: Planet Earth Was Deep Sea Covered

Earlier, Genesis 1:2 describes a water-covered Earth:

Now the earth was formless and empty, darkness was over the surface of the deep (Gen 1:2, NIV 1984).

The "deep" (*tᵉhôm*) was the deep worldwide ocean.

Command: Let the Waters Be Gathered and Dry Land Appear

The Bible does not say God "created" (*bārā'*) land (Gen. 1:9–10). Instead, He commanded the waters to "be gathered" (*qāvāh*, imperfect) and the dry land to "appear" (*rā'āh*, imperfect). The imperfect may suggest a "habitual"[190] ongoing action.

And God said, "Let the waters under the heavens be gathered together [*qāvāh*] into one place, and let the dry land [*ha-yabāshâh*] appear [*rā'āh*]" (Gen. 1:9).

"Gathered" and "appear" are passive,[191] so a force outside the sea and land acted on the already created materials of the water and Earth. God caused the gathering of the sea and the appearing of the first dry land out of the sea.

---

190 Gary D. Pratico and Miles V. Van Pelt, *Basics of Biblical Hebrew,* 129–130.
191 *Niphal* indicates either passive or reflexive, and because God commanded these, they are passive.

Consequence: The First Dry Land Appeared

At God's command, the waters were gathered, and a continental landmass appeared out of the deep sea water. The Hebrew word used is *ha-yabāshâh,* "the dry land/ground." The idea that the land was "dry land" suggests a larger body of land that dried out over time, in contrast to small wave-swept temporary volcanic islands. The term "dry land" is singular, suggesting that at first there was a single continent. The verbs "be gathered" (*qāvāh*) and "appear" (*rā'āh*) in Genesis 1:9 are imperfect, indicating incomplete ongoing action, suggesting that the gathering of the waters and the appearing of the dry land need not have been completed immediately but may have continued over time. The generation between the command for an open air expanse and the command for vegetation would have provided that time.

Psalm 104:2–9 poetically records many of the same creation events reported in the parallel Genesis 1 narrative. "In the beginning God created the heavens and the earth" (Gen. 1:1). "He stretches out the heavens" (Psa. 104:2). "He set the earth on its foundations" (Psa. 104:5). "Darkness was over the surface of the deep" (Gen 1:2). "You covered it with the deep as with a garment; the waters stood above the mountains" (Psa. 104:6). Then God commanded, "Let the water under the sky be gathered to one place, and let the dry land appear" (Gen. 1:9), and "the waters fled" (Psa. 104:7).[192]

> But at your rebuke the waters fled,
> > at the sound of your thunder they took to flight;
> they flowed over ["upon" is a better translation] the mountains,
> > they went down into the valleys,
> > to the place you assigned for them (Psa. 104:7–8, NIV 1984).

At God's rebuke and command, "the waters fled" (Psa. 104:7) and were "gathered to one place" (Gen. 1:9) that was "assigned for them" (Psa. 104:8), and "dry land" (Gen. 1:9) appeared.

A massive water movement pushed outward as the land rose from the sea and appeared above the sea surface. Water flowed from the higher parts of the rising land down into the sea. Then the land dried out. Time between the described days would allow for drying.

Calling: God Named the Land and Seas

God named the land and seas, expressing His sovereignty over both:

---

192 An alternate translation in the NASB suggests mountain upthrust and valley formation, which also would fit plate tectonics, causing the rise of the first continental land in Genesis 1:9.

God called the dry ground "land," and the gathered waters he called "seas" (Gen. 1:10a, NIV 1984).

Commendation: After Land Rose, God Declared It Was Good

God evaluated His work of forming dry land and seas, and He declared it was "good." God was transforming the Earth from the uninhabitable conditions described in Genesis 1:2 into a functional planet suitable for future life.

And God saw that it was good (Gen. 1:10b).

Chronology: No Numbered Day

The Bible does not list a numbered day for this command unit. With no numbered day, the Scripture allows this command unit's events to take place over a Biblically unspecified amount of time between the command for open air on a second described day and the command for the start of green vegetation on a third described day.

The Bible Account and Evidence in Creation Fit Together

Each command unit further transformed Earth from uninhabitable to habitable. The Earth was covered with a deep ocean and wrapped in thinning, overcast cloud. God said, "Let there be light," and there was light, starting day one. On a second described day, God separated the sea water below from the cloud water above. Then God brought about this next good change—gathering the waters into one place and causing the rising of the first dry continental land. And God saw that it was good.

> *The truth of the Bible and the evidence in God's work in the created world correspond.*

From 1963 until 1967, a small volcanic island called Surtsey rose from the sea to become part of the island chain south of Iceland. Surtsey erupted until it reached a total area of about one square mile. Then sea water eroded it away until today it is only half that size. Geological evidence indicates Earth may have had such wave-swept temporary islands, but early Earth had no permanent dry continental land. A geology professor says about early Earth, "We are talking about a time when, if you were looking at the Earth from space, you would hardly see any land mass at all."[193]

Geologists discovered that a basalt rock layer, heavy with iron oxide (FeO), underlies the worldwide ocean. Geologists tell us that a new kind of lighter rock formed, made of lighter weight silicon oxide (SiO_2) and aluminum oxide (Al_2O_3)—granite. That lighter rock was relatively buoyant and tended to rise through the heavier basalt

---

193 Stanford Report, Louis Bergeron, news.stanford.edu/news/2009/november9/ancient-sea-temperature.

iron oxide mantle. At that time, "the mantle was much more fluid and the crust much thinner."[194] A vast mass (called a craton) of that lighter rock slowly rose through the heavier semi-molten mantle. The rising craton pushed the sea water aside and broke through the ocean surface. The water gathered into seas, and the first dry continental land appeared. Unlike the soft volcanic pumice of possible earlier temporary volcanic islands, the new craton cooled into tough lighter granite on top of heavy basalt that together withstood the sea's pounding. More cratons rose, adding to the continental land.[195] Geologists tell us that the one original continent made of multiple cratons would split and reform repeatedly until Earth has the present continents, each with one or more cratons at its core.

God commanded the water to be gathered into one place and dry land (singular) to appear, and now science proposes that Earth once had only one dry continent. The truth of the Bible and the evidence in God's work in the created world correspond. Scripture and creation—when both are understood correctly—will match, correspond, and be compatible.

---

194 "Craton," McGill University, www.cs.mcgill.ca/~rwest/wikispeedia/wpcd/wp/c/Craton.htm.

195 "Cratons—Old and Strong," *Metageologist*, Dec. 19, 2012, all-geo.org/metageologist/2012/12/cratons-old-and-strong.

Chapter 22

A Third Described Day: Earth Produced Green Vegetation

Step by step God was working out His good plan for planet Earth. Diffuse sunlight shone through the cloud layer to the surface of rotating Earth. An open atmosphere separated the sea water below from the thick cloud vapor above. But Earth had no green plants, and Earth's early atmosphere was not ready for animals or humans. Planetary scientists tell us that volcanoes had been spewing out an abundance of carbon dioxide, as well as nitrogen, sulfur dioxide, methane, ammonia, and water vapor—but no free oxygen. Earth's early atmosphere would have been deadly to animals and humans. It contained far too high a level of carbon dioxide (CO_2). Humans cannot live in an atmosphere with high levels of carbon dioxide.

In the *Apollo* voyages across the approximately 240,000 miles to the moon and then back to Earth, one mission had an almost fatal accident. *Apollo 13* had three modules: the cone-shaped Command Module in which the three astronauts rode into space, and which would reenter Earth's atmosphere and land in the ocean; the Service Module, which provided most of the power, oxygen, and water during the long trip to and from the moon; and the Lunar Lander Module.

On the way to the moon, an explosion occurred in the Service Module. The mission changed from the planned moon landing to the dramatic rescue of the three astronauts: Jim Lovell, Jack Swigert, and Fred Haise. The still-attached Lunar Lander Module, instead of landing on the moon, became their lifeboat.

One of many potentially fatal problems was the rising level of carbon dioxide (CO_2) breathed out by the astronauts now living in the lunar lander. The lander had only a few round CO_2-removing canisters, intended for two astronauts' short trip down to the moon and back into lunar orbit, and soon those round canisters were used up. The Command Module used square canisters (different companies made the two modules) but had only a little battery power left, not enough to run those square CO_2-removing canisters.

During the astronauts' long trip back to earth, the NASA engineers went into full crisis mode as the concentration of CO_2 reached near-fatal levels in the lunar lander. A team worked out a plan to use duct tape to attach the square CO_2-removing canisters from the shut-down command capsule to the lunar lander, reducing the CO_2 to normal levels and saving the astronauts' lives. The whole world followed the dramatic rescue.

Humans cannot live in air with high levels of carbon dioxide. Instead, we need moderate levels of oxygen and low levels of carbon dioxide.

Conditions on Earth: The Earth Had No Green Plants for Future Animals and Humans

Earth had no green vegetation. Green chlorophyll-containing cells not only produce food but also release something equally vital to life: oxygen. Plants take in carbon dioxide (CO_2) and release oxygen (O_2). But Earth had no green vegetation, and its atmosphere had too much carbon dioxide (as much as 30%) but no free oxygen (O_2).

Step by step God was preparing Earth according to His plan. On each described day, He started a new step in His work. By this time Earth had water, light, a carbon dioxide-laden atmosphere, and land. God had prepared Earth for vegetation.

Command: "Let the Earth Produce Vegetation"

On a third described day, God continued His transformation of Earth. He commanded the earth to start (imperfect verb) producing vegetation (*dāshā,* "grow green"), resulting in green vegetation (*deshe,* "green growth").

> Then God said, "Let the land produce vegetation: seed-bearing plants and trees on the land that bear fruit with seed in it, according to their various kinds." And it was so (Gen. 1:11, NIV 1984).

"Let the earth produce green vegetation" was God's command—a simple command but one that carried the absolute authority of the Creator. *The Brown-Driver-Briggs Hebrew and English Lexicon* defines the verb *dāshā* as "sprout, shoot, grow green."[196] God commanded the earth to start producing (*dāshā*) vegetation (*deshe*). And vegetation, *deshe* ("green-vegetation"), started to grow.

The verb *dāshā* and the noun *deshe* are cognates, two words from the same root word. These cognates intensify the idea of these two words, emphasizing that the core command was to cause the earth to start growing green vegetation.

> Let-start-producing-green-vegetation [*dāshā*] the earth [*ha-ārets*] green-vegetation [*deshe*] (Gen. 1:11, from Hebrew).

Consequence: At God's Command, Earth Produced Green Vegetation

God's command resulted in the earth producing green vegetation on that literal day:

---

196 Brown, Driver, Briggs, *Hebrew and English Lexicon,* 2235 (Strong's #1876), 205.

And-was so.

And-brought-forth [*yatsa'*] the earth green-vegetation [*deshe*],

  seed plants [*ēsev*] bearing seed according-to-its-kind [*min*, kind, singular]

  fruit trees [*ēts peri*] yielding fruit with seed inside according-to-its-kind [*min*].

And-saw God that *it was* good.

And-was evening, and-was morning, *a* third day (Gen. 1:11b–13, from Hebrew).

Both the command "Let-start-producing-green-vegetation" (*dāshā*) and the result, "And-brought-forth" (*yatsa'*), are imperfect, indicating "incomplete action," "action . . . for which the conclusion is not in view."[197] God caused (*hiphil*) the earth to start producing green vegetation that day, and the earth would continue to produce green vegetation.

Green Vegetation/Grass, Seed Plants, and Fruit Trees

The plant kingdom[198] includes vegetation with green photosynthesizing chlorophyll—from green algae to green apple trees:

- Green plants (corresponding to the broad sense of *deshe*)
  - o Blue-green algae (phylum Cyanobacteria)
  - o Green algae
  - o Spore-reproducing green plants such as mosses and ferns
  - o Seed plants
    - · Gymnosperms: naked seed plants, such as conifers, including pines, spruces, firs, cedars, yews, and redwood trees
    - · Angiosperms: encased seed plants, such as grasses, including grain plants (corresponding to a narrow sense of *deshe*); herbs and vegetable plants (corresponding to *ēsev*); and trees bearing fruit (corresponding to *ēts peri*).

The plants mentioned in verse 12 (grasses, seed plants such as herbs and vegetables, and fruit trees) are all enclosed-seed plants classified as angiosperms (from two Greek words meaning "enclosed seed"). Not included in the plants listed are gymnosperms (from two Greek words meaning "naked seed"), such as conifers, including pines, spruces, firs, cedars, yews, and redwood trees. Also not included are many simpler kinds of plants—algae (including giant kelp plants) in water and on land, horsetails, mosses, and ferns that reproduce by spores. Scripture does not preclude the possibility that God may have caused the earth to produce different kinds of plants before or after the third described day. But green vegetation did start that literal day.

To describe the vegetation, Genesis 1:11–12 uses three terms: green vegetation

---

197 Gary D. Pratico and Miles V. Van Pelt, *Basics of Biblical Hebrew*, 129–130.

198 The number of kingdoms in the classification of life has grown from two to five or six. I am using "plant kingdom" in the older sense as green vegetation. Today Cyanobacteria are classified in a different kingdom.

(*deshe*), seed plants (*ēsev*), and fruit trees (*ēts peri*). The Hebrew word *ēsev* refers to "seed-bearing plants": vegetable plants and herbs that produce enclosed seeds. For example, a pepper plant encloses pepper seeds in the pepper. The Hebrew words *ēts peri* refer to fruit trees that "bear fruit with seed in it" (Gen. 1:11, NIV 1984). For example, an apple tree encloses apple seeds in the apple.

How this passage is understood depends on how the first Hebrew plant term, *deshe*, is understood. The Hebrew word *deshe* can have a narrow sense of "grass" or a broad sense of "all green vegetation." The translation of *deshe* and the punctuation of the verse reflect how the translators understood *deshe*.

One possible way of understanding this text is to interpret the word *deshe* as "grass." Grasses range from common lawn grass to grains like wheat to tall prairie grasses. Grasses encase their seeds in seed coats, so grasses are angiosperms. If *deshe* means grasses, then God told the earth to bring forth three subclasses of angiosperm plants:

> Let the earth put forth [*dāshā*]
>> grass [*deshe*],
>> seed-producing plants [*ēsev*], and
>> fruit trees [*ēts peri*] (Gen. 1:11, CJB, arr. mine).

Hebrew Old Testament scholar Allen P. Ross suggests a second possible understanding: "This vegetation (*deshe*) seems to be the general term, and herbage (*ēsev*) and trees (*ets*) seem to be subdivisions of it (an interpretation supported by verses 29–30, which attest to only two kinds—seed-plants and trees)."[199] Many Bible scholars agree, concluding that *deshe* in Genesis 1:11 refers to the broad category of green vegetation.[200] With this second understanding, Genesis 1:11 would be punctuated and translated:

> Then God said,
> "Let the land produce [*dāshā*] vegetation [*deshe*, green vegetation]:
>> seed-bearing plants [*ēsev*] and
>> trees on the land that bear fruit with seed in it" (NIV 1984, arr. mine).

According to the second translation (above) of this verse, God told the earth to start producing green vegetation on the third described day. The verse lists the two important kinds of angiosperm plants—seed-bearing plants and fruit trees—that would produce food for humans in the future (Gen. 1:29). Vegetables and fruit are vital food for humans.

---

199 Allen P. Ross, *Creation and Blessing* (Grand Rapids: Baker, 1996), 110. I transliterated the Hebrew terms the same way as elsewhere in the book to avoid confusion. I am not claiming he agrees with all my ideas.

200 Holladay, *Lexicon*, 1911, 75.

Genesis 1:11–12 states that the seed-bearing plant (*ēsev*) will reproduce seed according to its kind (*min*, singular), and the fruit-bearing tree (*ēts peri*) will reproduce seed according to its kind (*min*, singular). Seed-bearing plants will remain seed-bearing plants, and fruit trees will remain fruit trees.

These two kinds of plants—seed-bearing plants (*ēsev*) and fruit trees (*ēts peri*)—would provide future humans with food:

> Then God said, "I give you every seed-bearing plant [*ēsev*] on the face of the whole earth and every tree that has fruit [*ēts peri*] with seed in it. They will be yours for food (Gen. 1:29, NIV 1984).

On that third described literal day, God commanded the earth to start producing either three kinds of covered-seed angiosperm plants: grasses, seed-bearing plants, and fruit trees. Or God commanded the earth to start producing green vegetation and lists two kinds of angiosperm plants—seed-bearing plants and fruit trees—that would produce food for humans.

Commendation: The Green Vegetation Was Good

The Creator God evaluated His work. He saw that the vegetation He had made was good:

> And God saw that it was good (Gen. 1:12).

Green vegetation would carry out the God-given good function of providing food for animals and humans (Gen. 1:29–30). In addition, the green plants would use up the excess carbon dioxide and produce oxygen.

Chronology: A Third Day

God caused the earth to start producing green vegetation on one literal day—the third described day. Then the evening started night, and morning ended night of the third described day.

> And-was evening, and-was morning, *a* third day (Gen. 1:13, from Hebrew).

God Was Preparing the Earth for the Next Great Changes

Botanists describe a breakthrough in vegetation—the start of blue-green and then green vegetation, both with chlorophyll ($C_{55}H_{70}O_6N_4M_g$).[201] Chlorophyll enables photosynthesis, which produces food for animals and humans. The Earth's early atmosphere contained as much as 30% carbon dioxide (CO_2) but 0% free oxygen

---

201 There are several varieties of chlorophyll. This is only one of the varieties.

(O_2). Botanists say the first blue-green chlorophyll-containing cells formed in the shallow water at the edges of the newly risen land.[202] The chlorophyll-containing cells began taking in the excess carbon dioxide and releasing vast amounts of oxygen. As a result, trillions of tons of oxygen was released, first into the ocean water and then into the atmosphere. That oxygen would have a dramatic effect.

Free oxygen in the water removed iron from the water, clearing the water. In the air, free oxygen began to oxidize the methane and ammonia that formed a haze in the atmosphere. Eventually chlorophyll-containing cells would produce enough oxygen to clear the sky. Oxygen began forming a protective ozone (O_3) layer in the upper atmosphere, stopping most of the UV radiation that would have been deadly to land plants, animals, and humans. Oxygen began to transform Earth's atmosphere into the "just right" good air with 21% oxygen and .04% carbon dioxide suitable for oxygen-breathing future life. Those changes were part of God's plan for a cleared sky, good air, and food for animals and humans.

On a third described day, God caused the earth to bring forth vegetation that would serve as food and produce oxygen, both essential to future animals and humans. Thus, the truth of the Bible and the evidence in God's work in the created world correspond, match, and are compatible.

---

202 Botanists propose that early chlorophyll-containing cells may have formed stromatolites at the continent edge.

Chapter 23

A Fourth Described Day: Luminaries Rule Day and Night

Miss Hall was a tall, athletic English teacher and coach of the girls' basketball team in my small high school. She was tough on the team and very tough on bad English! I loved basketball, but my interest in grammar was a different story. Yet, to my great benefit, Miss Hall's English classes forced me to learn grammar and vocabulary, teaching me about verbs and nouns and how they worked. Later I learned Hebrew grammar and vocabulary. Grammar and word meanings became vital to me in the very complex process of understanding and putting together all the Bible creation texts.

A pair of those challenging Bible texts are Genesis 1:1 and Genesis 1:14–19. When did God create the stars? On day four (Gen. 1:14–19) or in the beginning (Gen. 1:1) as part of the heavens?

Some people today would answer that God created the heavens as space on day one.[203] Then on day four of seven consecutive days (a "Creation Week"), God created the sun, moon, and stars. This view would mean that God created the galaxies two days before Adam. Genealogies can date Adam to about 6,000 years ago, so these people conclude that the universe is 6,000 years old. Problems arise with this answer—both exegetical problems and scientific problems, both conflicts with the Hebrew text and conflicts with evidence in the creation.

> The Bible says God created the heavens and earth "in the beginning" (Gen. 1:1). Then on a fourth described day, He gave the luminaries, which He had created "in the beginning," new functions in the expanse of Earth's sky.

The alternative is that the Bible says God created the heavens and earth "in the beginning" (Gen. 1:1). Then on a fourth described day, He gave the luminaries, which He had created "in the beginning," new functions in the expanse of Earth's sky.

Distinguished Hebrew and Old Testament professor Allen P. Ross discusses

---

203 Ken Ham says space (heaven) was created on the first day. "He made time (beginning), space (heaven), and matter (earth). This was the beginning of our universe, all part of the first day in time" (Ken Ham, *Dinosaurs in Eden*, 9). Defining *ha-shāmāyim* ("heavens") as "space" is incorrect.

both views: (1) God created the luminaries on day four. (2) God already created the luminaries in the beginning. Then, on a fourth day, God made the luminaries carry out "their functions to dominate the day and the night, to serve as signs for the fixed seasons, and to rule over the heavens."[204]

The Bible says God created the heavens in the beginning (*bᵉreʾshît*, in the beginning time/phase of unspecified length). The Hebrew phrase "the heavens and the earth" (*et ha-shāmāyim vᵉet ha-ārets*) is a Hebrew merism—two contrasting words that refer to the entirety. An English example of a merism would be "she looked high and low," meaning she looked everywhere. The merism *ha-shāmāyim vᵉet ha-ārets* means the entire universe, including the luminaries—the sun, moon, and stars. The Bible teaches that God *bārāʾ*, "created," the heavens and planet Earth "in the beginning."

Hebrew professor John Sailhamer says, "The whole of the universe, including the sun, moon, and stars, was created 'in the beginning' (1:1) and thus not on the fourth day."[205] God had already created the stars, including our sun, and the moon during the extensive beginning time.

Initial Conditions on Earth: Cloudy Overcast Sky

At the end of the beginning time, Genesis 1:2 switches the perspective to planet Earth: "Now the earth." Genesis 1:2 describes the Earth as uninhabitable and uninhabited, and "darkness was on the surface of the deep." The Bible does not say darkness was across the heavens. The darkness was "on the surface of the deep," the deep ocean that covered Earth's surface. The luminaries were shining across space, but they were not yet functioning to Earth's dark surface. Then at God's command, diffuse sunlight penetrated to the place that had just been declared dark, Earth's surface, starting day one on rotating planet Earth. But the sky was still overcast and the source of light was not visible from the surface of Earth. No luminaries were distinguishable from the surface of Earth. God created the luminaries in the beginning, but until a fourth day, they were not yet fully functioning to Earth's surface.

Command: Let Luminaries Separate Day and Night, Mark Seasons, Function as Lights

Genesis 1:14 records God's command. God commanded the luminaries, which He had created in Genesis 1:1, to carry out three new functions. These new functions were not in outer space. These new functions were in the "expanse of the sky" (*rāqîa ha-shāmāyim*), the same expanse of the sky formed on a second described day between the cloud water above and sea water below (Gen. 1:6), the same expanse of the sky (*rāqîa ha-shāmāyim*) in which winged creatures would fly (1:20). This command was not about the creation of the distant luminaries in space. Instead, God's command

---

204 Allen P. Ross, *Creation and Blessing*, 111.
205 John Sailhamer, *The Pentateuch as Narrative*, 92–93.

was for three new functions in Earth's sky: to separate and rule day and night, to be signs for seasons and days and years, and to be lights "in the expanse of the sky."

John Sailhamer explains, "Though our English translations of Genesis often suggest that God created the sun, moon, and stars on the fourth day, the Hebrew text does not demand, *or even allow for,* such an interpretation. The overall sense of Genesis 1 assumes that by the fourth day, the sun, moon, and stars are already in place. . . . According to the Hebrew text, God said, 'Let the lights in the expanse be for separating the day and night.' . . . God's command, in other words, *assumes that the lights already exist*" (emphasis his).[206] Sailhamer explains that on the fourth day, the luminaries "were given new functions, 'to separate the day and night' and 'to serve as signs to mark seasons and days and years.'"[207]

> *Since day one, diffuse sunlight had penetrated the overcast cloud covering Earth's surface. From the perspective of Earth's surface, the sun, moon, and stars were not functioning as individual distinguishable lights, as the cause of day and night in the expanse of the sky. So on this fourth described day, God commanded the already-created luminaries to carry out their new functions in the expanse of Earth's sky.*

God did not create the galaxies of stars in the universe on a fourth described day. He commanded the already-created luminaries to carry out new functions in the expanse of Earth's sky.

"Let the luminaries be in the expanse of the sky" for three purposes:
    "to separate the day from the night;
    for signs, and for seasons, and for days and years;
    to give light on the earth" (Gen. 1:14–15).

The Genesis 1 account of a fourth described day never uses the word *bārā',* "created." The words used in the command are about causing new functions of the already created luminaries in the expanse of the sky of planet Earth.

Here is where the Hebrew grammar comes in. *Yᵉhî,* "let be," does not mean "let

---

206 John Sailhamer, *Unbound,* 30–32, 132.
207 John Sailhamer, *The Pentateuch as Narrative,* 92–93.

come into existence *ex nihilo*" in the sense of *bārā'*, "create." God's command *y*ᵉ*hî*, let-be, is a mild (jussive) command connected to three purpose clauses, indicating that God caused three new functions of the luminaries in the expanse of Earth's sky. It is a command to let these three new functions be carried out, starting on that literal fourth described day.

> Then-said God,
>   "Let-be [*y*ᵉ*hî*] lights/luminaries in *the* expanse of the sky
>   <u>for-to-cause-to-separate</u> between the day and the night,
>   and-let-them-be [*y*ᵉ*hî*]
>   <u>for-signs</u>, and for seasons and days and years,
>   and-let-them-be [*y*ᵉ*hî*] for-lights in *the* expanse of the sky
>   <u>for-to-cause-to-give-light</u> on the earth."
> And-was so (Gen. 1:14–15, from Hebrew).

God's command in Genesis 1:14 is the mild command *y*ᵉ*hî*, *"let-be,"* plus the infinitive "let be ... to separate" between day and night in the expanse of the sky. *L*ᵉ*habedîl*, "to-cause-to-separate," is a hiphil infinitive, a Hebrew construction expressing the cause of the action. A hiphil is objectively recognized by its Hebrew construction (the Hebrew hiphil stem). "The hiphil stem is used to express *causative* action with the *active* voice" (emphasis theirs).[208] God said, "Let the luminaries separate between day and night, and be for signs and seasons and days and years, and to give light to the Earth." In verse 15 the verb is also a hiphil infinitive "to cause to give light on the earth," the final causal clause in the command.

Hebrew Old Testament professor and author John Walton explains that God's work on a fourth day was about the functions of the luminaries. Walton explains that the Hebrews thought in terms of "human-oriented functions." All three clauses are about causing new "human-oriented" functions "in the expanse of the sky" of planet Earth. The new luminary functions, begun on the fourth described day, are important to humans. For example, seasons were very important to the Hebrews: sowing season, harvesting season. The fourth day was not about God creating a trillion galaxies but about giving the already-created luminaries new functions pertinent to future humans on Earth.[209]

Since day one, diffuse sunlight had penetrated the overcast cloud covering Earth's surface. From the perspective of Earth's surface, the sun, moon, and stars were not functioning as individual distinguishable lights, as the cause of day and night in the expanse of the sky. So on this fourth described day, God commanded the already-created luminaries to carry out their new functions in the expanse of

---

208 Gary D. Practico and Miles V. Van Pelt, *Basics of Biblical Hebrew*, 126.
209 John Walton, *The Lost World of Genesis One*, 63, 64.

Earth's sky—to rule day and night, be signs for seasons and days and years, and be lights in the expanse of the sky to give light on planet Earth.

Consequence: The Skies Cleared and the Luminaries Carried Out Three New Functions

The creation text in Job 26:7–14 describes God's works of spreading out the northern heavens, suspending Earth on nothing, forming thick clouds that cut off the light of the full moon, marking out a boundary on the sea surface between the light of day and darkness of night (day one), and churning the sea presumably as dry land rose. Then 26:13 explains a change in Earth's sky:

By his breath the skies became fair (Job 26:13, NIV 1984).

God "cleared" (NASB) the skies, and they "became fair." By clearing the sky on a fourth described day, God enabled the luminaries—the sun, moon, and stars—to "rule," "give light," and "separate the light from the darkness" in the expanse of Earth's sky:

And God made [*asâh*, "do, make, . . . work"[210]] the two great lights—
    the greater light to rule the day and
    the lesser light to rule the night—and the stars.
And God set [*natan*, "give, put, set"[211]] them in the expanse of the heavens ["sky"]
    to give light on the earth,
    to rule over the day and over the night, and
to separate the light from the darkness.
And God saw that it was good (Gen. 1:16–18).

The verb *asâh* ("do, make, . . . work") is used in verse 16, narrating the results or consequence of God's command. Some in YEC have claimed that *asâh* means "created," that God created the luminaries on day four. But God's command was for three new functions of the luminaries to start in Earth's sky, not for the creation of a trillion galaxies in outer space. *Asâh* is connected to "govern/rule." God made the already created luminaries govern the day and night in Earth's sky on the fourth described day.

Some translations of the phrase about the stars (Gen. 1:16) unfortunately expand the verse by adding the verb "made" ("He also made the stars"), as if He created the stars on that day. But the Hebrew phrase has no verb. The Hebrew text does not report, "He also made the stars." This seemingly small expansion in some English translations confuses readers into thinking God created a trillion galaxies of stars on a fourth day. The end of verse 16 simply says, "and the stars." The Hebrew text

---

210 Brown, Driver, *Briggs, Hebrew and English Lexicon,* (Strong's #6213), 793–794.
211 Brown, Driver, Briggs, *Hebrew and English Lexicon,* (Strong's #5414), 678–681.

says, "the lesser light to rule the night, and the stars." The text reports function, not creation. God commanded the moon and stars to do their new function: rule the night. Nowhere in the command or consequence of a fourth described day does the Bible text say God created (*bārā'*) the stars on that day. The trillion galaxies, each with billions of stars, had already been created (*bārā'*) as part of the heavens in the Genesis 1:1 beginning time of unspecified length (*b^{e}re'shît*).

In verse 17, the verb *natan* ("to give, put, set") is related to the three purpose clauses, giving the consequence of God's command—to cause to give light on the earth, to rule day and night, and to cause to separate the light from the darkness.

> And God worked-on/made [*asâh*, "do, make, . . . work"] the two great lights/luminaries—
>> the-greater light/luminary for-rule-of-the-day and
>> the-lesser light/luminary for-rule-of the-night—and-the-stars.
> And gave/set [*natan*, "to give, put, set"] them God in-expanse-of the-sky
>> to-cause-to-give light on the-earth,
>> and-to-rule over-day and-over-night,
>> and-to-cause-to separate between the-light and the-dark.
> And-saw God that *it was* good (Gen. 1:16–18, from Hebrew).

The consequences (Gen. 16—18) of God's command was that God did (v. 16, *asâh*, "do") and gave (v. 17, *natan*, "give") three results. In both the command section and the consequence section, "to-cause-to-give-light" and "to-cause-to-separate" are Hebrew hiphil verbs. "The hiphil stem is used to express *causative* action with the *active* voice."[212] The Hebrew objectively states what God did (*asâh*) and gave (*natan*) on a fourth described day. Neither the command section (Gen. 1:14–15) nor the consequence section (Gen. 1:17–18) says God created (no *bārā'*) the universe with its trillion galaxies of billions of stars each two days before Adam. What God did was make the luminaries function in the expanse of Earth's cleared sky from the perspective of Earth as the cause of separation between the light and the darkness. The fourth described day of God's work was a literal day when God cleared the sky and commanded the already created luminaries to do their three new functions in the expanse of the sky.

Commendation: The Three New Functions of the Luminaries Were Good

God commanded the luminaries to carry out their three new functions to Earth's surface: ruling and separating day and night, being for signs and seasons and days and years, and being lights in the sky. And He saw that His great work causing the luminaries to carry out three new functions to Earth was good.

---

212 Gary D. Practico and Miles V. Van Pelt, *Basics of Biblical Hebrew*, 126.

And God saw that it was good (Gen. 1:18).

Chronology: A Fourth Day

Like the other numbered days, this fourth described day of God's work was a literal day.

Then-said God, "Let-be lights/luminaries in *the* expanse of the sky." ...
And-was so. ...
And-was evening,
and-was morning, *a* fourth day (Gen. 1:14–15, 19, from Hebrew).

These three functional changes began on a single literal day on Earth. However, the Bible does not say how much time passed before or after a fourth described day. Therefore, the work of a fourth described day is Biblically undated.

The Bible Account and Evidence in Creation Fit Together

"In the beginning God created the heavens" (with its luminaries). Then on a fourth described literal day, God commanded the already-created luminaries to carry out three new functions in Earth's cleared sky. The Bible text and the evidence God built into the creation match. The Genesis 1:1 creation of the heavens in the beginning time allows the sun and moon and stars to be however old they are.

Young Earth Creationism (with the view that the stars were created about 6,000 years ago, two days before Adam) has what it calls a "distant starlight problem."

One of the innumerable examples illustrating this massive problem for YEC is a discovery at the center of our galaxy. A century ago, Bell Laboratories researchers were experimenting with sending telephone conversations by radio waves, which is how our cell phones work today. Those researchers discovered a troublesome radio hiss coming from the Sagittarius constellation. They narrowed it down to what they called Sagittarius A* at the center of our Milky Way galaxy. But what caused this strange hiss? For decades no one knew. Albert Einstein's theory of relativity predicted the possibility of a supermassive object, far more massive than any star. It was called a black hole. A black hole cannot be seen, because even light cannot escape its immense gravity, but its effects on nearby stars can be seen and its presence can be detected by radio waves. Could a black hole be the source of the radio wave hiss from the center of our galaxy? In 1974 Stephen Hawking and fellow physicist Kip Thorne made a famous bet about the reality of black holes. Hawking bet against black holes. This was one bet Hawking would lose.

It took the precise instruments of the Keck Telescope on Mona Kea in Hawaii to discover the evidence. The Keck astronomers observed stars racing in tight orbits around what appeared to be nothing at the center of our Milky Way galaxy. However, their tight orbits and high speed indicated an immensely massive object with huge gravity at the center of the orbits. The astronomers plotted the orbit of one of the stars as it raced every sixteen years around what appeared to be nothing at the center of our Milky Way galaxy. They named that star S2. From S2's high-speed orbit, astronomers calculated the existence of a supermassive black hole about four million times the mass of our sun and lurking at the center of our galaxy. The center of our galaxy is about 26,700 light-years from Earth. Because light from the star S2 takes about 26,700 years at the constant speed of light to travel across 26,700 light-years distance, astronomers are seeing the past actions of S2 as it was when it orbited the black hole Sagittarius A* 26,700 years ago. If the star S2 had been created only 6,000 years ago, then that orbiting action we now see that appears to have occurred 26,700 years ago never actually happened. God would be making a "light show" of a star orbiting that never occurred. If so, then God created a deception. But our always truthful God created the heavens to reveal truth, to His glory (Psa. 19:1–2).

God created the heavens, including our Milky Way galaxy, "in the beginning," a Biblically unspecified amount of time ago. Then, on a fourth described sequential literal day, He cleared Earth's sky so that the luminaries could carry out their full functions to the surface of planet Earth. Thus, the light from S2 traveling 26,700 years to reach Earth is real and not a problem.

When we recognize that "in the beginning" (*b^{e}re'shît*) was the extensive beginning time when God created the galaxies, including our Milky Way with our solar system, and that on a fourth described day the sky cleared so the luminaries could fully function to Earth's surface, then we can see that God's Word and the evidence in God's creation, when both are correctly understood, match. And what a beautiful match it is!

Chapter 24

A Fifth Described Day: Air-Breathing Aquatic Life and Flying Life

In Oxford University is a marble bust of a mining surveyor, the son of a blacksmith. His name was William Smith. Today there is also a crater on Mars named for him. What did he do?

It was the late 1700s during the industrial revolution in England, and the newly invented coal-burning steam engines powered much of industry. They needed a great deal of coal. Coal is heavy, and railroads were still in the future. So an inventive Scottish engineer devised an ingenious canal system with lifts, locks, and even a tunnel so narrow boats could transport coal from the mines to factories and cities.

William Smith was a surveyor for the construction of the Somerset Coal Canal. He saw various horizontal strata layers of sedimentary rock in the canal cuts, tunnels, and mines and began collecting fossils from the different strata. He discovered that the unique set of fossils in each layer could identify that stratum of rock. As he traveled around England, he realized that the same strata of rock layers in the same order continued horizontally across much of England. He published the first geologic map of England. Called "Strata Smith," he was not given much honor until late in life, when he was called the "Father of English Geology," and to his surprise, he received an honorary doctorate.

> *We can recognize that the geologic layers, each with their unique fossils, form a reliable record of past life and events on Earth, yet reject blind chance evolution as the cause of the fossils in the successive geologic layers.*

The recognition of horizontal sedimentary rock strata, each with its unique set of fossils, was not developed to bolster evolution; after all, Darwin's *Origin of Species* would not be published until twenty years after Smith's death. We can recognize that the geologic layers, each with their unique fossils, form a reliable record of past life and events on Earth, yet reject blind chance evolution as the cause of the fossils in the successive geologic layers.

Conditions on Earth: Earth Ready for Animal Life

There was a time when the animals we know today did not exist. With land, plants, oxygen in the atmosphere, and full sunlight, planet Earth was ready for air-breathing animals.

Command: God Made Air-Breathing Water-Dwelling Creatures and Flying Creatures

On a fifth described day of His work, God commanded the start of air-breathing water-dwelling animals (*nephesh hāyāh*) and winged flyers (*ōph*) that fly across the expanse of the sky.

> And-said God,
> "Let swarm the waters with swarms of breathing-living beings [*nephesh hāyāh*], and flyers [*ōph*] let fly above the earth across the face of the expanse of the sky [*rāqîa ha-shāmāyim*]" (Gen. 1:20, from Hebrew).

By His command God created both air-breathing water-dwelling creatures and flyers on the same day, a fifth described day.

Consequence: God Created Air-Breathing Water-Dwelling Animals and Flyers

The Bible narrative says God created air-breathing (*nephesh*) water-dwelling creatures and winged flyers (*ōph*). So God, not blind evolution, is the source of these living creatures.

> And-created God
> the great water-creatures [*tanninim ha-gedolim*], and
> every breathing-living moving being that swarms [*sharetz*] the waters [*māyim*],
> according-to-their-kinds, and
> every winged flyer [*ōph kanaph*]
> according-to-its-kind.
> And-saw God that *it was* good (Gen. 1:21, from Hebrew).

On a fifth described day, God created great sea creatures (*tanninim gedolim*) and other air-breathing (*nephesh*) moving creatures that swarm the waters. He also created winged flyers (*ōph kānāph*).

The Hebrew words *tanninim* ("sea creatures") and *māyim* ("water," without specifying whether salt or fresh) in Genesis 1:20–21 indicate that this first group lived in water. *Tanninim gedolim* are great aquatic creatures. The Hebrew word *tannin* (plural *tanninim*) with *gadol* ("great," plural *gedolim*) is translated in the KJV as "great whales," in the ESV as "great sea creatures," and in the NASB as "great sea monsters." They were large air-breathing water-dwelling creatures. The creatures that swarmed the waters were *nephesh*, air-breathing animals. *Nephesh hāyāh* is often translated "living" but is more literally translated "breath [*nephesh*] of life [*hāyāh*]," and is so translated in Genesis 1:30 by the ESV and NIV 1984. Thus, *nephesh hāyāh* has the sense of air-breathing living animals. *The Brown-Driver-Briggs Hebrew and English Lexicon* defines *nephesh* as a "living being," "breathing."[213]

The Hebrew word *ōph* means "flying creatures"[214] and is broader than just birds. *Ōph* means flyers in general and can also include bats and flying reptiles like pterosaurs.

Not mentioned in the animals listed in Genesis 1:20–22 or 1:24–25 are non-air-breathing water-dwelling creatures such as fish (*dāg*), crustaceans, and mollusks. Yet in Genesis 1, God gave the two humans rule over the fish, mentioning fish (*dāg*) twice by name (Gen. 1:26, 28). Scripture does not preclude the possibility that God may have made these other kinds of animal life before and after the highlights account of a fifth described day.

God made great air-breathing sea creatures according to their kinds (plural). And He made flyers according to its kind (singular). God created both of these kinds on the same day—a fifth described literal day.

Two Possible Pairings of Great Air-Breathing Aquatic Creatures and Flyers

Genesis 1:20–24 states that God created air-breathing water-dwelling creatures and flyers on a fifth described day. The fossil layers reveal two times when air-breathing water-dwellers and flyers began about the same time: (1) Water-dwelling air-breathing reptiles are seen in fossil layers at the same time as the first flying reptiles. (2) The earliest kind of whale (cetacean) is seen in the fossil layers about the same time as the first bats and modern birds.

Some older Bible versions translate *tanninim* as "dragons." This was before the word "dinosaur" was coined in 1842. "Dragons" may have been the closest English word to what today we call dinosaurs on land, pterosaurs in the air, and pliosaurs in the water.

Paleontologists explain that the fossil record reveals that the first fully air-breathing water-dwellers and flyers (other than insects) were reptiles. Although most reptiles today live on land, many extinct reptiles seen in the fossil record lived in water. Air-breathing water-dwelling reptiles included ichthyosaurs (which resembled dolphins) and pliosaurs, with four large flippers and long necks. Both ichthyosaurs and pliosaurs had to surface to breathe in air. They were aquatic air-breathing animals.

The Hebrew word *ōph* ("flyers") is broader than just birds, allowing the possibility that the flyers created on a fifth described day were pterosaurs, flying reptiles. Examples of flying pterosaurs include pterodactyl and the huge quetzalcoatlus, with a wingspan of up to 33 feet (10 m) and weighing as much as 220 pounds (100 kg).

---

213 Brown, Driver, Briggs, *Hebrew and English Lexicon*, 6251, p. 659.

214 Brown, Driver, Briggs, *Hebrew and English Lexicon*, 6895, p. 733.

The first marine pliosaurs and the first flying pterosaurs are found in the fossil record in the same era. Therefore, the account of a fifth described day (Gen. 1:20–21) may include God's creation of the first marine pliosaurs and the first flying pterosaurs.

A second possibility suggests more familiar animals. We naturally think of air-breathing water-dwellers like the great whales and dolphins (cetaceans). Whales and dolphins live in the water yet must surface regularly to breathe air. And we naturally think of the flyers as like birds and bats. The fossil record indicates that the earliest members of the whale family and the first bats began about the same time. Modern birds may appear in the fossil record about the same time as cetaceans (whales, dolphins) and bats, although fossils of ancient birds, starting with Archaeopteryx and Confuciusornis, appear in significantly older layers. Thus, the account of the fifth described day (Gen. 1:20–21) may report God's creation of the earliest whales (cetaceans), bats, and modern birds.[215]

Scripture may not give enough details to determine with certainty which pairing of air-breathing water-dwelling creatures and flyers is referred to by Genesis 1:21–23. Whichever pairing is correct, the Bible indicates that they were started (Heb. imperfect verb indicating ongoing action[216]) on the same day—a fifth described day of God's work.

According to Their Kinds

Neither of these kinds would evolve into a new kind. Whether the plesiosaur kind or the cetacean kind, the great air-breathing sea creatures will not evolve into another kind. Whether the pterosaur kind or the bird kind and bat kind, the flyers will not evolve into a new kind.

Commendation: Good

God saw that His work making great air-breathing aquatic animals and flyers was good.

And God saw that it was good (Gen. 1:21, NIV 1984).

Chronology: A Fifth Day

Although geologists' and paleontologists' studies of rock strata with fossils may give an approximate date, Scripture does not date this fifth described day.

And-was evening, and-was morning, *a* fifth day (Gen. 1:23, from Hebrew).

How much time passed between a fourth described day and this fifth described

---

215 Flying insects pollinate flowering plants. But flying insects apparently started earlier than the first air-breathing sea creatures. The highlights account in Genesis 1 may not reveal when God made insects. The fossil record shows insects were made well before flowering plants, so were able to fulfill their role as pollinators of flowers.

216 Technically called "incomplete action."

day, and between this fifth described day and the sixth described day, the Bible does not say. But God began (Heb. imperfect) the great air-breathing sea creatures and flyers on the same literal day.

The Bible Account and Evidence in Creation Fit Together

God's inerrant Word and the reliable evidence He created are always in accord. God built truth-revealing evidence into the creation, including into the fossil layers. So the fossil layers are a reliable record of past life and events throughout the geologic history of planet Earth. That reliable evidence matches the order of events in Genesis 1.

With their unique sets of fossils, the rock layers reveal the same broad order recorded in the highlights account in Genesis 1. The lowest layers reveal no life, fitting the beginning time. Then layers start to contain sea fossils and plant fossils. Then layers contain fossils of air-breathing water-dwelling life and flying life that God began on a fifth described day. Upper layers contain fossils of modern land mammals. Finally, the top layers contain fossils of humans that God began on the sixth described literal day. Thus, the geologic layers match the highlighted events of the beginning and the six described literal days listed in Genesis 1.

Chapter 25

God Made Livestock, Small Animals, and Wild Animals

At Wheaton College is the skeleton of a great mastodon prominently displayed in the new science building. The skeleton is huge. When did God make the great grazing animals like the mastodons and mammoths, the scrambling animals like the raccoons, and the wild animals like the saber-toothed cats?

The account of a fifth described day ended with the chronology statement (with a *vav* consecutive, indicating events in sequence) "And-was evening, and-was morning, *a* fifth day." So this next command unit for land animals was after a fifth described day.

This command unit for land animals includes command, consequence, and commendation—indicating an independent command unit. The text allows this land animal command unit to have occurred during the generation of time after a fifth described day and before the sixth. Thus, these events need not be limited to one day. The making of land animals narrated in this passage could have extended over that entire generation of time between a fifth described day and the sixth described day (or could have occurred on the sixth described day).

Conditions on Earth: Animal Creation Not Complete

On a fifth described day, God made air-breathing aquatic and flying animals. But modern land mammals were still not present.

Command: God Commanded the Land to Produce Three Kinds of Land Animals

God commanded the land to produce three kinds of air-breathing (*nephesh*) land animals: large grazing animals, animals that scramble along the ground, and wild animals.

And God said,
"Let the land produce living creatures [*nephesh hāyāh*] according to their kinds:
    livestock [*behēmâh*],
    creatures that move along the ground [*remes*],
    and wild animals [*hāyāh hā'ārets*],
each according to its kind [*min*, kind, singular]" (Gen 1:24, NIV 1984, arr. mine).

Consequence: God Made Three Kinds of Land Animals

God caused the land to produce three kinds of air-breathing land animals. The first kind (*behēmâh*) was large plant-eating quadruped livestock.[217] This kind included large plant-eating quadrupeds, such as elephants, giraffes, cattle, and now-extinct plant-eating mammals such as mastodons and mammoths. The second kind included low scrambling four-legged animals (*remes*),[218] like raccoons, squirrels, and hyrax (conies). The third kind were wild beasts of the earth (*hāyāh hā'ārets*),[219] like present-day lions and tigers and bears and the now-extinct saber-toothed cats. These were air-breathing *nephesh* animals. They were included in "everything that has the breath of life [*nephesh*] in it" (Gen. 1:30). These were not insects or worms but air-breathing land animals. Thus, in the time between the fifth and sixth described days, God made air-breathing *nephesh* grazing quadrupeds, *nephesh* scrambling animals, and *nephesh* wild animals.

God made the three kinds of animals, each "according to its kind [*min*, singular]." Each of these three kinds—the large herbivore kind, the smaller scrambling animal kind, and the wild animal kind—will reproduce after its own kind.

And God made the beasts of the earth after their kind [*min*, singular], and
the cattle after their kind [*min*, singular], and
everything that creeps on the ground after its kind [*min*, singular] (Gen. 1:25, NASB).

During that time, one of the amazing mammals He made was the great mastodon, a reddish-brown-haired elephant-like mammal living in North America during the Ice Age. When one of them died, it became buried near Wheaton College in Illinois.

Commendation: Good

God evaluated His work and saw that what He had done was good: "And God saw that it was good" (Gen. 1:25, NIV). This separate commendation emphasizes the point that this creation unit is a separate section. Yet there is no numbered day, suggesting that this unit may well have been between described day five and described day six.

Calling: God Gave Adam the Authority to Name the Animals

In previous command units, God named the created item. God would give Adam the authority to name the animals (Gen 2:19–20). In addition, God would delegate authority and responsibility to Adam to care for the Garden (Gen. 2:15), both the plants and the animals. Finally, God would tell Adam and Eve to be fruitful, multiply,

---

217 Brown, Driver, Briggs, *Hebrew and English Lexicon*, 1044, p. 96–97, Strong's #0929–0930.
218 Harris, Archer, Waltke, *Theological Wordbook of the Old Testament*, 2177a.
219 Gordon Wenham, *Word Bible Commentary, Genesis 1–15*, 25.

and fill the Earth, subdue it, and have dominion over every living thing that moves on Earth (Gen. 1:28), including these animals.

Chronology: No Numbered Day

God commanded the land to produce three kinds of land animals: large herbivores, smaller scrambling animals, and wild animals. This command unit included a command, consequence, and commendation, indicating it is an independent command unit. However, this command unit has no numbered day, so it is not limited to one specific day but may have occurred over a significant amount of time between the fifth and sixth described days. Thus, the start of these land animal kinds is Biblically undated.

Chapter 26

How Did Animal Death Begin?

Charles Doolittle Walcott (1850–1927), head of the Smithsonian Institute, and his wife, Helena, were horseback riding along a trail, seeking fossils in the Canadian Rockies. The year was 1909. As the story goes, a large rock from an outcrop above had slid down and blocked the trail. Charles dismounted and moved the rock to clear the trail for himself and his wife. Instead of discarding the rock, they split it open with a rock hammer and found a beautifully preserved yet strange fossil. The Walcotts had discovered the Burgess Shale fossil bed, called the source of "the world's most important animal fossils."[220] The whole Walcott family worked on these rocks for years, collecting sixty-five thousand fossils that the family brought to the Smithsonian. Instead of finding fossils of great sea reptiles, dinosaurs, fish, or whales, the Walcotts found only ancient Cambrian period primitive sea animals—trilobites, brachiopods, and echinoderms.

These are among the oldest fossils on Earth, fossils of the Cambrian explosion of life. These fossils are also a record of the death of those early animals.

Paleontologists have called the early competition between predator and prey the Cambrian arms race. Fossils from this period show evidence that animals suffered violent injuries and death. One of the fossils the Walcotts found was Anomalocaris. That ancient predator was one to two meters (three to six feet) long. Paleontologists named it the "T Rex of the Cambrian" because it crunched its trilobite prey. Evidence of bite marks on broken trilobite pieces matches the hard circular mouth of Anomalocaris.

◀ **Anomalocaris—Fearsome Predator of the Cambrian Sea**

Yinan Chin, http://www.goodfreephotos. com/Wikimedia Commons

---

220 www.smithsonianmag.com/history/how-the-burgess-shale-changed-our-view-of-evolution-3678444.

Even the mighty tyrannosaurus suffered violent injuries, diseases, and death. Displayed at Chicago's Field Museum is the huge tyrannosaurus dinosaur named Sue, dating back to the Cretaceous period. When paleontologists did a postmortem examination of her fossilized skeleton, they found that several ribs had been broken and healed, and one toe and her jaw had been severely infected.[221]

▼ **Tyrannosaurus "Sue"—Powerful Predator of the Cretaceous**

By Christophe Hendrickx, Own work, CC BY-SA 3.0, https://commons.wikimedia.org/w/index.php?curid=12573427

In California, the La Brea Tar Pits from the Pleistocene epoch contain hundreds of skeletons of carnivores—huge dire wolves and saber-toothed cats with seven-inch saber-like fangs. The Tar Pits also contain the skeletons of herbivores the carnivores ate: Columbian mammoths, Pacific mastodons, bison, ground sloths, antelope, and many other species that had become trapped in the sticky tar and died. The skeletons contain evidence of diseased and injured bones and teeth. Just a few meters into the deep tar, the only human skeleton was found, the small La Brea woman, dated to around 10,000 years ago.[222] The Tar Pits appear to have been trapping animals in the tar for many millennia.

The Cambrian arms race fossils, the Cretaceous fossilized bones of Sue, and the Pleistocene La Brea Tar Pit skeletons contain major evidence of animal disease and violent animal death. British poet Tennyson, a contemporary of Darwin, described the violence as "red in tooth and claw." From the Cambrian period onward, the fossil record reveals animal death and violent carnivorism.

---

221 "Sue postmortem reveals extensive injuries," New Scientist, DAILY NEWS, 8 October 2001.
222 Fuller, Benjamin T., et al., "Tar Trap . . . 'La Brea Woman,'" 3/9/2016), *PaleoAmerica* 2 (1): 56–59.

Agreement: All God Did Was Good; All Human Death Was by Adam's Sin

Bible believers agree on several key ideas. The Bible teaches that all God is and does is good but Adam by his sin brought human death.

Bible Believers Agree That God and All God Does Is Good

The one and only Creator God, who made the heavens and earth, is absolutely good.

> Sing to the LORD, all the earth!
> Tell of his salvation from day to day. . . .
> For all the gods of the peoples are worthless idols,
> but the LORD made the heavens. . . .
> Oh give thanks to the LORD, for he is good (1 Chron. 16:23–26, 34).

Everything God is and everything God does is good, reflecting His completely good character. Yet the fossil record reveals that animal death was universal in extent, was often violent in character and massive in amount, started with the earliest animals, and extended over a long time.

Bible Believers Agree Adam's Sin Caused All Human Death

When Satan tempted the first human pair, Eve was deceived (Gen. 3:13; 1 Tim. 2:13–14), but Adam deliberately disobeyed his Creator's good command. Therefore, Adam is held responsible. Since Adam is the ancestor of all humans, he, by his sin, started human death for himself and all his descendants, all future humans:

> Therefore, as through one human [Adam] the sin entered into the world, and through the sin the death, and so the death passed into all humans [*anthrōpŏs*] because all [humans] sinned" (Rom. 5:12, from Greek).

> For as in Adam all die, so also in Christ shall all be made alive (1 Cor. 15:22).

Scripture reveals two falls: first the fall of Lucifer/Satan, then the Fall of Adam.

The context of both Romans 5:12 and 1 Corinthians 15:22 is about human death and human salvation. Both verses teach that Adam's sin brought human death. Romans 5:12 states that death spread to all humans because all sinned. *Anthrōpŏs* means a human, "a person of either sex, with focus on participation in the human race, *a human being.*"[223] Romans

---

223 Fredrick Danker/Walter Bauer, *A Greek-English Lexicon of the New Testament*, 81.

5:12 teaches that Adam, by his sin, passed "the death" (Greek text has the article "the") to all his descendants, to all humans. Thus, death in Romans 5:12 is human death passed down to all humans. And we all, by our sin, confirm that verdict of death.

First Corinthians 15:22 establishes an equation between "in Adam all die" and "in Christ shall all be made alive." All who are "made alive" in Christ Jesus are human believers in Him. So all who die in Adam are also humans. Both verses declare that all human death is through Adam's sin.

> *The Bible teaches that Adam's sin started all human death (Rom. 5:12; 1 Cor. 15:22), but the Bible does not say Adam's sin started animal death.*

Most Bible Believers Agree That Satan's Sin and Fall Preceded Adam's Sin and Fall

Scripture reveals two falls: first the fall of Lucifer/Satan, then the Fall of Adam. The first fall, the first rebellion, the first sin was not Adam's. The first sin and fall was the fall of Satan.

Disagreement on Animal Death: Three Views

God's Word reveals that God is good and truthful. His Word, the Bible, is inerrant, and the evidence He built into the creation is reliable. The fossil record reveals apparent evidence of violent animal death before Adam. How does the fact that God is good and the apparent evidence from paleontology of violent animal death before humans, before Adam's Fall, fit together? Bible believers suggest three possible sources of animal death.

View 1: Adam, by His Sin, Started Animal Death

Young Earth Creationism teaches that all human and animal death resulted from Adam's Fall about 6,000 (to at most 10,000) years ago. A leading Young Earth creationist wrote, "Originally [until Adam's Fall] everything was perfect. . . . There was no death of animals or humans in the original creation." Adam's Fall "affected EVERYTHING in the entire universe" (emphasis his).[224] According to this view, all animal death—and evidence of death in the fossil record—came about after Adam's Fall. YEC claims most fossils are from a single event: the global Flood, dated by Ussher to 2348 BC.

Proponents of this view often base their claim—that Adam's sin started all animal

---

224 Ken Ham, *Dinosaurs of Eden*, 21, 24.

death about 6,000 years ago—largely on the two verses that show Adam's sin began all human death, Romans 5:12 and 1 Corinthians 15:22:

> Therefore, as through one human [Adam] the sin entered into the world, and through the sin the death, and so the death passed into all humans [*anthrōpŏs*] because all [humans] sinned (Rom. 5:12, from Greek[225]).

> For as in Adam all die, so also in Christ shall all be made alive (1 Cor. 15:22).

Response: *The Bible Teaches That Adam, by His Sin, Started Human Death*

The context of both Romans 5:12 and 1 Corinthians 15:22 is about human death and human salvation. The Bible teaches that Adam's sin started all human death, but the Bible does not say Adam's sin started animal death. Neither Romans 5:12 nor 1 Corinthians 15:22 is about animals. Romans 5:12 states that death spread to all humans because all sinned. In this context, "the world" in Romans 5:12 ("through one man sin entered into the world") is "the world of people, the human race, not the physical earth." Romans 5:12 does not say that through Adam's sin, death passed down to all animals.[226]

All who are "made alive" in Christ Jesus are all human believers in Him. So all who die in Adam are also humans. Both verses declare that all human death is through Adam's sin. Neither verse says Adam's sin started all animal death. The curse on Adam does not mention animal death.

The view that Adam began all animal death also has a fossil problem. Animal fossils indicate animal death. Sequential layers, each with their unique kinds of fossils, fit the order of creation events listed in Genesis 1. Most fossils are below the top layers that contain human fossils, indicating violent animal death before humans—before Adam.

The YEC view that Adam's Fall started all animal death about 6,000 years ago is not proven by Genesis 3 or Romans 5:12 or 1 Corinthians 15:22, and it does not fit the fossil record. Thus, the idea that Adam started all animal death about 6,000 years ago lacks support from Scripture and from the creation.

View 2: God Started Animal Death as Part of His Good Work

Some Old Earth creationists teach that God started animal death. They say the fossil record displays evidence that animal death began millions of years ago. OEC advocates explain that the Bible states that all God did was good, concluding that animal death and carnivorism are beneficial and part of God's good plan and work.

Is animal death good? While my children were growing up, they loved the friendly

---

225 Young's Literal Translation also correctly includes "the" in "the sin" and "the death."

226 Leon Morris, *Romans*, 229. Also Murray, *Romans*, 181, "sphere of human existence;" Cranfield, *Romans*, 113, "mankind"; Hodge, *Romans*, 146, "mankind"; Moo, *Romans 1—8*, 331, "the world of humanity."

cat that our family rescued. They gave that cat lots of love and attention year after year. Our cat had a good life but eventually grew old. One day our cat lay down on the green grass in the warm sunshine, went to sleep, and never woke up. I buried him under the apple tree. If all animal death were like this, one might argue that animal death is within the realm of good. The idea that animals were created to live a mortal life and then die a peaceful death might be reconcilable with Scripture.

Consider rabbits. If each original and new rabbit lived forever, Earth would be overrun by rabbits, not to mention mice and rats. Rabbit death keeps the rabbit population at a reasonable level, preventing overpopulation, which would lead to starvation. The rabbit species is benefited by predators that weed out weak animals and regulate the rabbit population, even though weeding out involves animal death. This view concludes that animal death is "necessary and good for survival,"[227] part of God's good work.[228]

Response: Violent Animal Death Does Not Seem to Fit God's Work

The fossil record reveals suffering and violent animal death. How can animal suffering and violent death be considered good?

Our good Lord allows the beings He has created to make choices, but He is not to blame for those choices and their consequences. Theologian John Feinberg points out that God created "agents [angels and humans] who can act: He did not create their acts (good or evil)."[229] If an agent God created started animal death, God is not at fault.[230] Although animal death is within God's overall sovereign plan, God Himself does not seem to have started the violent animal death and carnivorism seen in the fossil record.[231]

---

227 Bethany Sollereder, "Predators and Prey: Was Death Part of God's Plan All Along?" *Christianity Today*, October 2019.

228 Mark S. Whorton, *Peril in Paradise*, (2005).

229 John S. Feinberg, *The Many Faces of Evil*, 1994, 127. I am not implying that Dr. Feinberg would or would not agree with this third view of animal death.

230 An example is found in the book of Job. Satan asked God to strike "all that he [Job] has." Although taunted by Satan to harm Job, God refused. Instead, God permitted Satan to do harm. The results were terrible. Satan used natural elements and wicked human agents to bring death to Job's children, servants, and animals (Job 1:12–22). Job laments deeply: "'Then Job arose and tore his robe and shaved his head and fell on the ground and worshiped. And he said, "Naked I came from my mother's womb, and naked shall I return. The Lord gave, and the Lord has taken away; blessed be the name of the Lord.' In all this Job did not sin or charge God with wrong" (Job 1:20–22). At first God did not allow Satan to touch Job's body. Later Satan asked God to harm Job's body, but God did not do so. Instead, God allowed Satan to cause Job intense physical disease. The book of Job teaches that God does not do wrong but allows Satan to cause undeserved disease and death. God apparently allowed Satan to introduce animal death and disease.

231 God's goodness in creation is upheld, despite Satan apparently starting violent animal death, then Adam starting all human evil and human death. Two ways of seeing God's goodness have been suggested:

Free-Will (Arminian) Defense of God's Goodness

• Free creatures (in a libertarian sense of no constraints at all) can 100 percent freely choose to do good or evil.

• This freedom of angels and humans is very good.

• God cannot both create free creatures and guarantee they will do no evil. God chose to create free creatures.

View 3: Satan Started Animal Death

Evidence in the fossil record reveals massive violent animal death. The Bible does not explicitly say who started animal death or when it started. (Animal death is not a significant subject in the Bible.) However, the Bible tells us who sinned first and who "has the power of death." Distinguished Old Testament scholar Walter Kaiser suggested that the devil, Satan, seems to have been the cause of the start of animal death during the time before Adam's Fall.[232]

The View of Two Stage Biblical Creation

Adam's sin started all human death. Based on cumulative Bible evidence, Two Stage Biblical Creation makes a Bible-based theological deduction that Satan started the violent animal death seen in the fossil record.

The Bible clearly states that all God did was good. "The Lord is good to all, and His tender mercies are over all His works" (Psa. 145:9, NKJV). Adam's sin was not the first sin, the first rebellion. Could the first sin, the less-mentioned sin, have led to the start of violent animal death? What if Satan, after his fall, started animal death and then, later, Adam's Fall caused all human death?

God created Lucifer and his fellow angels as perfect beings. Job 38 describes God laying the foundations of the earth while "the morning stars sang together and all the sons of God shouted for joy" (Job 38:7). Angels, including Lucifer, the light bearer, rejoiced at God's work. God had already created Lucifer as a perfect being before He laid Earth's foundations (Job 38:4–7).

Ezekiel 28 interweaves references to Lucifer and the wicked king of Tyre, a double reference recognized since the early church.[233]

• Satan and Adam and his descendants have freely chosen to do evil, so they and we (not God) are guilty.

Sovereign-God (Augustinian/Moderate Calvinist) Defense of God's Goodness

• God is sovereign, so all created beings act within the constraints of His design and overall purpose.

• God designed angels and Adam and Eve as agents able not to sin and able to sin (*posse non peccare et posse peccare*), unlike all humans since, who are unable not to sin (*non posse non peccare*).

• God's omnipotence does not include doing two contradictory things. God has no blame for what He cannot do.

• God cannot both create angels and Adam and Eve with choice and not allow them to choose evil.

• Lucifer and Adam chose to sin, so they, not God, are guilty of starting moral and natural evil. Satan started animal death and Adam started human death. Their choices were within God's plan but not forced.

• God is defeating evil. Jesus, God the Son, paid for our sin and offers us eternal life with Him. When we believe in the Lord Jesus, He enables us on any occasion not to sin, although we will not live our entire Christian life with no sin. When we do sin, we confess our sin to God and He cleanses us from all sin. In the future, God will end and judge all evil. In the New Creation, believers will no longer be able to sin (*non posse peccare*). Thank God!

• God is good. He is not to blame for Satan's choice that apparently started animal death or Adam's choice that started all human evil and human death. Jesus has triumphed over and will end sin and death!

232 Walter Kaiser in "The Great Debate," Ken Ham and Jason Lisle vs Hugh Ross and Walter Kaiser, Ankerberg, #3, suggested Satan started animal death.

233 Philip Schaff, *Early Church Fathers*, Confessions of Cassian, Part 1, I–X; Adam, Satan, and the King of Tyre.

You were the model of perfection,
        full of wisdom and perfect in beauty....
You were blameless in your ways
        from the day you were created
        till wickedness was found in you.
Through your widespread trade [trafficking]
        you were filled with violence, and you sinned....
So I [the Sovereign LORD God] threw you to the earth (Ezek. 28:12–17, NIV 1984).

Lucifer made the horrible choice of rebelling against his Creator. In righteous response to Lucifer's wickedness, God expelled him, the devil, from Heaven and threw him down to Earth.

A theological deduction: God apparently allowed Satan—who "has been sinning from the beginning," who "was a murderer from the beginning," who was "filled with violence," who is "the prince of this world," who is "like a roaring lion, seeking someone to devour"—to introduce violent animal death, parasitism, disease, and carnivorism from the time of the very earliest of animals. Scripture explicitly identifies only one created being who has "the power of death." He is identified as "the one who has the power of death, that is, the devil" (Heb. 2:14).

This deduction is not denying God's sovereignty over death. God decrees death as the just penalty for wrongdoing, yet even then, He does not take pleasure in the death of the wicked (Ezek. 18:23, 32). Satan started animal death not out of justice but out of his own evil nature and sinful desires. Apparently God allowed Satan to have been the agent to introduce violent animal death. Satan, who has "the power of death," apparently triggered a terrible change. Satan brought violent animal death, parasitism, disease, and carnivorism. Evidence of violent animal death is in the fossil record.

After His fall, Satan apparently started the violent animal death seen in the fossil record. Adam, by his sin, certainly started all human death (Rom. 5:12; 1 Cor. 15:22). Death is an enemy, the last enemy Jesus conquers. But the completion of that conquest is still in the future.

How could Satan have started carnivorism when God gave animals plants for food?

How could Satan have started carnivorism when the Bible says that on the sixth day God gave animals every green plant for food?

The answer is both happened, each when the Bible says. Satan was "sinning from the beginning" and "was a murderer from the beginning," and it appears that he added violent death and carnivorism to the good animals God made. On the sixth described day, God gave humans seed plants and fruit for food. On the same day, He gave animals "every green plant for food," making them all vegetarian on the sixth described day.

> Then God said, "I give you [Adam and Eve] every seed-bearing plant . . . for food. And to all the beasts and all the birds of the air and all the creatures that move on the ground—everything that has the breath of life in it—I give every green plant for food." And it was so.
>
> God saw all that He had made, and it was very good. And there was evening, and there was morning—the sixth day (Gen. 1:29–31, NIV 1984).

On the sixth described day, God gave "every green plant for food" to all land animals and flyers, thus ending carnivorism from the sixth described day. For a short time God made Earth a paradise with no carnivorism.[234]

In Acts 3 Peter addresses the people, declaring that they had delivered Jesus over to Pilate, but God has glorified Him. "You killed the Author of life, whom God raised from the dead. . . . Repent, . . . that your sins may be blotted out." Peter continues in verse 21, declaring that "heaven must receive [Jesus] until the time for restoring [*apokatastasis,* "restoration"] all things about which God spoke by the mouth of his holy prophets." Isaiah spoke of that future time: "The wolf shall dwell with the lamb, and the leopard shall lie down with the young goat, and the calf and the lion and the fattened calf together; and a little child shall lead them" (Isa. 11:6). "The wolf and the lamb shall graze together; the lion shall eat straw like the ox" (Isa. 65:25).

This future restoration (*apokatastasis*) in the Millennium restores conditions similar to those on the sixth described day. As in the Millennium, God must have made lions vegetarian on the sixth described day when He gave them all vegetation to eat (Gen. 1:30). Revelation 20:1–2 says Satan will be bound for one thousand years in the future Millennium and God will restore conditions similar to the brief paradise of the sixth described day.

How could God evaluate His work on the sixth day as "very good" if Satan had already started violent animal death?

On the sixth described day, God made Earth "very good," giving animals (and humans) only vegetation to eat (Gen 1:29–30), so ending any animal violence and carnivorism that Satan had added earlier. Just as the Lord Jesus will restore (Acts

---

234 Genesis 1:29–30 declares that God said, "I give you [Adam and Eve] every seed-bearing plant . . . for food. And to all the beasts and all the birds of the air and all the creatures that move on the ground—everything that has the breath of life in it—~~I give~~ <u>every green plant for food</u>" (NIV 1984). In the inspired Hebrew text, there is no verb in this last clause, no "I give," and certainly no "I have given" as if 1:30 were saying all animals had always been vegetarian. The verb is in Genesis 1:29, "I give you," Adam and Eve, vegetables and fruit for food, and that verb also applies to "every green plant for food" to animals on that same sixth described literal day. God gave vegetation to air-breathing land animals and birds, including, apparently, previously carnivorous animals, on the sixth described literal day.

3:21) peaceful conditions in the future Millennium, so He made Earth a very good paradise on the sixth described day. Thus, God could say at the end of the sixth day, "very good." "God saw everything that he had made, and behold, it was very good" (Gen. 1:31). On the sixth described day, God made Earth a vegetarian paradise and evaluated everything He had done, and it was "very good."

YEC advocates ask, How could Adam and Eve be considered in a "very good" paradise with stacks of fossils under their feet? In response, fossils bear witness to the fact of animal death. The fossil layers are a historical record of what actually happened.

With all that sin and death, is there hope?

Although the first peaceful time in Eden is gone, there is hope for humans, for with God's judgment was mercy. God promised to send a Redeemer, a male offspring of Eve who would crush Satan's head, but at great cost to Himself (Gen. 3:15): death on the cross to pay the penalty for our sin. Through that act of our sinless Creator (who chose to become fully human by the virgin birth), dying in our place on the cross and three days later rising from the dead, we can receive eternal life in Him.

In the future Millennium, God will restore (Acts 3:21) a peaceful paradise. Satan will be bound at the start of the future Millennium, and animal violence and carnivorism again will cease. In that future restoration of paradise, the lion will again become vegetarian (Isa. 65:25). After the Millennium, God will create the eternal New Heavens and New Earth with no sin, no sorrow, no sickness, no death, and no end.

History has two falls, each followed by death: The first fall, by Satan's sin, apparently started animal death. The second Fall, by Adam's sin, certainly added all human death.

History has two times of peaceful paradise when God stops carnivorism and makes animals vegetarian: The first was the "very good" sixth described day and an (apparently brief) time thereafter. The second will be the "restoring" in the Millennium.

Conclusion: Bible Implies Satan Started Animal Death from the Beginning

All that God made was "good." But another individual, a created individual, a fallen, sinful, violent individual, was lurking in the background.

A theological deduction: God apparently allowed Satan—who was "filled with violence," who "has been sinning from the beginning," who "was a murderer from the beginning," "who has the power of death," who is "the prince of this world," who is "like a roaring lion, seeking someone to devour"—to introduce universal animal death and violent carnivorism to the good animals God made during the time of the six described days. Later, Adam's sin started all human death.

Chapter 27

The Sixth Described Day: Humans; The Seventh Day: Rest

Plants covered much of the land. Water-dwelling creatures filled the sea. Flying creatures swept across the sky. Land animals roamed the Earth. But God had not finished His creation work.

Conditions on Earth: Earth Ready, but No Humans

God saw everything He had created and evaluated it as "good." But there were no humans to be loved by God and respond with love to God, to worship and fellowship with their Creator. God's work on the sixth described day would be making humans in the image of God, able to fellowship with their Creator.

The Garden

In the East, in a place called Eden, no wild or cultivated plants had grown. The Lord God had not yet sent rain on the land or made humans to cultivate the ground (Gen. 2:4b-5). In that land God caused water to rise up as mist (Gen. 2:7, ESV) or bubbling springs (NIV 1984) and water the ground. There the Lord God (YHVH *Elohîm*) planted a beautiful Garden (Gen. 2:8). The Hebrew word for garden is *gan*, "enclosure, garden,"[235] indicating an enclosed, protected, fruitful garden area. God planted the beautiful Garden inside that safe and secure enclosure (Gen. 2:4b–25). A river flowed through the Garden, watering it. That Garden would produce abundant, delicious fruit that would be food for Adam and Eve.

Command: God Created the Human Pair in His Image

On the sixth described day, God created the first humans, Adam and Eve, in His image. God's work on the sixth day was unique, and the command unit is equally unique: "Then-said God, 'Let-us-make man, in-our-image [*b^{e}tsalem*], to-our-likeness [*k^{i}demot*]'" (Gen. 1:26, from Hebrew).

Then God said, "Let us make man in our image, after our likeness. And let them have dominion [*rādāh,* "rule, have dominion"] over the fish of the sea and over

---

235 Brown, Driver, Briggs, Hebrew and English Lexicon, 1879-1880, p. 171, Strong's #1558.

the birds of the heavens and over the livestock and over all the earth and over every creeping thing that creeps on the earth" (Gen. 1:26).

Humans are not another kind of animal. Humans, both male and female, were created uniquely in the image of God. God created humans to be His representatives, responsible for caring for the Earth and its animal life.

Consequence: Humans in the Image of God

Humans were not created *ex nihilo*. God made Adam from the dust of the ground (Gen. 2:7) and gave him a living soul, making him a living being:

> And-formed the L ORD God the man *from* dust of the ground
> and breathed into his nostrils *the* breath of life,
> and the man became a living being [*nephesh hāyāh*] (Gen 2:7, from Hebrew).

God uniquely created both Adam and Eve equally in the image of eternal God:

> So God created man in his own image,
> in the image of God he created him;
> male and female he created them (Gen. 1:27).

Zechariah 12:1 explains that Almighty God formed the spirit of humans, Adam and Eve, within them.

> Thus declares the L ORD,
> who stretched out the heavens
> and founded the earth
> and formed the spirit of man within him (Zech. 12:1, arr. mine).

The first two humans, Adam and Eve, were given a spiritual nonmaterial component. God uniquely made Adam and Eve "in His own image." Humans are not the product of chance-based blind evolution; humans were created uniquely with an eternal spirit. God made humans able to relate to Him in continual love, worship, and praise and serve Him as His representatives with dominion over the animals on Earth.

> And God blessed them. And God said to them, "Be fruitful and multiply and fill the earth and subdue it [*kābash*, "subdue"], and have dominion [*rādāh*] over the fish of the sea and over the birds of the heavens and over every living thing that moves on the earth" (Gen. 1:28).

God gave humans the responsibility of being His representatives and administrators over the Earth. God blessed Adam and Eve. In turn, they were to be a blessing to the Earth and all its life. God also told them to subdue (*kābash*) the Earth and have dominion (*rādāh*) over its creatures. As God's representatives on Earth, humans are to rule Earth and all its animals for good. We are not to misuse that dominion. God also told Adam and Eve to increase and multiply and fill the Earth.

On the sixth described literal day, God gave Adam and Eve seed-bearing vegetables and seed-bearing fruit to eat (Gen. 1:29). "And to every beast of the earth and to every bird of the heavens and to everything that creeps on the earth, everything that has the breath of life" God gave "every green plant for food. And it was so" (Gen. 1:30).

In summary, on the sixth described day of His work, God created humans, both male and female, uniquely in His image and told them to be fruitful, reproduce, and fill the Earth. He gave them rule over the fish, birds, and every living thing that moves. God gave those humans food from seed plants and fruit trees (Gen. 1:29). And on that same sixth described day, God gave animals "every green plant for food."

Commendation: God's Work Was "Very Good"

Bible believers agree that everything God is and everything God does is always good and right. On day one, God evaluated the light and declared the light was good. Next, He evaluated His other sovereign creation works, and He saw that they were "good." Finally, at the end of the sixth described day, God looked at all He had done and evaluated His work not just as "good" but "very good."

And-saw God all that He had done [*asâh*], and-behold *it was* very good.
And-was evening and-was morning the sixth day (Gen. 1:31, from Hebrew).

Acts 3:21 says God will restore (*apokatastasis*, "restoration") all things. That restoration is in the future Millennium. For a restoration in the future, there must have been a past time when Earth was Millennium-like. Earth was not in a Millennium-like condition when it was uninhabitable, uninhabitable, sea covered, and dark (Gen. 1:2). But at the end of the sixth described day, when God had made both Adam and Eve in His image, instructed and blessed them, and given to every beast of the earth and every bird and everything that creeps on the earth every green plant for food, God evaluated all His work as "very good."

Chronology: The Sixth Day

God made the first two humans uniquely in His image on the sixth described day.

And there was evening, and there was morning—the sixth day (Gen. 1:31, NIV 1984).

The sixth day, with the creation of Adam[236] and Eve, is the only numbered day

---

236 Various manuscripts have lists with some differences in the genealogies. Also, "son of" may mean

of the six that the Bible enables us to roughly date. To estimate Adam's date, people have added the years in the genealogies of his descendants. But trying to date the universe (created in the beginning time) using Adam's date is claiming far more than the Bible says. Adam may be dated to thousands, not millions, of years ago. But previous events remain Biblically undated.

The Seventh Described Day: God Rested

On the seventh described day, God rested. He rested, not because He was weary, for He never grows weary (Isa. 40:28), but because He had completed His creation work and evaluated it as "very good." From that glorious seventh described day onward, Earth, life, and Adam and Eve enjoyed a brief "very good" world in the presence of their Creator.

> Thus the heavens and the earth were finished, and all the host of them. And on the seventh day God finished his work that he had done, and he rested on the seventh day from all his work that he had done. So God blessed the seventh day and made it holy, because on it God rested from all his work that he had done in creation (Gen. 2:1–3).

Six Great Days of Creation and One Day of Rest

At the end of the extensive "in the beginning" time (the first stage of creation), the Earth was uninhabitable, uninhabited, cloud darkened, and sea covered (Gen. 1:2). Then God worked six described literal days making Earth lighted, habitable, and inhabited. Finally, He rested on the seventh day. Each described day was a literal day:

- Day one: God commanded, "Let there be light" (1:3–5), lighting Earth's dark sea.
- *A* second day: God made an expanse between sea below and cloud above (1:6–8).
    - o Then God gathered the waters and made dry land appear (1:9–10).
- *A* third day: God caused the Earth to produce green vegetation (1:11–12).
- *A* fourth day: God caused the luminaries to perform three new functions for Earth (1:14).
- *A* fifth day: God made air-breathing water-dwelling animals and flyers (1:20–22).
    - o Then God made three kinds of air-breathing land animals (1:24–25).
- The sixth day: God made Adam and Eve in His image. (1:26–31).
- The seventh day: God rested (2:1–3).

The six described days completed the second stage of God's creation work. "These

---

descendant. Therefore, an exact date even for Adam is questionable.

[*are the*] generations of the heavens and the earth when [*they were*] created" (Gen. 2:4a, from Hebrew).

Chapter 28

The Perfect Human Pair in the Protected Garden Chose Sin

In a land that had been without rain, barren of wild and cultivated plants, in the east of Eden, the LORD God (YHVH *Elohîm*) planted a beautiful Garden with bountiful fruit trees. The Hebrew word for "garden" (*gan*, "enclosure, garden") indicates an enclosed fruitful area of land.

The Garden was a paradise, the perfect protected place for the perfect couple. Then God brought the man and formed the woman in that protected paradise, the Garden of Eden.

God Gave Adam and Eve the Rule over Paradise

In that wonderful sixth described day, the culmination of God's creation work, the Bible says God blessed Adam and Eve and gave them dominion and rule:

And God blessed them. And God said to them, "Be fruitful and multiply and fill the earth and subdue it and have dominion over the fish of the sea and over the birds of the heavens and over every living thing that moves on the earth" (Gen. 1:26–28).

God told Adam and Eve to "be fruitful and multiply and fill the earth and subdue it and have dominion" over the animals (Gen. 1:28).

God gave Adam and Eve seed-bearing fruit and vegetables as food.

"I give you every seed-bearing plant on the face of the whole earth and every tree that has fruit with seed in it. They will be yours for food. And to all the beasts of the earth and all the birds of the air and all the creatures that move on the ground—everything that has the breath of life in it—I give every green plant for food" (Gen. 1:29–30, NIV 1984).

Thus, it seems the whole Earth could have continued to be a paradise under the leadership of Adam and Eve.

Satan's Temptation Led to Human Sin and Human Death

God created angels and humans with the ability to choose. The ability to choose is good. But with that ability came the ability to choose evil. Would Adam and Eve choose to trust God, their Creator, and gladly obey Him, or would they rebel like Satan? The Garden contained a choice, a belief-in-God decision. Adam and Eve could choose to obey God by not eating of the "tree of the knowledge of good and evil" or choose to rebel.

> And-commanded the Lord God [YHVH *Elohîm*] the man saying, "From any tree of the Garden you may eat. But from the tree of the knowledge of good and evil you must not eat! For when [*bᵉyôm*, "in-day, when"] you eat of it, dying you-will-die" (Gen. 2:16–17, from Hebrew).

The command "not eat . . . !" is similar to the Ten Commandments' negative commands: "Not kill!" "Not steal!" "Not commit-adultery!" The "not eat" command was given explicitly to Adam, and he is held responsible. The phrase "dying you-will-die" (*mōt,* infinitive meaning to die or dying; *tamut,* ingressive imperfect meaning you-are-already-starting-to-die-and-will-die) has the sense of death invading immediately, but not necessarily completing its terrible work immediately. The freedom of human choice was a great gift with great responsibility, but with that choice came the potential of an appalling consequence—"you will die." Genesis 2:17 says nothing about animals dying.

Then fallen Satan, in the form of a serpent, tempted Eve to disobey God's good command not to eat the fruit of the tree of the knowledge of good and evil. Satan, making sin sound so tempting (Gen. 3:1–7), deceived Eve into disobeying God's good command (Gen. 3:13; 1 Tim. 2:13–14). But Adam deliberately chose to disobey God's clear command. Adam deliberately sinned. By his sin, Adam—the ancestor of all humans—started human death for all his descendants.

> Therefore, *just* as through one man [Adam] the sin entered into the world [of all humans], and through the sin the death, and so the death passed into all humans [*anthrōpŏs*] because all *humans* sinned (Rom. 5:12, from Greek).

> For as in Adam all die, so also in Christ shall all be made alive (1 Cor. 15:22).

Adam followed Satan into sin, brought death to himself, and passed death to all his descendants. Yet by God's immeasurable mercy, all humans who put their trust in Jesus, our Creator and Savior, receive eternal life in Him.

God's Plans for Us Are Good

All God did was good. He created a wonderful world and the perfect couple, making them in His own image and likeness. He gave them the honor of representing Himself on earth. He provided the human pair with a beautiful Garden protected from evil. And in the center of the Garden, He caused the tree of life to grow. Above all else, He gave the human couple the capacity to know and fellowship with Him, their Creator. All God did was good.

Yet God also gave both angels and humans a real choice. Earlier, Satan sinned, and now Adam sinned. Both introduced suffering and death into the good world God had made. The Bible declares, "All have sinned" (Rom. 3:23); we've all broken God's good law.

God planned a way for us to have our sin forgiven so we can again know Him. The problem is that "all have sinned," and "the wages of sin is death" (Rom. 3:23; 6:23). God Himself provided the amazing, perfect solution—His only Son, the God-Man, Jesus. Jesus is the only human with no sin of His own to pay for, so He alone could take the full penalty for the wrong we do. "But God shows his love for us in that while we were still sinners, Christ died for us" (Rom. 5:8). Jesus was buried, but on the third day, He rose from the dead. Now He offers the gift of eternal life to all who believe in Him. And "everyone who calls on the name of the Lord [Jesus] will be saved" (Rom. 10:13).

Chapter 29

Have Advocates of Two Stages Already Solved the Creation Puzzle?

Have Bible believers before us who held two stages of creation, starting with the early church fathers, and Jewish teachers of the Torah like Rabbi Moses ben Naḥman (known as Nachmanides or Ramban) already largely solved the great creation puzzle? Let's hear what the Bible says and how they responded:

Hear God's inerrant Word, the Bible: "In the beginning God created [*bārā'*] the heavens and the earth. Now the earth was uninhabitable and uninhabited [*tōhû v^abōhû*]" (Gen. 1:1–2). Then "for six days the LORD did-work on the heavens and the earth, the sea, and all that *is* in them" (Exod. 20:11, from Hebrew). God created the heavens and the earth "in the beginning" (Gen. 1:1); then He worked six literal days on the earth making it lighted, habitable, and inhabited (Gen. 1:3–31).

> *Belief in two stages of creation, the second stage having six literal days, is a historical belief of Jewish and Christian Bible believers. Two Stage Biblical Creation is a back-to-the-Bible effort.*

Hear Rabbi Moses ben Naḥman (Ramban): "*In the beginning G-d created.*" "We have in our holy language no other term for the bringing forth of something out of nothing but *bārā'*." God *bārā'*, "created," from "total and absolute nothing." He continues, "With one command [Gen. 1:1] G-d created at first the heavens and the earth and all their hosts. . . . Scripture returns to explain that the earth after this creation was *tohu*." During the six days, God put things "into a finished condition."[237]

Hear church father Basil: "In the beginning God created the heavens and the earth." That time was the "epoch when the formation of this world began."[238] But the earth was "still incomplete" and "waiting for the appointed time" for God to complete the work. When the "appointed time" arrived, God's first command, "Let

---

237 Ramban (Nachmanides), *Commentary on the Torah: Genesis*, trans. Chavel (NY: Shiloh, 1971), 17, 23.
238 Basil the Great, *Hexaemeron Homilies*, trans, Blomfield Jackson, Sermon one, 8.

193

there be light," began day one on earth. Each of the six days was "a day and of a night."[239] Basil taught there were two parts of creation, and in the second part, the six days were literal days.

Hear medieval theologian Hugo St. Victor: God created "time" and "the first substance" "in the beginning" in Genesis 1:1. Genesis 1:2 says the world was unfinished. "But how long it continued in this state … Scripture does not clearly show."[240] Then God put the earth into an orderly arrangement in the six literal days.

Hear the great pre-Reformation theologian Thomas Aquinas: "It seems better to maintain that the creation [Gen. 1:1] was prior to any of the days."[241]

Hear theologian Charles Hodge: "Some understand the first verse of Genesis to refer to the original creation of the matter of the universe in the indefinite past, and what follows [the six days] to refer to the last reorganizing change in the state of our earth to fit it for the habitation of man."[242]

Hear modern Bible teachers: Bernard Northrup, William Lane Craig, Paul Copan, John Sailhamer, and Gorman Gray believe the Bible teaches two stages or parts of creation.

Belief in two stages of creation, the second stage having six literal days, is a historical belief of Jewish and Christian Bible believers. Two Stage Biblical Creation is a back-to-the-Bible effort founded on what the Bible in the original languages has taught all along: "In the beginning God created the heavens and the earth," then God worked in the six literal days. This understanding fits the Bible and matches the creation.

Two Stage Biblical Creation from the Bible

The one eternal triune holy God of the Bible is the Creator of the universe and everything in it (Gen. 1:1). God is truthful, and the Bible is His inspired, inerrant Word (in the original Hebrew and Greek autographs). The evidence He built into the creation is reliable, so the Bible and creation match. Genesis 1 was written as history (indicated by the Hebrew *vav* consecutives) and records the actual sequential historical events of the creation in the order in which they occurred. Two Stage Biblical creationists believe in two stages because they are in the Bible.

First, "in the beginning God created the heavens and the earth" (Gen. 1:1), but Genesis 1:2 describes the Earth as unfinished: uninhabitable, uninhabited, sea covered, and dark. Second, Genesis 1:3–31 records God's works in six literal described days during which God finished the earth, started green plants, created animals, and made the first human pair—Adam and Eve—in His image (Gen. 1:3–31).

---

239 Basil the Great, *Hexaemeron Homilies*, trans, Blomfield Jackson, Sermon two, 14.

240 Hugo St. Victor, *De Sacramentis Christianae Fidei*, 21.

241 Thomas Aquinas, *Sententiarum*, Book II, Distinction xiii, Article 3, "Ad Terium"; trans. Custance, *Void*, 22.

242 Charles Hodge, *Systematic Theology, Abr.*, 210.

Some ideas suggested in this book (such as generations, ordinal numbers indicating unnumbered days between the six described days, or Satan initiating the violent carnivorism seen in the fossil record) are exegetically only probable. But the Hebrew Bible text evidence for the two biggest ideas—two stages (in the beginning, then the six described days) and "in the beginning God created the heavens and the earth" as the Biblically undated beginning time when God created *ex nihilo* the actual universe—seem to be approaching exegetical certainty.

Although some details still needed to be worked out, it seems many past theologians understood that "in the beginning God created the heavens and the earth" (Gen. 1:1). Genesis 1:2 turns from the universe to the earth. Now earth was uninhabitable, uninhabited, sea covered, and dark (Gen. 1:2). Then Genesis 1:3–31 records the six day-night days when God made the Earth lighted, inhabitable, and inhabited.

Chapter 30

Bible Concepts of Two Stage Biblical Creation

The great Biblical creation puzzle is not simple. It has many parts to be fitted together. Once all the pieces are fitted together, the creation picture is beautiful.

1. **The Bible alone is God's Word; its every statement, as originally written, is true.**

God's inspired, inerrant Word, the Bible, as originally written in Hebrew and Greek, is 100 percent true (Psa. 119:160; 2 Tim. 3:16). God, the ultimate Author, is 100 percent truthful. A creation theory should be based on, be proven by, and match the inspired, inerrant Hebrew and Greek Bible text.

2. **The inerrant text of the Bible is the basis of Two Stage Biblical Creation.**

Biblical authority of the inerrant Hebrew and Greek Bible text is the foundation and basis of Two Stage Biblical Creation. "In the beginning God created [*bārā'*] the heavens and the earth" (Gen. 1:1), but Earth was uninhabitable, uninhabited, sea covered, and dark (1:2). Then God worked six day-night described days making Earth lighted, habitable, and filled with life (Gen. 1:3–31). These two stages are in the Bible and have been recognized and taught by past and present Jewish and Christian Bible scholars.

3. **The Genesis 1 narrative requires a plain literal interpretation.**

Genesis 1 is historical narrative (indicated by the *vav* consecutive series) and should be interpreted by the plain literal sense. God created the literal heavens and literal Earth "in the beginning." Planet Earth is described in verse 2 as uninhabitable, uninhabited, dark, and sea covered at the conclusion of the beginning time. Genesis 1:3–31 reports that God worked six literal sequential days making Earth lighted, habitable, and full of life. Two Stage Biblical Creation takes all of Genesis 1 literally.

4. **God's Word and God's creation, both accurately understood, match.**

God's inspired Word, the Bible, is inerrant and is our highest authority. God also built reliable evidence into the creation (Psa. 19:1; Rom. 1:20). When the inspired, inerrant Hebrew and Greek Bible texts on creation are understood accurately and are correlated with each other, connections with evidence that God built into the creation will naturally follow, because both God's Word and His creation are from the same 100 percent truthful Creator.

5. **Genesis 1:1 is a declaration that God created the heavens and the earth in the beginning. Genesis 1:1 is not just a title or summary.**

Genesis 1:1 is not merely a title, a summary of the six days, a metaphor, or the start of day one, but is a declaration that God created *ex nihilo* not only space-time-energy-matter but from these the literal heavens (the star-filled universe) and the literal planet Earth in the literal beginning.

6. **Eternal God the Father through eternal God the Son created the universe** *ex nihilo*.

In the beginning, eternal God the Father through eternal God the Son by His command "created the heavens and the earth" *ex nihilo*, out of nothing (Gen. 1:1; John 1:1–3; Rev. 4:11). The universe is not eternal, nor was there preexisting eternal chaos. Only God is eternal. Eternal God created the universe starting with absolutely nothing.

7. *B^{e}re'shît*, **"in the beginning," means a beginning time or phase.**

When referring to time, *b^{e}re'shît*, "in the beginning," means in a beginning time or phase. The length of time is unspecified by the word *b^{e}re'shît* itself. Zedekiah's beginning was over four years of his eleven-year reign: "In the beginning (*b^{e}re'shît*) of the reign of Zedekiah king of Judah, in the fourth year, in the fifth month" (Jer. 28:1, NASB). Job's beginning (*re'shît*) was all his years prior to the time of his troubles (Job 8:7; 42:12). In Genesis 1:1, *b^{e}re'shît* should be taken literally as the beginning time before the six days.

8. **God created the heavens and earth "in the beginning," before the six days.**

The Hebrew perfect aspect of the verb *bārā'*, "created," indicates God completed the *ex nihilo* creation of the actual universe and earth during that beginning time. "The heavens and the earth" is a Hebrew merism meaning the universe with its starry host and planet Earth. The Hebrew *vav* consecutive construction (and-then/and-next) found throughout Genesis chapter 1 indicates that the command starting day one on planet Earth occurred *after* the creation of the heavens and the earth reported in Genesis 1:1. Two Stage Biblical Creation takes Genesis 1:1 literally—that God created the heavens with its host of stars and planet Earth in the beginning time. That was stage one of creation.

9. **God created and expanded the heavens.**

The Bible declares that "in the beginning God created the heavens" and that "God . . . created the heavens and stretched them out" (Gen. 1:1; Isa. 42:5). Only the

Creator could have known these two facts—that the universe had a beginning and is expanding—long before modern science discovered the same facts, robust evidence that the eternal God of the Bible is the one and only Creator. The sudden beginning and precisely right expansion of the universe indicate these events were not by chance but were designed and carried out by the all-powerful, infinitely intelligent Creator, the God of the Bible.

10. At the end of stage one, Earth was uninhabitable, uninhabited, sea covered, and dark.

Genesis 1:1 is about the universe, the creation of "the heavens and the earth." Genesis 1:2, "Now the earth" (*vav*-disjunctive-prefixed initial noun), switches perspective from the universe to planet Earth. Genesis 1:2 describes planet Earth at the end of the events of Genesis 1:1 as uninhabitable, uninhabited, sea covered, and dark. Genesis 1:2 does not say the universe was dark. Darkness "was over the face of the deep," over the surface of Earth's dark, cloud-wrapped deep sea. In Job 38:9, God explains, "I made the clouds its [the sea's] garment and wrapped it in thick darkness" (NIV 1984).

11. "Let there be light" was to the place just declared dark—Earth's dark sea surface.

God already had created the heavens, the universe with its stars, including our star, the sun, during the beginning (Gen. 1:1). But on planet Earth, "darkness was on the surface of the deep" because of the thick clouds (Job 38:9). Then God commanded, "Let there be light." In context, the light shone to the place just declared dark: Earth's sea surface. The penetration of diffuse sunlight to the surface of rotating planet Earth started day and night of literal day one on Earth.

12. The plain sense of *yôm* with a number and evening and morning is a literal day.

Genesis 1 is historical narrative (indicated by the series of *vav*-consecutive-prefixed verbs). The plain sense of *yôm* in historical narrative, in the context of a number and evening and morning, is a literal day. In the Old Testament, when the Hebrew word *yôm* ("day") appears with a number (three days, seventh day), morning, or evening, it always means a day-night day. God worked in six described literal days.

13. On a fourth day, God gave the luminaries three new functions to Earth's surface.

God created (*bārā'*) the heavens with the galaxies, including the Milky Way with our solar system, in the beginning time (Gen. 1:1). Since day one, diffuse sunlight lit the daylight side of rotating planet Earth. Planet Earth was still cloud covered (Job

26:8, 9; 38:9); no distinct luminaries were visible in the sky from the perspective of the surface of the Earth's deep waters.

Job 26:13 explains the change in Earth's sky: "By his breath the skies became fair ["cleared," NASB]" (Job 26:13, NIV 1984). On a fourth described day, God cleared the sky and caused the already created sun, moon, and stars to carry out three new functions to planet Earth: separate and govern day and night, mark seasons and days and years, and be lights in the cleared expanse of the sky.

The Hebrew text of the end of Genesis 1:16 does not say "He also made the stars"— as if He created the stars on that day. The end of verse 16 says, "The lesser light [the moon] to rule the night, and the stars." This text reports a new function of the moon and stars from the perspective of Earth's surface: to rule/govern the night on rotating Earth. God had *bārā'* ("created") the stars as part of the heavens in the Genesis 1:1 beginning time. Then on a fourth described literal day, He made the already-created luminaries fully functional to Earth's surface by clearing the sky (Job 26:13).

14. Hebrew ordinal numbers without articles indicate six described sequential days.

Cardinal numbers (one, two, three) count total quantity. In the Hebrew text, day one has a cardinal number, indicating a total quantity of one day. Then the text switches to ordinal numbers: *a* second day, *a* third day, *a* fourth day, *a* fifth day, the sixth day, the seventh day. Ordinal numbers indicate the position in a series (first, second, third). The ordinal number, especially without a definite article, tells us that a "second day" of God's work was sometime after "day one" in the series and before "*a* third day." The ordinal numbers indicate that the seven days in Genesis 1 were in chronologically sequential order, but do not require that all seven days be consecutive, following one immediately after the other.

15. God created in two stages: in the beginning, then six literal days.

God created in two stages or parts or phases. In stage one, in the beginning God created the heavens (the star-filled universe) and planet Earth (Gen. 1:1). But Earth was unfinished (Gen. 1:2).

In stage two, God worked in six described literal sequential days making Earth lighted, habitable, and inhabited (Gen. 1:3–31)."For six days the LORD worked" (Exod. 20:11, from Hebrew). God started (Hebrew imperfect verbs) each day's work on its literal day. God started daylight-nighttime days on Earth's surface on day one. On a second described day, God started an open expanse of air between the sea water below and cloud water above. On a third described day, He started green vegetation. On a fourth described day, He started three new functions of the luminaries for Earth's surface. On a fifth described day, He created air-breathing sea creatures and flyers. On the sixth described day, He created the first human pair in His image. Each item started on its literal day. That was stage two of creation.

16. Adam can be roughly dated, but events earlier than Adam are Biblically undated.

Bible genealogies can roughly date Adam and Eve and the sixth day to thousands, not millions, of years ago. But because the beginning was an extensive time and the Hebrew ordinal numbers without articles indicate the six described days were sequential (not necessarily consecutive), the beginning and all creation events before Adam are Biblically undated.

17. All God did was good. But first Satan rebelled and then Adam chose to disobey.

Adam's sin was not the first sin. There were two falls: first Satan's sin and fall, then later Adam's sin and Fall.

The Bible describes Satan as "sinning from the beginning" (1 John 3:8), "a murderer from the beginning" (John 8:44), "filled with violence," and thrown "to the Earth" (Ezek. 28:12–17, NIV 1984). From these verses we can deduce that Satan started the violent animal death seen in the fossil record in the time of the six days.

18. On the sixth described day, God created Adam and Eve and gave vegetation for food.

On the sixth described day, God created Adam and Eve in His image and likeness. God blessed them and told them to multiply; He gave them rule over the fish of the sea, the flyers in the air, and every animal that scampers on the ground; and He gave the man and woman every covered-seed-bearing fruit and vegetable plant for food.

On that same sixth described day, God gave all green vegetation to every air-breathing (*nephesh*) wild beast of the earth (former carnivores), every flyer in the air, and every scrambling animal for their food. Thus, God ended carnivorism of all air-breathing *nephesh* land and flying creatures on that sixth described day. At the end of the sixth described day, He evaluated all that He had done as "very good."

19. Adam chose to sin, beginning all human death.

When God created Adam and Eve, He created them sinless. The two unique trees and God's command not to eat from the second tree show that God gave Adam and Eve a choice: they could choose to trust God and obey, or they could rebel and disobey God and eat of the tree of the knowledge of good and evil.

Adam deliberately chose to sin and, by his sin, passed down sin and death to all humans (Gen. 3; Rom. 3:23; 5:12). Human sin preceded and caused all human death. "The wages of sin is death" (Rom. 6:23). The all too brief paradise of human fellowship with God and no human sin or death ended with Adam's sin and the curse on Adam and Eve.

20. The Genesis 1 order of events and the order in the fossil record match.

The concise order of events in Genesis 1 and the broad order of the fossil layers match. The lowest layers lack fossils; the next layers have sea fossils and plant fossils; the next layers have fossils of air-breathing sea creatures, flying creatures, then land animals. Only the top layers have human fossils. This sequence corresponds to the order of events in Genesis 1: the sea-covered Earth, then plants, then air-breathing aquatic and flying creatures, then modern land animals, and finally humans.

21. "In the beginning" followed by six sequential days allows a Biblically undated creation.

The Hebrew word $b^e re'sh\hat{\imath}t$, "in the beginning," when referring to time, means a beginning time of unspecified length. "The heavens and the earth" is a Hebrew merism meaning the universe with its stars and planet Earth. God created the universe with its galaxies and planet Earth in the extensive beginning time. The Hebrew ordinal numbers without definite articles indicate that the six described days were sequential, allowing an unspecified number of unmentioned days between the six described days.

The extensive beginning time and sequential (rather than consecutive) days allow all events before Adam to be Biblically undated. Thus, the universe, planet Earth, and life are all however old they are. Adam's descendants' genealogies roughly date Adam, not the universe. Two Stage Biblical Creation recognizes that the Bible creation texts do not date any creation event before Adam, so all creation events before Adam are Biblically undated. A Biblically undated creation allows (but does not confirm) the older ages proposed by science discoveries for the universe, the Earth, and life.

22. God's answer to human sin is belief in our Creator and Savior—the Lord Jesus Christ.

By the Father's plan, eternal God the Son—our Creator and Savior the Lord Jesus, the God-Man—overcame sin and death by His own substitutionary death on the cross, paying for our sin, and His physical bodily resurrection from the dead. He gives eternal life to all who repentantly believe who Jesus is and what He did and put their faith in Him. The Good News is: Jesus "died for our sins in accordance with the Scriptures, that he was buried, that he was raised on the third day" (1 Cor. 15:3–4). "Believe on the Lord Jesus Christ, and you will be saved" (Acts 16:31, NKJV) and live forever with Him in the New Creation.

My prayer is that to God's glory these ideas, to the degree that they are Bible based, may be recognized as Biblical, accepted, and improved upon by sincere students of the Bible.

Chapter 31

The Drama of Creation

Before telescopes gazed into the universe, before aircraft knifed through the blue sky, before railroads crossed the land, before ships sailed across the seas, before the pyramids rose into the sky, before the first human pair walked in the Garden, before animals spread across the sea and land, before the moon lit the night, before the Earth spun through space, before the nuclear furnaces of great suns burst into fiery power, before space stretched out, before time began—there was only God in perfect holiness, beauty, and love.

God alone.

God alone through all eternity past—

    eternal God the Father,

    eternal God the Son,

    eternal God the Holy Spirit,

Triune, unchanging, everlasting, holy, full of love, perfect in goodness,

complete in wisdom, possessing all power, everywhere at once,

    existing in unending glory and joy beyond all that we can imagine.

Stage One of Creation

Then, "In the beginning God created the heavens and the earth." Suddenly, in an instant, God created *ex nihilo*, out of nothing, all the vast energy and substance of the entire universe. He created it all solely by His own power and mighty command, making a trillion galaxies, fashioning planet Earth, and making it fit for life. All was for the delight and glory of the three Persons of the one eternal God.

In the beginning time, eternal God the Father through eternal God the Son created the *aionas*—the universe, the vastness of space, the start of the eons of time, all the matter-energy that exists.

In the beginning was the Word, and the Word was with God, and the Word was God. He was in the beginning with God. All things were made through him, and without him was not any thing made that was made. . . . And the Word became flesh and dwelt among us, and we have seen his glory, glory as of the only Son from the Father (John 1:1–3, 14).

For by Him all things were created that are in heaven and that are on earth, visible and invisible . . . All things were created through Him and for Him. And He is before all things, and in Him all things consist (Col. 1:16–17, NKJV).

God [the Father] . . . has spoken to us by his Son, whom he appointed heir of all things, and through whom he made the universe [*aionas*] (Heb. 1:2, NIV 1984).

In the beginning time, God created all the fixed laws of the universe—unchanging laws, perfect from the first instant, precisely crafted to guide the heavens and the earth under His sovereign control. God created "the fixed laws of heaven and earth" (Jer. 33:25, NIV 1984).

God fitted the universe together precisely right in the beginning time.

By faith we understand that the universe [*aionas*] was formed [*katartidzo*, "form precisely, fit together just right"] at God's command so that what is seen was not made out of what was visible (Heb. 11:3, NIV 1984).

In the beginning time, God stretched out the heavens, expanding the universe that He had made. God created the heavens—the universe had a beginning. God stretched out the heavens—the universe has been expanding ever since.

Thus says the God, the LORD,
　　who created [*bārā'*] the heavens, and stretched them out (Isa. 42:5).

Thus declares the LORD,
　　who stretched out the heavens
　　and founded the earth
　　and formed the spirit of man within him (Zech. 12:1, arr. mine).

In the beginning time, God enveloped the universe in "light as with a cloak" (Psa. 104:2a). He filled the universe with light. As the universe expanded, the remnant of that ancient first light stretched out into long invisible microwaves, forming a background radiation all across the cosmos—the cosmic microwave background radiation. The remnant of that light is evidence that the universe had a beginning and has been expanding ever since, just as the Bible has said all along.

In the beginning time, God created the heavens, not empty, but creating all the material of the universe and forming the vast starry host—huge galaxies of billions of stars spinning across space. God created not just one galaxy but a trillion galaxies, each with billions of suns. God created the heavens, with their starry host spread across the universe.

You have made the heavens, even the highest heavens, and all their starry host (Neh. 9:6, NIV 1984).

By the word of the LORD were the heavens made, their starry host by the breath of his mouth (Psa. 33:6, NIV 1984).

In the beginning time, God put the stars into an organized array, into precise formations. The "starry host" was like a great army put into orderly array. God put the stars in galaxies, the galaxies in filaments of thousands of galaxies, the filaments in a web of a trillion galaxies spread across billions of light-years of the universe. Like a great and intricate building project, the stars are "the work of your fingers" (Psa. 8:3, NIV 1984).

In the beginning time, God created not only the universe but planet Earth.

In the beginning God created . . . the earth (Gen. 1:1).

Before the mountains were born
or you brought forth the earth and the world,
from everlasting to everlasting you are God (Psa. 90:2, NIV 1984).

God is everlasting. For the everlasting God who inhabits eternity, as He looked out at His unfolding works, what are years—whether thousands of years or billions of years? What are a billion years to Him? Might the unfolding creation events have been over billions of years and be to His glory?

But the Earth is not everlasting. Earth had a beginning. At the end of stage one, Earth was barren, desolate, empty of life.

Now-the-earth was uninhabitable and uninhabited [*tōhû v^abōhû*],
and-darkness *was* over *the* surface of *the* deep,
and-Spirit of God *was* hovering over *the* surface of the waters (Gen. 1:2, from Hebrew).

Planet Earth was uninhabitable, uninhabited, deep sea covered, and dark. Our star, the sun, shone across our solar system. But thick dark cloud enveloped our planet like a blanket wrapping a baby, shutting out the sunlight from planet Earth's darkened sea.

I made the clouds its [Earth's] garment
and wrapped it in thick darkness (Job 38:9, NIV 1984).

Stage one of creation was complete. But planet Earth was still uninhabitable, uninhabited, deep sea covered, and dark.

Stage Two of Creation

Then God began stage two of His magnificent work of creation. Step by step through six described sequential day-night days, God changed Earth from uninhabitable, uninhabited, sea covered, and dark to lighted during the day, with land covered by green vegetation, with life in the sea and air and land, and with two beautiful people.

At God's command, "Let there be light," diffuse sunlight penetrated the thick dark cloud and reached down to planet Earth's dark sea. "And there was light." The light shone in the place that had just been described as dark—the surface of Earth's deep sea waters. God saw the light, and it was good. He separated the light from the darkness and sovereignly named the light "day" and the darkness "night." As the Earth rotated, the diffuse sunlight gave way to evening and the darkness of nighttime, then hours later the first hint of morning light ended the literal day that God named "day one" on planet Earth.

Then, on a second described literal day, at God's command, an expanse of cleared air opened between the sea water below and the unbroken overcast cloud water above. God named the expanse "sky." Then evening faded into nighttime, and hours later, the night ended with the first streaks of dawn, completing a second sequential day of God's work.

During the generation of time that followed that second described day, at God's command, the waters of the worldwide sea were gathered into one place, and land appeared. The land dried out and became a dry continent. God named the dry ground "land" and the gathered waters "seas." No numbered day is attached to this command, so this event need not be limited to a single day. How long this gathering of waters and formation of dry land took, the Bible does not say. God saw what He had done, and it was good.

On a third described day, God commanded the earth to start producing green vegetation. God saw all that He had done that day, and it was good.

Earth had been a world of water and bare rock but now became a world with green plants growing in the diffuse sunlight. The sky above was still cloudy, no sun visible in the dull daytime sky, no moon or stars visible in the overcast sky at night. Those green plants would cause extraordinary changes by God's plan, producing something that would clear the sky, something that would allow future animal life to breathe—oxygen.

As time passed in the generation following the third described literal day, more and more free oxygen was produced through photosynthesis by the green plants. Oxygen combined with and eliminated the poisonous methane and ammonia that had been making the sky obscure. High in the atmosphere, ozone molecules, triple oxygen molecules, began blocking ultraviolet radiation that would have been deadly to land animals.

The vegetation would include seed-bearing plants and fruit trees, producing the most beautiful natural gourmet food for Adam and Eve and the animals. God was preparing Earth for His work on a fourth, a fifth, and the sixth described days.

On a fourth described literal day, the sky, which had been shrouded in cloud, cleared. At God's command, the luminaries that God had created as part of the heavens back in Genesis 1:1 now fully functioned in all their splendor in the cleared sky for the first time. They began to separate and rule day and night, mark seasons and days and years, and be lights in the expanse of Earth's sky. God saw what He had done, and it was good. The sunset and evening's last light faded into night, and for the first time in the sky above Earth, the moon's soft orb and the bright pinpricks of the stars lit Earth's night sky.

On a fifth described literal day, God created great air-breathing (*nephesh*) water-dwelling creatures and flyers. These may have been the first great water-dwelling reptiles and flying reptiles, or they could have been whales and birds. If the former, then in the following generation, pliosaurs would undulate through the world's seas, and great pterosaurs would fly overhead. Those great pliosaurs would reproduce only the pliosaurs kind, the flying pterosaurs only the pterosaur kind. Or if the latter, the first whales would have navigated the sea, and the first songbirds would have filled the air with their music. And God saw what He had done, and it was good. He blessed them and told them to be fruitful and increase. Evening's beautiful sunset ended the daytime, and the next morning's dawn ended the nighttime of a fifth described literal day of God's work.

Next God caused the land to produce land animals—large grazing animals, scrambling smaller animals, and wild animals of the earth. And God saw what He had done, and it was good.

On the sixth described literal day, God said, "Let us make man in our image, in our likeness." So God created humans—male and female—in His image and likeness. God gave them the rule over the fish of the sea, over the birds of the air, and over every living thing that moves on the Earth. God blessed the human pair and told them to be fruitful, increase, and fill the Earth. God gave them food from seed-bearing plants and fruit trees. On that same day, God gave all beasts of the Earth, flyers, and scramblers with the breath of life every green plant as food, making them all vegetarian. At the end of the day, God saw all He had made, and it was "very good"! The daytime ended with the evening, and hours later, the nighttime ended with the morning light, completing the sixth and final described day of God's magnificent work.

God finished His work of creation, and on the seventh described day, He rested from all His creation work. Next Scripture says, "These [*are the*] generations of the heavens and the earth when [*they were*] created" (Gen. 2:4a). Each described literal day began one of the "generations of the heavens and the earth."

God created in two stages—the "in the beginning" extensive time that began with the *ex nihilo* creation and resulted in the created heavens with the galaxies of stars and planet Earth. Then God worked six specific sequential days, making Earth lighted, habitable, and inhabited. How much time passed between each of the six described work days, we are not told. Bible genealogies roughly date Adam and the sixth described day to thousands, not millions, of years ago. The universe, planet Earth, and all life before Adam are Biblically undated so are however old they are.

Earlier, God also created magnificent angelic beings, including Lucifer, created as a perfect being. God gave angels choice, just as He would later give Adam and Eve choice. In pride, Lucifer chose to rebel against his Creator. Lucifer was filled with violence, and God righteously threw him down to Earth. The Cambrian Burgess Shale is a record of fossils of the first varieties of animals God made on the Earth. But those fossils are also evidence of death and carnivorism beginning before Adam. God is sovereign even over death. God apparently allowed Satan—who "has been sinning from the beginning," who "was a murderer from the beginning," who was "filled with violence," "who has the power of death," who is "like a roaring lion, seeking someone to devour"—to be the agent of death, introducing violent animal death from the beginning to the good animals God made.

All too soon after God made Adam and Eve, Satan came in the form of a serpent to Eve, tempting her. She was deceived, and then Adam deliberately sinned, starting all human death. Why did you do that, Adam? Why? Adam's sin began all human death, human suffering, human environmental destruction, human hatred, human murder, and human war. Satan's sin preceded and apparently started violent animal death. Adam's sin preceded and certainly started all human death.

God finished His great creation work. But another greater task lay ahead—the work of redeeming, of saving, all humans who would believe in His Son, the sinless Lord Jesus, who alone could and did pay for our sin. And that work would be a far more painful work, a far greater work than creating a trillion galaxies.

Now the good creation that God made has upon it all the marks of the sin and destructiveness of Satan and the sin and Fall of Adam. This creation is running down and wearing out. But God has planned and promised a perfect magnificent New Creation for His family of believing humans. If we believe in the Lord Jesus, we become part of that family, the everlasting family, the family of God. All who believe in Jesus will receive everlasting life in Him and will live forever in an unending relationship of perfect love and astounding joy and exalting worship with eternal God the Father and eternal God the Son, our Creator and Savior, the Lord Jesus in His everlasting New Creation.

Chapter 32

Can Two Stage Creation Be a Bridge Between YEC and OEC?

Through the early centuries of the church, Christians debated what the Bible says about God until they found a Bible-based understanding that God is one God in three eternal persons—Father, Son, and Holy Spirit. Through the next centuries of the church, Christians continued debating, this time about Jesus, until they found a Bible-based understanding that He has always been fully eternal God, the second Person of the Trinity, and that by His virgin conception and birth, He also became fully human—the God-Man.

Through the Reformation centuries, Christians debated what the Bible says about salvation until they rediscovered the Bible-based understanding that salvation is by God's grace alone through faith alone in Jesus alone (not by works but unto good works). Through recent centuries, Bible believers have debated what the Bible says about itself until they found a Bible-based understanding that all Scripture as originally written in the original documents (the autographs) is inspired by God and is infallible, inerrant, and authoritative in all it teaches.

With the rise of science, creation then became a major topic of debate. Can we come to a consensus on creation?

In recent times Christians have been debating creation. Today people who accept that Genesis 1 narrates the actual historical creation events often take one of two positions: Six-Day-Only Young Earth Creationism or Day-Age Old Earth Creationism. Yet these two positions are at an impasse. YEC affirms six literal days, concluding that the universe and Earth must be about 6,000 years old. OEC affirms that the Bible and creation (both accurately interpreted) will match, that the Bible does not date the creation, and that the evidence in the creation indicates an older universe and Earth.

OEC concludes that the six days must have been long day-ages, each lasting millions of years. Both sides assume their two big claims are linked. YEC affirms six literal days and a young 6,000-year-old universe. OEC affirms that the creation and the Bible match, allowing an older universe, and affirms six long day-ages. But the Bible evidence supports only one of each pair of claims: a Biblically undated creation (until Adam) and six literal days.

Two Stage Biblical Creation: Both an Undated Creation and Six Literal Days

Young Earth Creationism has faithfully upheld six literal days. Old Earth Creationism has wisely explored the evidence for God's work in a Biblically undated, apparently older creation. Two Stage Biblical Creation may provide a Bible-based bridge for a consensus between YEC and OEC. Two Stage Biblical Creation—taking both Genesis 1:1 and the six days literally—may be a bridge for a Bible-based reconciliation of Old Earth and Young Earth creationists. The goal of Two Stage Biblical Creation is to be precisely Biblical, taking Bible historical narrative literally. Just as we have found a Biblical consensus on previous great doctrines, is it possible that, with God's enabling, we may arrive at a Biblical consensus on creation? Could that consensus be by taking *both* of the following Bible-based beliefs literally?

1. Genesis 1:1–2: God created the heavens and the earth in the beginning time, at the end of which the Earth was uninhabitable, uninhabited, dark, and sea covered.

2. Genesis 1:3–31: God worked six literal days (the ordinal numbers without articles indicating sequential days) making earth lighted, habitable, and inhabited. A consensus on creation based on the inspired Hebrew text of the Bible and matching the evidence God built into the universe will be a compelling testimony to the world and to God's great glory.

Young Earth creationists rightly champion their three great Biblical concepts: God's Word, the Bible, is true; the God of the Bible is the Creator; the six days should be taken by the plain sense of the word *yôm* with a number as literal days. Will they be willing to leave behind the idea, based on an "in" added to Bible translations, that all creation was in six days, resulting in a necessarily young creation? Will they be willing to accept that "in the beginning God created the heavens and the earth," and then God worked on six sequentially numbered literal days?

Old Earth creationists rightly champion their Biblical understanding that "in the beginning God created the heavens and the earth," and their science discoveries are strong evidence that the God of the Bible is the Designer and Creator of the universe, Earth, and life. Will they be willing to back away from their millions-of-years-long days and instead recognize that God started each of the six described magnificent works on a Biblically undated sequential literal day?

Reconciliation Based on the Bible Is Important

"In the beginning God created the heavens and the earth" (Gen. 1:1), but at the end of that beginning time the Earth was uninhabitable, uninhabited, sea covered, and dark (Gen. 1:2). Then God worked six literal days (the ordinal numbers without articles indicating sequential days), each described day starting one of His great works making earth lighted, habitable, and inhabited (Gen. 1:3–5). A Biblical view results in a seamless match of the holy Bible and the creation—to the great glory of God!

It is hard to change a concept in one's view. But people need a truly Biblical worldview, starting with an accurate understanding of Biblical creation. A Biblical view of creation starts with the same truth the apostle John started his Gospel with: "All things were made through him" (John 1:3). God the Son is the Creator, who became also fully a Man, lived without sin, died in our place for our sin, and rose from the dead. A Biblical worldview and effective apologetics and evangelism need to be built on a truly Biblical view of creation. Only a truly Biblical view of creation will match first the Bible and then also the creation.

Conclusion

Question

Can six literal days and evidence of an older universe fit together?

My friend asked a good question: "How can the Bible account of six literal days of creation and the physical evidence of an older universe fit together?"

Answer

When Genesis 1 is taken literally—in the beginning God created the heavens and earth, then He worked six sequential literal days—the creation is Biblically undated and the evidence in the creation naturally harmonizes with the Bible.

Two Stage Biblical Creation strongly affirms that the Bible as originally written in the Hebrew Old Testament and Greek New Testament is 100 percent true. Also, God made the creation with reliable evidence. Because both the Bible and the creation are from the 100 percent truthful God, when both are understood accurately, they harmonize perfectly.

Two Stage Biblical Creation recognizes that Genesis 1 was written as a historical narrative (indicated by the Hebrew *vav* consecutives). Bible historical narrative should be interpreted literally. When we take all of the Genesis 1 Hebrew text literally—"In the beginning God created the heavens and the earth" (Gen. 1:1), but Earth was still uninhabitable (Gen. 1:2), then God worked six literal sequential days (Gen. 1:3–31)—then the text reveals two stages of creation (the beginning time and the six sequential days) and leaves the creation events before Adam Biblically undated. With a Biblically undated creation, the physical evidence in the creation harmonizes beautifully with the inspired, inerrant Genesis 1 historical narrative.

Genesis 1:1 says God created the heavens in the beginning (*bᵉre'shît*). The first word of the Hebrew text of the Bible, *bᵉre'shît*, or the unprefixed *re'shît*, when referring to time, consistently means a beginning phase or time. The verb in Genesis 1:1, *bārā'*, emphasizes God created *ex nihilo*. The Hebrew phrase "the heavens and the earth" (*et ha-shāmāyim vᵉet ha-ārets*) means the universe. God created the universe, including the galaxies and planet Earth, starting with nothing during the beginning time. Genesis 1:2 describes planet Earth, after its creation in the beginning, as uninhabitable, uninhabited, sea covered, and dark.

Then Genesis 1:3–31 narrates God's six literal described days making Earth lighted, habitable, and inhabited. *Yôm*, "day," each with a number and evening and morning, indicates each described day was a literal day. The Hebrew ordinal numbers (second through seventh) and the first five numbers without definite articles (day one, *a* second day, *a* third day, *a* fourth day, and *a* fifth day) indicate that the six described days were sequential, in the order listed, not necessarily consecutive. This allows unnumbered days before and after the described days.

With *b*ᵉ*re'shît*, meaning a beginning phase or time, and ordinal numbers allowing unnumbered days between the six described days, the creation (until Adam) is Biblically undated, allowing but not affirming the older ages that science proposes.

With the Bible text allowing an older creation, the science discoveries—that the universe had a beginning and has been stretching out or expanding ever since—fit beautifully with what the Bible has been saying all along. Eleven times the Bible says God is stretching out the heavens. "God the LORD, . . . who created the heavens and stretched them out" (Isa. 42:5, NIV 1984). Now science has discovered that the universe had a beginning and is stretching out or expanding, just as the Bible said all along.

The order of events in Genesis 1 (with details from other Bible texts) and the order in the geologic layers match: the formation of Earth with its foundational layers, the cloud-darkened sea-covered condition of early Earth, diffuse light to Earth's surface, an open atmosphere, green plants, luminaries fully functioning to Earth's surface in the cleared sky, air-breathing aquatic and flying life, modern air-breathing land animals, and finally humans.

When the creation is understood as occurring in two stages—the "in the beginning" creation time, then six sequential described literal days—then the text leaves the creation events before Adam Biblically undated, so the universe and Earth and life are however old they are. With a Biblically undated universe and Earth and life before Adam, the evidence in the physical creation harmonizes beautifully with God's inspired, inerrant Word, the Bible, because both are from the same 100 percent truthful creator. Only the Creator could have known these facts long before they were discovered by modern science, strong evidence that the God of the Bible is the Creator and that the Bible alone is His written communication to us.

Appendix A
Fifteen Affirmations of Two Stage Biblical Creation

1. The Bible is true, so reliable evidence in the creation will match.

We affirm that God's Word, the Bible, as originally written, is 100 percent true (John 17:17; 2 Tim. 3:16). When understood accurately, God's Word and reliable creation evidence (Psa. 19:1; Rom. 1:20) will match, because both are from the same 100 percent truthful Creator.

We deny that our truthful God built false appearance of age into the universe, including planet Earth.

2. Bible historical narrative should be interpreted literally.

We affirm that Genesis 1 is historical narrative (as indicated by the *vav* consecutives) and should be interpreted literally. We interpret literally the Genesis 1:1 creation of the heavens and the earth, the 1:2 description of unfinished Earth, and the six described days of 1:3–31.

We deny that a creation theory is fully Biblical without taking all of Genesis 1 literally.

3. God created in two stages—in the beginning, then six literal days.

We affirm that in stage one, "in the beginning," God created the universe—the heavens and earth (Gen. 1:1)—but Earth was uninhabitable, uninhabited, sea covered, and dark (Gen. 1:2). In stage two, God worked six described literal days making Earth lighted, habitable, and inhabited (Gen. 1:3–31).

We deny that Genesis 1:1 is merely a title, summary, metaphor, or part of day one.

4. In the beginning eternal God created the universe out of nothing, *ex nihilo*.

We affirm that "in the beginning" the eternal God of the Bible created *ex nihilo*, out of nothing, the universe with its space, time, matter, energy, and natural laws (John 1:1–3; Rev. 4:11).

We deny that the universe is eternal. We deny that there was preexisting chaos.

5. God created the heavens and earth "in the beginning."

We affirm that the Hebrew word *bᵉreʾshît*, "in the beginning," when referring to time, means in the beginning time. (The length of time is unspecified by the word *bᵉreʾshît*.) "The heavens and the earth" is a Hebrew merism meaning the universe. God created the universe "in the beginning."

We deny that the Bible places the "in the beginning" creation events into day one.

6. **God created the heavens and stretched them out.**

We affirm that the Bible declares, "God . . . created the heavens and stretched them out" (Isa. 42:5). The universe had a beginning and is stretching out, expanding. Only the Creator could have known this before modern science. The God of the Bible is the Creator.

We deny that the universe began and expanded by chance to be precisely right for life.

7. **After the creation of the heavens and the earth in Genesis 1:1, Earth is described as uninhabitable, uninhabited, sea covered, and dark.**

We affirm that Genesis 1:2 describes planet Earth at the end of the events of Genesis 1:1 as uninhabitable, uninhabited, sea covered, and dark (caused by dark clouds, Job 38:9). "Now the earth" (Gen. 1:2) switches perspective from the universe to Earth. God commanded the light to the place declared dark, Earth's dark surface, starting day one on planet Earth.

We deny that Genesis 1:2 declares that the universe was dark.

8. **Each *yôm* ("day") with a number was a literal day.**

We affirm that each of the six described days was a literal day-night day.

We deny that the six described days were day-ages, each millions of years long.

9. **Hebrew ordinal numbers without articles indicate six sequential days.**

We affirm that the ordinal numbers without definite articles ("*a* second day") indicate that the six described work days were sequential, not necessarily consecutive.

We deny that the Hebrew text of Exodus 20:11 says God created everything "in six days."

10. **On a fourth described day, God gave the luminaries new functions to Earth.**

We affirm that on a fourth described day, God made the already-created luminaries carry out three new functions to planet Earth: to separate and govern day and night, mark seasons and days and years, and be lights in the expanse of the sky.

We deny that the Bible says God *bārā'*, "created," the luminaries on a fourth day.

11. **Creation events before Adam are Biblically undated.**

We affirm that Bible genealogies can roughly date Adam and the sixth day to thousands, not millions, of years ago. "In the beginning" was an extensive beginning time, and the Hebrew ordinal numbers without articles indicate that the six described days were sequential but not necessarily consecutive. All creation events before Adam are Biblically undated.

We deny that the Bible provides certain evidence for dating any creation event before Adam.

12. All God made was good. Satan has the power of death and could have started animal death.

We affirm that all God did was good. Satan "has been sinning from the beginning" (1 John 3:8), "was a murderer from the beginning" (John 8:44), was thrown "to the Earth" (Ezek. 28:12–17), and "has the power of death" (Heb. 2:14). From these verses we deduce that God allowed Satan to start universal animal death in the six days.

We deny that Scripture says Adam's Fall started all animal death.

13. Adam, by his sin, began all human death.

We affirm that the Bible teaches that Adam and Eve were created sinless and in the image of God. Adam deliberately disobeyed God. Adam, by his sin, passed down death to all humans (Gen. 3; Rom. 3:23; 5:12).

We deny that any human created in the image of God lived and died before Adam.

14. The order of events in Genesis 1 and the order of the geologic layers match.

We affirm that the order of events in Genesis 1 and the order of the geologic layers match: a sea-covered Earth, plants, air-breathing aquatic and flying life, modern land animals, and finally humans.

We deny that the fossil layers are a record of chance evolution or that chance evolution created the physical laws, the universe, and life.

15. God's answer to human sin and death is salvation and eternal life in His Son.

We affirm that eternal God the Son, our Creator and Savior the Lord Jesus, provides salvation by His substitutionary atoning death on the cross and bodily resurrection from the dead (1 Cor. 15:3–4). He gives eternal life to all who believe in Him (Acts 16:31).

We deny that we can earn salvation by good works (Titus 3:5).

Appendix B

The Events of the Two Stages of Creation

Stage One of Creation: In the Beginning

"In the beginning God created the heavens and the earth" (Gen. 1:1).

- The eternal perfect God—Father-Son-Spirit—exists forever.
- God "in the beginning" created *ex nihilo,* out of nothing (Gen. 1:1, John 1:3).
- God "in the beginning" created the *aionas*—the time-space-energy-matter universe.
- God has been stretching out the heavens, expanding the universe (Isa. 42:5).
- God enveloped the heavens in light in the beginning time (Psa. 104:2).
- God created the heavens, setting the host of stars in an organized array (Neh. 9:6).
- God made the primeval dusts of the world (Prov. 8:26).
- God created the Earth (Gen. 1:1; Prov. 8:26).
- God made Earth's outliers (Prov. 8:26), probably including the moon.
- God set Earth on its foundations, forming its layered interior (Psa. 104:5; Isa. 48:13).
- God fashioned planet Earth to be inhabited (Isa. 45:18).
- God made hills on the Earth and settled the mountains in place (Psa. 104:8; 90:2).
- God caused Earth's growing clouds to conceal the moon from view (Job 26:9).
- God wrapped Earth in thick dark clouds, shutting out the light (Job 38:9–12).
- God filled the clouds with water (Job 26:8) and made springs bursting with water.
- God made the deep sea, covering Earth's first mountains (Gen. 1:2; Psa. 104:6).
- At the end of the beginning time, "now the earth was uninhabitable and uninhabited, and darkness was on the surface of the deep" (Gen. 1:2).
  - o Earth was uninhabitable (Gen. 1:2).
  - o Earth was uninhabited, empty of life (Gen. 1:2).
  - o Earth was dark, wrapped in thick dark cloud cover (Gen. 1:2; Job 38:9).
  - o Earth was deep sea covered, even over the mountains (Gen. 1:2; Psa. 104:6).

Satan was "sinning from the beginning" and thrown to Earth, Biblically undated.

Stage Two of Creation: Six Described Sequential Days

Then God worked six literal sequential days making Earth lighted, habitable, inhabited.

- Day one, God commanded, "Let there be light" (Gen. 1:3–5), lighting Earth's surface.
- A second day, God made an expanse between sea below and cloud above (Gen. 1:6–8).
  o God gathered the sea waters and made dry land appear (Gen. 1:9–10).
- A third day, God commanded the earth to produce green vegetation (Gen. 1:11–12).
- A fourth day, God caused luminaries to fully function to Earth (Gen. 1:14).
- A fifth day, God made air-breathing aquatic creatures and flyers (Gen. 1:20–22).
  o God made three kinds of air-breathing land animals (Gen. 1:24–25).
- The sixth day, God created Adam and Eve in His image (Gen. 1:26–29).
  o God gave animals plants to eat, and God saw everything He had made and declared it to be "very good" (Gen. 1:30–31).
- The seventh day, God rested (Gen. 2:1–3).

  "These [*are the*] generations of the heavens and the earth when they were created" (Gen. 2:4a).

Appendix C

Bible Texts Declaring God Stretched Out the Heavens

Bible texts indicate God has been stretching out or expanding the universe from the beginning to the present. The Bible said this long before science did. Before modern science discoveries, only the Creator could have known about the expanding universe. Each of these verses is in a creation context:

1. **Isaiah 42:5** God created the heavens and stretched them out:

> Thus says the God, the LORD,
>> who created [*bārā'*] the heavens, and <u>stretched them out</u> [*nātāh*],
>> who spread out [*rāqa'*] the earth and what comes from it,
>> who gives breath to the people on it and spirit to those who walk in it.

2. **Psalm 104:1–2** God enveloped in light and stretched out the heavens:

> Bless the LORD, O my soul!
> O LORD my God, You are very great.
> You are clothed *with* splendor and majesty.
>> Enveloping *in* light as with a cloak,
>> <u>Stretching</u> [*nātāh*] <u>out the heavens like a tent</u> (from Hebrew).

3. **Isaiah 51:13** God stretched out the heavens and founded planet Earth:

> The LORD your Maker,
>> <u>stretching out</u> [*nātāh*] <u>of the heavens</u> and
>> founding [*yasad*] earth (from Hebrew).

4. **Zechariah 12:1** God stretched out the heavens and founded planet Earth:

> Thus declares the LORD,
>> <u>stretching</u> [*nātāh*] <u>out the heavens</u>,
>> founding [*yasad*] the Earth, and
>> forming [*yātsar*] the spirit of man within him (from Hebrew).

5. **Isaiah 48:13** God founded planet Earth and stretched out the heavens:

> My hand founded [*yasad*] the earth,
> And My right hand <u>spread out</u> [*tāpha^{k}h*] <u>the heavens</u> (NASB).

6. Jeremiah 10:12 God made the Earth and stretched out the heavens:

But God made [*asâh*] the earth by his power;
    he founded [*kun*] the world by his wisdom
    and <u>stretched out</u> [*nātāh*] <u>the heavens</u> by his understanding (NIV 1984).

7. Jeremiah 51:15 God made the Earth and stretched out the heavens:

He [God] made [*asâh*] the earth by his power;
    he founded [*kun*] the world by his wisdom
    and <u>stretched out</u> [*nātāh*] <u>the heavens</u> by his understanding (NIV 1984).

8. Job 9:7–8 God sealed off light from Earth; He stretches out the heavens:

He speaks to the sun and it does not shine;
    he seals off the light of the stars.
He alone <u>stretches</u> [*nātāh*] <u>out the heavens</u>
    and treads on the waves of the sea (NIV 1984).

9. Isaiah 44:24 God stretched out the heavens and spread out the Earth's land:

Thus says the LORD, your Redeemer, who formed you from the womb:
"I the LORD who made all things,
    <u>who alone stretched out</u> [*nātāh*] <u>the heavens,</u>
    who spread out [*rāqaʹ*, "beat thin/spread like gold overlay"] the land by myself."

10. Isaiah 40:21–22, 26a After founding Earth, God continued stretching out the heavens:

Has it not been told you from the beginning [*rōsh*]?
    Have you not understood since the Earth was founded [*mōsad*]?
He sits enthroned above the circle [*ᵏhug*] of the Earth,
    and its inhabitants are like grasshoppers,
He <u>stretches out</u> [*nātāh*] <u>the heavens like a canopy,</u>
    <u>and spreads</u> [*māthaᵏh*] <u>them out like a tent to live in.</u> . . .
Lift your eyes and look to the heavens:
    Who created [*bārāʹ*] these? (NIV 1984).

11. Isaiah 45:12 After creating humans, God stretched out the heavens:

I made [*asâh*] the Earth and created [*bārāʹ*] humans on it;

I with my hands stretched out [*nātāh*] the heavens, and
I commanded all their host (from Hebrew).

12. **Job 26:7** Before suspending planet Earth in orbit, God spread out the northern skies:

He spreads out [*nātāh*] the northern skies over empty space;
he suspends the earth over nothing (NIV 1984).

God has continually stretched out the heavens from the moment of *ex nihilo* creation.

Appendix D

Does Animal Death before Adam's Fall Undermine Jesus' Atonement for Humans?

YEC claims that we must believe that Adam's sin started all animal death about 6,000 years ago, because any animal death before Adam's sin would undermine Jesus' atonement[243] and make the Christian faith all in vain. YEC advocates state, "The Bible plainly teaches that 'the wages of sin is death' (Romans 6:23). . . . Adam's sin brought death on all creation. . . . If death existed before Adam, then death is not the penalty for sin. How, then, did Jesus' death pay the penalty for our sin? If death is not tied to Adam's sin, then life is not tied to Jesus' death and resurrection, and the Christian faith is all in vain."[244]

YEC also claims that to accept animal death and bloodshed before Adam's sin "is to destroy the basis of the Gospel message."[245] "Now if there was death and bloodshed of animals before sin, then this undermines the atonement. Also, if there were death, disease, bloodshed, and suffering before sin, then such would be God's fault—not our fault!"[246]

YEC claims that any animal death before Adam's sin would "destroy the basis of the Gospel message" and "undermines the atonement," and as a result "the Christian faith is all in vain." Does this claim agree with what the Bible teaches?

The Bible teaches that Adam's sin preceded and caused all human death: The inspired Greek text reports the result of Adam's sin, using the article "the" in the words "the sin" and "the death":

Therefore, as through one man [Adam] the sin entered into the world, and through the sin the death, and so the death passed into all humans [*anthrōpŏs*] because all sinned (Rom. 5:12, from Greek).

"The sin" is very specific—Adam's sin. And "the death" is equally specific—the *human* death that was "passed into all humans." That death was passed down through Adam to his descendants, to humans. We inherit his sin nature. We sin, and "the wages of sin is death," our human death. Jesus' atoning substitutionary death is for humans. Romans 5:12 says by one man's sin, "the death passed to all humans [*anthrōpŏs*]." Romans 5:12 is explicitly about human sin and human death. Animals are not mentioned in this verse.

---

243 Ken Ham, *The Answers Book 1*, 99–100.

244 John D. Morris, "Death before Sin," Institute for Creation Research, 2001, https://www.icr.org/article/18303.

245 Ken Ham, "Billions, Millions, or Thousands: Does It Matter?" *Acts & Facts*, May 1, 1991.

246 Ken Ham, "Millions of Years—Are Souls at Stake?" *Answers Magazine*, Jan. 1, 2014.

The Bible teaches that "the wages of sin" is death, human death: Alluding to Romans 6:23, "the wages of sin is death," some YEC advocates claim that Adam's sin caused animal death.[247] But Romans 6:23 ("For the wages of sin is death, but the free gift of God is eternal life in Christ Jesus our Lord") applies only to humans, not animals. Romans 6:23 is only about human sin causing human death.

In the phrase "the wages of sin is death," the word "death" refers to human death, not animal death. Yet YEC claims, "If death [emphasizing animal death] existed before Adam, then death [referring to Romans 6:23, which uses the word to mean human death] is not the penalty for sin." This switch from animal death to human death is a fallacy, making the YEC argument invalid.

The Bible makes a distinction between animal death and human death: The Bible teaches a qualitative difference between animal death and human death. In Genesis 9:3–6, God permitted Noah to kill animals but not humans, because humans are made in God's image. Murdering a human is a sin.

Animal death and human death are two different categories. "For it is impossible for the blood of bulls and goats to take away sins" (Heb. 10:4). Jesus had to become a human because only the substitutionary death of the only perfect human, the God-man Jesus, can take away human sin. Biblically, there is an immense difference between animal death and the death of humans, created in the image of God.

The Bible teaches that the atonement is for humans: "Christ died for our sins" (1 Cor. 15:3). His atonement is for human sin and is applied to believing humans—judicially applying His payment to our sin, restoring our relationship with God, giving us eternal life in Jesus, and enabling our adoption into God's family (John 1:12). Adam's sin preceded and caused all human death. Jesus' atonement is for human sin and results in human salvation and eternal life.

"Christ died for our sins." Jesus' atonement is about humans, not animals. Therefore, YEC's argument, that there could not have been animal death before Adam's sin because it would nullify the atonement, is invalid and is not backed by the Bible.

Two Stage Biblical Creation's Conclusion

Does the presence of violent animal death in the fossil record undermine Jesus' atonement for humans? No. Adam's sin preceded and caused all human death. Because the first human sin (the cause) preceded the first human death (the consequence), Jesus' atonement (the payment for the cause, ultimately ending the consequence) is not undermined in the slightest. Adam's sin caused all human death; Jesus' atonement provides all humans who believe in Him everlasting life.

The atonement by Christ's substitutionary death is only for humans, not animals. Thus, Jesus' atonement for humans by His substitutionary death paying for our sin remains effective. There was no human death (the result) before sin (the cause),

---

247 John D. Morris, "Death before Sin."

specifically no human death before Adam's sin. Therefore, Jesus' atonement paying our death penalty for our human sin is not undermined at all, but remains 100 percent effective!

Appendix E

Do Jesus' Words against Divorce Date Creation to 4000 BC?

Divorce—divorce was a huge controversy among the Pharisees of Jesus' time. The dispute was not whether a man could divorce his wife (the Pharisees assumed that), but whether he could divorce her "for any cause" (Matt. 19:3). The Law of Moses in Deuteronomy 24:1–4 reluctantly allowed a written divorce if a man found "some indecency" (*ervat dābār*, "some indecency, nakedness"), a serious sexual indecency, in his wife. However, the two schools of the Pharisees, the school of Shammai and the school of Hillel, disagreed on how far "cause" extended, Hillel stretching its meaning to include even serving the husband "an improperly cooked meal."[248]

The Pharisees tested Jesus with their question, followed by Jesus' profound answer:

"Is it lawful to divorce one's wife for any cause?" (Matt. 19:3).

He [Jesus] answered, ". . . He who created them from the beginning [*archēs*] made them 'male and female'" (Matt. 19:4).

And Jesus said to them, . . . "But from the beginning [*archēs*] of creation [*ktiseōs*], 'God made them male and female. Therefore, a man shall leave his father and mother and hold fast to his wife, and the two shall become one flesh.' So they are no longer two but one flesh. What therefore God has joined together, let not man separate" (Mark 10:5–9).

The Matthew 19:4 version reports only Jesus' words "from the beginning." But the Greek word *archēs* by itself "does not delineate what beginning."[249]

The Mark 10:6 version includes Jesus' clarifying word "creation," explaining what beginning—*namely* creation. From the beginning, namely creation, God made male and female, a perfect couple. Therefore, a man is to leave his father and mother and stick to his wife in an intimate, monogamous, one-male-one-female lifetime marriage. The pair God has joined together, let no man separate (referring to Genesis 1:27 and 2:24).

ἀπὸ	δὲ	ἀρχῆς κτίσεως	ἄρσεν καὶ θῆλυ	ἐποίησεν αὐτούς.
apó	*de*	*archēs ktiseōs*	*arsen kai thalu*	*epoiasen autous.*
from	But	beginning creation	male and female [*God*]	made them.

---

248 D. A. Carson, "Matthew," *The Expositor's Bible Commentary*, vol. 8 (Grand Rapids: Zondervan, 1984), 411; R. Kent Hughes, *Mark* (Wheaton, IL: Crossway, 1989), 46.

249 Spiros Zodhiates, *The Complete Word Study Dictionary New Testament* (Chattanooga, TN: AMG Publishers, 1992), #746, 260–261.

Two Views of Jesus' Words in Mark 10:6

In Mark 10:6, does Jesus teach Adam and Eve were <u>at</u> the beginning/<u>at</u> the start of creation, so the universe can be dated by Adam's genealogies to about 6,000 years old? Or does Jesus teach (nothing about the age of the universe, but) that <u>from</u> the beginning, (*namely*) creation, God made them male and female, so from the creation onward God's principle is that couples should stay united in marriage?

YEC's Trick Question

YEC uses a trick question that supposedly "devastates" belief in an older creation: "In the context of the first marriage between Adam and Eve, do you think Jesus was wrong in Mark 10:6 when He said that God made them male and female <u>at</u> the *beginning of creation*? Or do you believe that the creation has been around for 13 billion years and marriage first came about at the *end of creation* a few thousand years ago with Adam and Eve?"[250] (italics his, underline mine).

YEC assumes *apo'* ("from") in Mark 10:6 means "at,"[251] claiming Adam and Eve were "at the *beginning of creation*"[252] in the sense of at the start of creation. They claim that *archēs* ("beginning") *ktiseōs* ("creation") means "<u>at</u> the *beginning of* [in the sense of at the start of] *creation*."[253] If Adam and Eve were at the start of creation, YEC says that it would seem absurd to say that thirteen billion years had passed before Adam and Eve were created. If Adam and Eve on the sixth day were <u>at</u> the start of creation, then the universe can be dated by Adam's descendants' genealogies (plus a few days) to about 4000 BC.

Greek NT text response: Jesus said, "But from the beginning, [*namely*] creation, 'God made then male and female,'" so stay married.

In response, *apo'* means "*from, away from*,"[254] not "at." The Greek experts Bauer, Danker, et al. in their standard *A Greek-English Lexicon of the New Testament* (known for their use of abbreviations) say, "W[ith] the prep[osition] *ap' archēs* [means] *from the beginning*."[255] Native Greek speaker and NT Greek expert Spiros Zodhiates, in *The Complete Word Study Dictionary New Testament,* says, "With a prep[osition] preceding: *apo'* (575), from, *ap' archēs,* [means] from the beginning," and he lists both Mark 10:6 and Matthew 19:4.[256] Jesus did not say He made Adam and Eve "at" the beginning/

250 Bodie Hodge, "Jesus Devastates an Old Earth," Answers in Genesis, Dec. 30, 2014, accessed 9/8/21, answersingenesis.org/theory-of-evolution/millions-of-years/jesus-devastates-an-old-earth.

251 Hodge, "Jesus Devastates an Old Earth," "male and female <u>at</u> the beginning of creation" (my underline).

252 Hodge, "Jesus Devastates an Old Earth."

253 Hodge, "Jesus Devastates an Old Earth."

254 Fredrick Danker and Walter Bauer, *A Greek-English Lexicon of the New Testament*, 105.

255 Danker and Bauer, *Greek-English Lexicon*, 138.

256 Spiros Zodhiates, *The Complete Word Study Dictionary NT* (Chattanooga: AMG Publishers, 1992), 261.

start of creation. He said, "But <u>from</u> [*apo'*] *the* beginning [*namely*] creation [*archēs ktiseōs*] [*God*] made them male and female."

o **From the beginning:** In Mark 10:6 *apo'* is genitive followed by two genitive nouns. *Apo'* with the genitive has the "basic sense of 'separation from' someone or something.'"[257] Because *apo'* has the basic sense of 'separation from,' it should be translated *"from, away from"*[258] (not "at," with the incorrect sense of at the start). Jesus is saying God made them male and female <u>from</u> the beginning. Therefore, couples are to stay together. *Apo'* means "from,"[259] and most Bible versions correctly translate *apo'* in Mark 10:6 as "from"—ESV, KJV, NASB, NKJV, Young's Literal, and many more.

o **Beginning:** *Archēs*, a Greek genitive noun, means the "commencement of something as an action, process, or state of being, *beginning*."[260]

o **Creation:** *Ktíseōs*, a genitive noun, means the "act of creation, *creation*."[261] The act of creation started with the *ex nihilo* creation of the heavens and the earth "in the beginning" and finished with the creation of male and female on the sixth described day.

o **Beginning, *(namely)* creation:** *Archēs* ("beginning") and *ktíseōs* ("creation") form a genitive of apposition, in which the first word (beginning) is clarified by the second word (creation). By using the genitive of apposition, Jesus is clarifying which beginning, not the beginning of the Law that the Pharisees were appealing to, but the original beginning, the creation.

How the two nouns, "beginning" and "creation," fit together grammatically is crucial for understanding what Jesus said. "Beginning" and "creation," *archēs ktiseōs*, are consecutive genitive nouns. Of the over a dozen uses of the Greek genitive, the one that fits all the factors in Mark 10:6 is the genitive of apposition. "To test whether the genitive in question is a genitive of apposition, replace the word *of* with the paraphrase *which is* or *that is, namely*. . . . If the paraphrase makes sense, a genitive of apposition is likely."[262] "But from *the* beginning [*namely*] creation, 'God made them male and female.'" In the genitive of apposition (also called the genitive of definition or clarification), the first noun is defined or clarified by the second. The first noun, called the head noun, is "beginning," and the second or clarifying noun is "creation." "The genitive of apposition . . . is frequently used when the head noun is ambiguous."[263] The Matthew 19:4 version includes only the head noun "beginning." Which beginning? Was this the beginning of the Law that the Pharisees appealed

---

257 Danker/Bauer, *Greek-English Lexicon*, 105.
258 Danker/Bauer, *Greek-English Lexicon*, 105.
259 Danker/Bauer, *Greek-English Lexicon*, 105.
260 Danker/Bauer, *Greek-English Lexicon*, 137.
261 Danker/Bauer, *Greek-English Lexicon*, 572–573; Friberg, *Analytical Greek Lexicon*; Barclay-Newman, *Greek-English Dictionary*; Louw-Nida, *Greek English Lexicon of the NT*; Liddell Scott, *Greek-English Lexicon*, Thayer, *Greek-English Lexicon of the NT*.
262 Daniel B. Wallace, *Greek Grammar Beyond the Basics* (Grand Rapids: Zondervan, 1996), 95.
263 Daniel B. Wallace, *Greek Grammar Beyond the Basics* (Grand Rapids: Zondervan, 1996), 95.

to? Or was the beginning the creation events in Genesis 1 and 2 when God created the male and female pair?

Jesus responded with a principle the rabbis of that day used: "The more original, the weightier."[264] Jesus went back to the original beginning, the creation, by referring to Genesis 1:27 and 2:24. Jesus clarified any ambiguity in the head noun "beginning" by adding the genitive of apposition identifying which beginning, namely the "creation."[265] In the consecutive pair of genitive nouns *archēs ktíseōs*, "beginning, *namely*, creation," the second noun clarifies the first. From (*apó*) the beginning (*namely*) creation (*archēs ktiseōs*), God created male and female, and God's principle from the beginning is that a couple should stay married.

If Adam and Eve were <u>at</u> the start of creation, perhaps then the universe could be dated by Adam's descendants' genealogies (plus a few days) to about 6,000 years ago. But Jesus did not say Adam and Eve were <u>at</u> the beginning of creation. YEC's argument is founded on its English translation of *apó* as "at," "at the beginning." Instead Jesus said, "But from [*apo'*] the beginning [*namely*] creation, *God* made them male and female. Therefore, a man shall . . . hold fast [*proskóllo*] to his wife" (Mark 10:6–7, from Greek Majority/Byzantine Text). *Proskóllo* means to glue or stick together permanently. I use double-stick tape (sticky on both sides) to hold my carpet in the right place even through the rough treatment of family life. Jesus' teachings on marriage, the wedding vow, and the continued commitment of our union are like double-stick tape for lifelong marriage, holding the couple together even as they learn how to truly love each other through not only the fun times but also all the rough times of family life.

---

264 D. A. Carson, "Matthew," *The Expositor's Bible Commentary*, vol. 8, 412.

265 Colin Brown, "*ktísis*" *NIDNTT*, vol. 1 (Grand Rapids: Zondervan, 1975), 378–387; "*ktísis*," "act of creation," BDAG, 572–573; "*ktísis*," "the act of creating," *Thayer's Greek Lexicon*; "*ktísis*," "God's creative action," Friberg, *Analytical Greek Lexicon*.

Abbreviations

Creation Theories, Organizations, and Other Common Abbreviations

AiG	Answers in Genesis (Ken Ham)
ANE	Ancient Near East
ASA	American Scientific Affiliation
CMB	Cosmic microwave background
CMI	Creation Ministries International (Carl Wieland)
Gap	Gap or Creation-Ruin-Restoration Theory
ICR	Institute for Creation Research (Henry and John Morris)
ID	Intelligent Design
LXX	Greek Septuagint Old Testament
NT	New Testament
OEC	Old Earth Creationism
OT	Old Testament
RTB	Reasons to Believe (Hugh Ross)
YBC	Young Biosphere Creation (Gorman Gray)
YEC	Young Earth Creationism (Henry and John Morris, Ken Ham, Carl Wieland)

Bible Versions

ASV	American Standard Version (1901)
CJB	Complete Jewish Bible (1998, 2016)
ESV	English Standard Version (2001)
KJV	King James Version (1611)
LXX	Septuagint Greek Old Testament translation
NASB	New American Standard Bible (1960)
NIV 1984	New International Version (1984)
NIV	New International Version (2011)
NKJV	New King James Version (1982)
YLT	Young's Literal Translation (1862)

Reference Works

BAG/BDAG	Bauer Arndt and Gingrich; Rev. Danker Greek-English Lexicon of the NT
BDB	Brown-Driver-Briggs-Gesenius Hebrew-English Lexicon of the OT
ICC	International Critical Commentary
NIBC	New International Biblical Commentary
NICOT	New International Commentary on the Old Testament
NIDOTTE	New International Dictionary of Old Testament Theology and Exegesis
TWOT	Theological Wordbook of the Old Testament
WBC	Word Bible Commentaries

Hebrew, Greek, and Latin Transliterations

Hebrew Terms (in English rather than Hebrew alphabetical order)

Adonai (LORD) — 77

'āphār/'āpherōt (dust/dusts) — 100, 107, 109

āretz/eretz/ha-āretz (earth/the earth) — 88

asâh (to "do, make, . . . work") — 39, 40, 41, 42, 102, 132, 163, 164, 187, 219

bārā' (to create) — 3, 41, 42, 44, 66, 70, 71, 80, 86, 87, 88, 90, 91, 96, 102, 117, 141, 142, 144, 149, 160, 161, 162, 164, 193, 196, 197, 198, 199, 203, 211, 214, 218, 219

bᵉ (in-, prefix) — 40, 42, 83, 84

behēmâh (livestock, large land animal) — 172, 173

bᵉreʾshît (in-beginning) — 3, 42, 43, 44, 46, 65, 68, 75, 83, 84, 85, 91, 109, 141, 160, 164, 166, 197, 201, 211, 212, 213

bᵉtsalem (in-image) — 185

bᵉyôm (in-day, when) — 191

dāg (fish) — 169

dāshā (to grow-green) — 154, 155, 156

deshe (green-vegetation) — 154, 155, 156

ehād (one) — 35, 36

Elōhîm (God) — 3, 77, 79, 80, 81, 83, 84, 141, 185, 190, 191

ēsev (seed plants) — 156, 157

ēts peri (fruit trees) — 155, 156, 157

gan (enclosure, garden) — 185, 190

hāyāh (to be) — 144, 169

hāyāh hāʾāretz (wild animals of the-earth) — 172, 173

ᵏhōshek (darkness) — 114, 121

ᵏhul (to writhe, whirl, travail) — 101

ᵏhuqqah/ᵏhuqqōt (fixed law/s) — 92

kābash (to subdue) — 186, 187

kî shêshet yāmîm (for six days) — 40

kun (to establish) — 102, 103, 219

maʾaseh (works) — 97

makoun (foundation) — 102, 103

māthaᵏh (to spread out) — 219

māyim (waters) — 114, 121, 168

min (kind of plant or animal) — 155, 157, 172, 173

mōsad (foundation) — 219

mōt (to die) — 191

nātāh (to stretch out) — 218, 219, 220

nephesh (soul, breath) — 168, 169, 172, 173, 200, 206

Greek Terms

ktiseōs (creation) – 224, 225, 226, 227
poiéo (do, make) – 81
proskóllo (glue together) – 227
themellioo (to lay a foundation) – 102, 103

Latin Terms

ex nihilo (out of nothing) – 26, 38, 41, 42, 44, 45, 64, 70, 71, 74, 83, 86, 87, 88, 90, 91, 93, 102, 110, 112, 162, 168, 195, 197, 202, 206, 211, 213, 216, 220, 226
inclusio (literary bracketing) – 136
posse non peccare et passe peccare (able not to sin and able to sin) – 181

Authors and Prominent People

Scripture Index

Subjects

Bibliography

Anderson, Francis I. 1984. *Job.* Downers Grove: InterVarsity Press.

Ankerberg, John and John Weldon. 1998. *Darwin's Leap of Faith.* Eugene, OR: Harvest House Publishers.

Arnold, Thomas Patrick. 2008. *Two Stage Biblical Creation: Uniting Biblical Insights Uncovered by Ten Notable Creation Theories.* Arlington Heights, IL: Thomas Arnold Publishing.

Basil. 1895. "Hexaemeron Homilies." In *Nicene and Post-Nicene Fathers*, by Philip and Henry Wace Schaff. Buffalo, NY: Christian Literature Publishing Co.

Bauer, Danker, Arndt, Gingrich. 1979. *A Greek-English Lexicon of the New Testament.* Chicago: University of Chicago Press.

Behe, Michael J. 1996. *Darwin's Black Box: The Biochemical Challenge to Evolution.* New York: The Free Press.

Behe, Michael J; William A Dembski; Stephen C. Meyer. 2000. *Science and Evidence for Design in the Universe.* San Francisco: Ignatius Press.

Benner, Jeff A. 2005. *Ancient Hebrew Lexicon of the Bible.* College Station, TX: Virtualbookworm Publishing.

Blocher, Henri. 1984. *In the Beginning: The Opening Chapters of Genesis (Framework Hypothesis).* Downers Grove: InterVarsity Press.

Bozung, Douglas C. 2005. "An Evaluation of the Biosphere Model of Genesis 1." *Bibliotheca Sacra 162* 406-423.

Bradley, Walter L. 2018. "The Fine Tuning of the Universe: Evidence for the Existence of God?" *Perspectives on Science and Christian Faith* 147-160.

Brown, Colin. 1975. *Dictionary of New Testament Theology.* Grand Rapids: Zondervan.

Brown, Driver, Briggs. 1906. *Hebrew and English Lexicon.* Oxford: Clarendon Press.

Brown, Walt. 2001. *Compelling Evidence for Creation and the Flood.* Phoenix: Center for Scientific Creation.

Calvin, John. 1975. *Commentary on Genesis.* Edinburg: Banner of Truth Trust.

Carlson, Richard F. 2000. *Science and Christianity: Four Views.* Downers Grove: InterVarsity Press.

Carson, D. A. 1984. *Exegetical Fallacies.* Grand Rapids: Baker.

Carson, D. A. 1984. "Matthew." In *The Expositor's Bible Commentary, Vol. 8*, by Frank E. Gaebelein, 1-599. Grand Rapids: Zondervan.

Cassuto, U. 1961. *Commentary on the Book of Genesis.* Jerusalem: Magnes Press.

Clines, David J. A. 1989. *Job 1–20.* Waco, TX: Word .

Clinton, Bobby. 1977. *Interpreting the Scriptures, Hebrew Poetry.* Coral Gables, FL: WorldTeam.

Cohen, Gary G. 1964. "Hermeneutical Principles and Creation Theories." *Grace Journal 5:3* 17-28.

Collins, John C. 2010. "Adam and Eve as Historical People and Why It Matters." *Perspectives on Science and Christian Faith* 147-165.

—. 2006. *Genesis 1–4, A Linguistic, Literary, and Theological Commentary.* Phillipsburg, NJ: P & R Publishing.

Copan, Paul and William Lane Craig. 2004. *Creation Out of Nothing.* Grand Rapids: Baker.

Copan, Paul. 1996. "Is Creatio Ex Nihilo a Post-Biblical Invention? An Examination of Gerhard May's Proposal." *Trinity Journal* 77-93.

Craig, William Lane and Quentin Smith. 1995. *Theism, Atheism, and Big Bang Cosmology.* Oxford: Oxford University Press.

Craig, William Lane. 1979. *The Existence of God and the Beginning of the Universe.* San Bernardino, CA: Here's Life Publishers.

Craigie, Peter C; Marvin E. Tate, and Leslie C. Allen. 1983. *Psalms.* Waco, TX: Word Books.

Custance, Authur. 1970. *Without Form and Void.* Brockville, Canada: Doorway Papers.

Dahood, Mitchell. 1981. "Eblaite i-du and Hebrew 'ed, 'Rain-Cloud'." *Catholic Biblical Quarterly 43* 534-538.

—. 1966. *Psalms I, Anchor Bible.* Garden City, NY: Doubleday.

Davidson, Gregg and Ken Wolgemuth. 2018. "Testing and Verifying Old Age Evidence: Lake Suigetsu Varves, Tree Rings and Carbon-14." *Perspectives on Science and Christian Faith* 75-89.

Davidson, Richard M. 1994. "In the Beginning: How to Interpret Genesis 1." *Dialogue 6:3* 9-12.

Davidson, Richard M. 2015. "The Genesis Account of Origins." In *The Genesis Creation Account,* by ed. Gerald A. Klingbeil, 57-129. Berrien Springs, MI: Andrews University Press.

Davies, Paul. 2007. *Cosmic Jack Pot.* New York: Orion Publications.

Davis, John J. 1975. *Paradise to Prison, Studies in Genesis.* Grand Rapids: Baker.

Delitzsch, Franz. 1968. *Biblical Commentary on the Book of Job.* Grand Rapids: Eerdmans.

—. 1968. *Biblical Commentary on the Proverbs of Solomon.* Grand Rapids: Eerdmans.

Dembski, William A. 1999. *Intelligent Design: The Bridge Between Science & Theology.* Downers Grove: InterVarsity Press.

—. 2004. *The Design Revolution: Answering the Toughest Questions about Intelligent Design.* Downers Grove: InterVarsity Press.

Dembski, William A., ed. 1998. *Mere Creation: Science, Faith & Intelligent Design.* Downers Grove: InterVarsity Press.

Dill, Stephen E. 2010. *In the Beginning (Gap Theory).* Maitland, FL: Xulon Press.

Erickson, Millard J. 1985. *Christian Theology.* Grand Rapids: Baker.

Faulkner, Danny. 2004. *Universe by Design.* Green Forest, AR: Master Books.

Feinberg, Jeffrey Enoch. 1996. *Walk Genesis!* Dallas: UMJC Press.

Feinberg, John S. 1994. *The Many Faces of Evil.* Grand Rapids: Zondervan.

Feinberg, John S. 1984. "Truth: Relationship of Theories of Truth to Hermeneutics."

In *Hermeneutics, Inerrancy, and the Bible,* by Earl Radmacher and R. D. Preus. Grand Rapids: Zondervan.

Fields, Weston W. 1976. *Unformed and Unfilled, A Critique of the Gap Theory.* Collinsville, IL: Burgener Enterprises.

Finley, Thomas J. 2008. "Genesis 1 and Ancient Egyptian Creation Myths." *Bibliotheca Sacra* 178-194.

Fischer, Dick. 1990. "Days of Creation: Hours or Eons." *Perspectives on Science and Christian Faith 42.*

—. 1996. *The Origins Solution (OEC).* Lima, OH: Fairway Press.

Fonts, David M. 2003. *Genesis 1–11.* Colorado Springs: Victor.

Fruchtenbaum, Arnold. 2009. *The Book of Genesis.* San Antonio: Arial Ministries.

Futato, M. D. 1998. "Because It Had Rained: A Study of Gen. 2:5-7 with Implications for Gen. 2:4-25 and Gen. 1:1-2:3." *WTJ 60* 1-21.

Ganssle, Gregory E., ed. 2001. *God and Time: Four Views.* Downers Grove: InterVarsity Press.

Geisler, Norman L. 2002. *Systematic Theology.* Minneapolis: Bethany House.

Geisler, Norman L., ed. 2001. *The Genesis Debate.* Mission Viejo, CA: Crux Press.

Geisler, Norman L., J. Kerby Anderson. 1987. *Origin Science: A Proposal for the Creation-Evolution Controversy.* Grand Rapids: Baker.

Gish, Duane T. 1985. *Evolution: The Challenge of the Fossil Record.* El Cajon, CA: Master Books.

Gray, Gorman. 2015. *Genesis Chapter One: Scientifically Accurate and Surprisingly Simple.* Washougal, WA: Morningstar Publications.

—. 1996. *The Age of the Universe: What Are the Biblical Limits?* Washougal, WA: Morningstar Publications.

Grudem, Wayne. 1994. *Systematic Theology.* Grand Rapids: Zondervan.

Ham, Ken. 2007. "Did Jesus Say He Created in Six Days?" *answersingenesis.org/.* December 20. Accessed Oct. 6, 2019. https://answersingenesis.org/days-of-creation/did-jesus-say-he-created-in-six-literal-days/.

—. 2001. *Dinosaurs in Eden.* Green Forest, AR: Master Books.

—. 1998. *The Great Dinosaur Mystery Solved!* Green Forest, AR: Master Books.

—. 2006. *The New Answers Book 1.* Green Forest, AR: Master Books.

—. 2006-2010. *The New Answers Book 1–4.* Green Forest, AR: Master Books.

Ham, Ken; Andrew Snelling; Carl Wieland. 1990. *The Answers Book.* Glen Forest, AR: Master Books.

Hamilton, Victor P. 1990. *The Book of Genesis, Chapter 1–17.* Grand Rapids: Eerdmans.

Hansen, David G. 1998. "A Study of the Hebrew Word *Yom* in the Creation Narrative." *Bible and Spade 11:2* 35-44.

Harris, Archer, Waltke. 1980. *Theological Wordbook of the Old Testament.* Chicago: Moody Press.

Hartley, John E. 2000. *Genesis.* Peabody, MA: Hendrickson.

—. 1988. *The Book of Job*. Grand Rapids: Eerdmans.

Hasel, G. F. and M. G. Hasel. 2000. "The Hebrew Term ed in Gen. 2:6 and Its Connection in Ancient Near Eastern Literature." *Zeitschrift für die Alttestamentliche Wissenschaft 112* 321-340.

Hodge, Charles. 1988. *Systematic Theology, Abridged Edition*. Grand Rapids: Baker.

Holladay, William L. 2000. *A Concise Hebrew and Aramaic Lexicon of the Old Testament*. Leiden, Holland: Brill.

Howe, Frederic R. 1985. "The Age of the Earth: An Appraisal of Some Current Evangelical Positions, Parts 1–2." *Bibliotheca Sacra* (565) 23-37, (566) 114-129.

Humphreys, Russell. 2005. *Starlight and Time*. Madison: Evidence Press.

Johnson, Philip E. 1991. *Darwin on Trial*. Downers Grove: InterVarsity Press.

Kaiser, Walter C. 1981. *Toward an Exegetical Theology*. Grand Rapids: Baker.

Kelley, Page H. 1992. *Biblical Hebrew, An Introductory Grammar*. Grand Rapids: Eerdmans.

Kidner, Derek. 1967. *Genesis*. Downers Grove: Intervarsity Press.

—. 1975. *Psalms 73-150*. Downers Grove: InterVarsity Press.

—. 1964. *The Proverbs*. Downers Grove: InterVarsity Press.

Kline, Meredith G. 1958. "Because it had not rained." *WTJ 20:2* 146-157.

Klingbeil, Gerald A. 2015. *The Genesis Creation Account*. Berrien Springs, MI: Andrews University Press.

Lennox, John C. 2011. *Seven Days That Divide the World*. Grand Rapids: Zondervan.

Lewis, C. S. 1947. *Miracles: A Preliminary Study*. London: Collins.

Louw, Johannes and Eugene A. Nida. 1988. *Greek-English Lexicon*. New York: United Bible Societies.

Lubenow, Marvin L. 1992. *Bones of Contention: A Creationist Assessment of Human Fossils*. Grand Rapids: Baker.

McCabe, Robert V. 2000. "A Defense of Literal Days in the Creation Week." *Detroit Baptist Seminary Journal 5* 97-123.

McQuilkin, Robertson. 1983. *Understanding and Applying the Bible*. Chicago: Moody Press.

Miller, Hugh. 1857. *The Testimony of the Rocks*. Edinburgh: Constable.

Miller, Johnny V. 2012. *In the Beginning . . . We Misunderstood: Interpreting Genesis 1 in Its Original Context*. Grand Rapids: Kregel.

Miller, Keith B. 2003. *Perspectives on an Evolving Creation*. Grand Rapids: Eerdmans.

Mohler, Albert. 2010. "albertmohler." *albertmohler.com*. Accessed Oct. 11, 2019. albertmohler.com/2010/10/11/science-and-religion-arent-friends/.

Moo, Douglas. 1991. Wycliffe Exegetical Commentary Romans 1–8. Chicago: Moody.

Moreland, J. P. 1994. *The Creation Hypothesis (ID)*. Downers Grove: InterVarsity Press.

Moreland, J.P. and John Mark Reynolds, ed. 1999. *Three Views on Creation and Evolution*. Grand Rapids: Zondervan.

Moreland, Meyer, Shaw, Gauger, Grudem. 2017. *Theistic Evolution: A Scientific, Philosophical, and Theological Critique*. Wheaton: Crossway.

Morris, Henry M. 1993. *Biblical Creationism.* Grand Rapids: Baker.

—. 1982. *Men of Science; Men of God.* Green Forest: Master Books.

—. 1988. *Remarkable Record of Job.* Santee, CA: Master Books.

—. 1951. *The Bible and Modern Science.* Chicago: Moody Press.

Morris, Henry. 1974. *Scientific Creationism.* San Diego: Creation-Life Publishers.

—. 1976. *The Genesis Record.* Grand Rapids: Baker.

Mortenson, Terry. 2010. "Six Literal Days." *answersingenesis.org.* Accessed April 1, 2019. https://answersingenesis.org/days-of-creation/six-literal-days/.

Murphy, Roland E. 1998. *Proverbs.* Grand Rapids: Zondervan.

Newman, Robert C. and Herman J. Eckelmann, Jr. 1977. *Genesis One and the Origin of the Earth (Day-Age).* Downers Grove, IL: InterVarsity Press.

Northrup, Bernard E. 2003. *Recognizing Messiah in the Psalms.* Fairfax, VA: Xulon Press.

Osborne, Grant R. 1991. *The Hermeneutical Spiral.* Downers Grove: InterVarsity Press.

Overman, Dean L. 1997. *A Case Against Accident and Self-Organization.* New York: Rowman & Littlefield Publishers.

Payne, J. Barton. 1965. "Theistic Evolution and the Hebrew of Genesis 1–2." *Bulletin of the Evangelical Theological Society 8* 85-90.

—. 1962. *Theology of the Older Testament.* Grand Rapids: Zondervan.

Pember, G. H. 1876. *Earth's Earliest Ages.* London: Hodder and Stoughton.

Pratico, Gary D. and Miles V. Van Pelt. 2001. *Basics of Hebrew Grammar.* Grand Rapids: Zondervan.

Price, George McCready. 2006. "Genesis Vindicated." In *The Creationists,* by Ron Numbers, 91-92. Cambridge, MA: Harvard University Press.

Ramm, Berard. 1954. *The Christian View of Science and Scripture.* Grand Rapids: Baker.

Rana, Fazale and Hugh Ross. 2004. *Origins of Life.* Colorado Springs: NavPress.

Rana, Fazale with Hugh Ross. 2005. *Who Was Adam?* Colorado Springs: NavPress.

Ratzsch, Del. 1996. *The Battle of Beginnings.* Downers Grove: InterVarsity Press.

Rees, Martin. 1999. *Just Six Numbers.* New York: Basic Books.

Ridderbos, N. H. 1957. *Is There a Conflict Between Genesis 1 and Natural Science.* Grand Rapids: Eerdmans.

Rooker, Mark. 1992. "Genesis 1:1–3: Creation or Re-Creation?" *Bibliotheca Sacra 149* Part 1 (595) 416-419; Part 2 (596) 411-427.

Ross, Allen P. 1996. *Creation & Blessing.* Grand Rapids: Baker.

Ross, Allen P. 1991. "Proverbs." In *Expositor's Bible Commentary 5,* by Frank E. Gaebelein, 881-1134. Grand Rapids: Zondervan.

Ross, Hugh. 2004. *A Matter of Days.* Colorado Springs: NavPress.

—. 1996. *Beyond the Cosmos.* Colorado Springs: NavPress.

—. 1994. *Creation and Time.* Colorado Springs: NavPress.

—. 2006. *Creation as Science.* Colorado Springs: NavPress.

—. 2011. *Hidden Treasures in the Book of Job.* Grand Rapids: Baker.

—. 2016. *Improbable Planet.* Grand Rapids: Baker.

—. 2016. *Improbable Planet.* Grand Rapids: Baker.

—. 2014. *Navigating Genesis.* Covina, CA: Reasons to Believe Press.

—. 1993. *The Creator and the Cosmos.* Colorado Springs: NavPress.

—. 2001. *The Creator and the Cosmos.* Downers Grove, IL: NavPress.

—. 1989. *The Fingerprint of God.* New Kensington, PA: Whitaker House.

—. 1998. *The Genesis Question.* Colorado Springs: NavPress.

—. 2001. *The Genesis Question.* Colorado Springs: NavPress.

—. 2008. *Why the Universe Is the Way It Is.* Grand Rapids: Baker.

Sailhamer, John. 1990. "Genesis." In *The Expositor's Bible Commentary, Vol. 2,* by Frank E. Gaebelein, 19-284. Grand Rapids: Zondervan.

—. 1996. *Genesis Unbound.* Sisters, OR: Multnomah Books.

—. 1992. *The Pentateuch as Narrative.* Grand Rapids: Zondervan.

Samples, Kenneth Richard. 2012. *7 Truths That Changed the World (#3 A Fine Tuned Cosmos with a Beginning).* Grand Rapids: Baker.

Sarfati, Jonathan. 2004. *Refuting Compromise.* Green Forest, AR: Master Books.

Schaeffer, Frances A. 1972. *Genesis in Space and Time.* Downers Grove: InterVarsity.

Schicatano, Jim. 2001. *The Theory of Creation (OEC).* Lincoln, NE: Writer's Club Press.

Schroeder, Gerald L. 1990. *Genesis and the Big Bang.* New York: Bantam.

—. 2002. *The Hidden Face of God: Science Reveals the Ultimate Truth.* New York: Touchstone.

—. 1998. *The Science of God.* New York: Broadway Books.

Sewell, Curt. 1994. "The Tablet Theory of Genesis Authorship." *Bible and Spade.*

Simmons, Geoffrey. 2004. *What Darwin Didn't Know.* Eugene, OR: Harvest House Publishers.

Skinner, John. 1910. *A Critical and Exegetical Commentary on Genesis.* Edinburgh: T. & T. Clark.

Snoke, David. 2006. *A Biblical Case for an Old Earth.* Grand Rapids: Baker.

Stanbaugh, James. 1991. "The Days of Creation: A Semantic Approach." *CEN Tech. J. (Reprinted—Journal of Ministry & Theology)* 70-78.

Steinberg, Naomi. 1989. "The Genealogical Framework of the Family Stories in Genesis." *Semeia 46* 41-50.

Strobel, Lee. 2004. *The Case for a Creator.* Grand Rapids: Zondervan.

Tate, Marvin E. 1990. *Psalm 51–100.* Waco, TX: Word Books.

Tsumura, David Toshio. 1989. "The Earth and the Waters in Genesis 1 and 2." *Journal for the Study of the Old Testament Sup. Series 83.*

Van Bebber, Mark, and Paul S. Taylor. 1994. *Creation and Time: A Report.* Gilbert, AZ: Eden Communications.

Van Till, Howard. 1986. *The Fourth Day.* Grand Rapids: Eerdmans.

VanGemeren, Willem A. 1997. *New International Dictionary of Old Testament Theology and Exegesis, Vol. 1-5.* Grand Rapids: Zondervan.

Wallace. 1996. *Greek Grammar Beyond the Basics.* Grand Rapids: Zondervan.

Waltke, Bruce and M. O'Connor. 1990. *An Introduction to Biblical Hebrew Syntax.* Winona Lake, IN: Eisenbrauns.

Waltke, Bruce K. 1974. "Creation and Chaos." Portland, OR: Western Conservative Baptist Seminary. 1-72.

—. 2001. *Genesis A Commentary.* Grand Rapids: Zondervan.

Waltke, Bruce. 1975-1976. "The Creation Account in Genesis 1:1–3, Parts I–V." *Bibliotheca Sacra.*

Walton, John. 2009. *The Lost World of Genesis One.* Downers Grove: InterVarsity Press.

Ward, Peter and Donald Brownlee. 2004. *Rare Earth.* New York: Copernicus Books.

Weingreen. 1939. *Hebrew Grammar.* Oxford: Clarendon Press.

Wenham, Gordon J. 1987. *Genesis 1–15.* Waco, TX: Word.

Westermann, Claus. 1984. *Genesis 1–11, A Commentary.* Minneapolis: Augsburg Publishing House.

Whitcomb, John C. and Henry M. Morris. 1961. *The Genesis Flood.* Phillipsburg, NJ: P & B Publishing.

Whitefield, Rodney. 2003. *Reading Genesis One.* San Jose, CA: Rodney Whitefield Publisher.

Whorton, Mark S. 2005. *Peril in Paradise.* Waynesboro, GA: Authentic Media.

Wiseman, P. J. and D. J. Wiseman. 1985. *Ancient Records and the Structure of Genesis: A Case for Literary Unity.* Nashville: Thomas Nelson.

Wiseman, P. J. 1977. *Clues to the Creation in Genesis.* London: Marshall, Morgan & Scott.

—. 1948. *Creation Revealed in Six Days.* London: Marxhall, Morgan & Scott.

Woodbridge, John. 1988. *Great Leaders of the Christian Church.* Chicago: Moody Press.

Yahuda, A. S. 1933. *Language of the Pentateuch in Its Relations to Egyptian.* London: Oxford University Press.

Young, Edward J. 1964. *Studies in Genesis One.* Phillipsburg, NJ: P & R Publishing.

Youngblood, Ronald. 1990. *The Genesis Debate.* Eugene, OR: Wiph and Stock Publishers.

Zodhiates, Spiros. 1992. *The Complete Word Study Dictionary: New Testament.* Chattanooga, TN: AMG Publishers.